TEXTS & DOCUMENTS
A Series of The Getty Center Publication Programs

The TEXTS & DOCUMENTS series offers to the student of art, architecture, and aesthetics neglected, forgotten, or unavailable writings in English translation.
     Edited according to modern standards of scholarship and framed by critical introductions and commentaries, these volumes gradually mine the past centuries for studies that retain their significance in our understanding of art and of the issues surrounding its production, reception, and interpretation.
     Eminent scholars guide the Getty Center for the History of Art and the Humanities in the selection and publication of TEXTS & DOCUMENTS. Each volume acquaints readers with the broader cultural conditions at the genesis of the text and equips them with the needed apparatus for its study. Over time the series will greatly expand our horizon and deepen our understanding of critical thinking on art.

Julia Bloomfield, Kurt W. Forster, Thomas F. Reese, *Editors*
The Getty Center Publication Programs

THE GENIUS OF ARCHITECTURE

PUBLISHED BY THE GETTY CENTER FOR THE HISTORY OF ART AND THE HUMANITIES

DISTRIBUTED BY THE UNIVERSITY OF CHICAGO PRESS

TEXTS & DOCUMENTS

THE GENIUS OF ARCHITECTURE; OR, *THE ANALOGY OF THAT ART WITH OUR SENSATIONS*

Nicolas Le Camus de Mézières

INTRODUCTION BY ROBIN MIDDLETON

TRANSLATION BY DAVID BRITT

The Getty Center Publication Programs
Julia Bloomfield, Kurt W. Forster, Thomas F. Reese, *Editors*

TEXTS & DOCUMENTS

Architecture
Harry F. Mallgrave, Editor

The Genius of Architecture; or,
The Analogy of That Art with Our Sensations
Werner Szambien, Editorial Consultant
Lynne Kostman, Manuscript Editor

Published by The Getty Center for the History of Art and the Humanities,
Santa Monica, CA 90401-1455
© 1992 by The Getty Center for the History of Art and the Humanities
All rights reserved. Published 1992
Printed in the United States of America

98 97 96 95 94 93 92   7 6 5 4 3 2 1

Contents

Acknowledgments

I would like to thank Mary McLeod and Werner Szambien for making some good suggestions, Barry Bergdoll, Nina Rosenblatt, and Nicholas Savage for doing research on my behalf, and Jane Egan for typing my scrawls. I am also most grateful to Tony Vidler for having brought Jean-François de Bastide's *La petite maison* to my attention and to M. Arnaud de Vitry for allowing me to inspect his library and to consult his copy of Le Camus de Mézières's book on the Halle au Blé. My thanks are due as well to M. Paul Bouteiller, who has done the first substantial research into Le Camus de Mézières's Hôtel de Beauvau. M. Bouteiller and the editor of the journal *L'administration* were extremely helpful in securing permissions to translate the contract document for the *hôtel* and to reproduce its plan.

—R.M.

Translator's Note

As Le Camus de Mézières himself is the first to say, he is no stylist. But he belongs to an age when, to some retrospective eyes at least, writers and builders alike seem to have had a natural gift of proportion and balance. He also writes as an expert, in the language of a technology and an ethic that are foreign to even the most nostalgic of moderns: "This is the palace of the Gods; these apartments that we have to decorate are theirs, and it is for us to impose our customs upon them."

A modern English idiom simply cannot accommodate such ideas. What is more, the terms of art have changed; the language of building has a complex and largely oral history, so that to this day no two regions of England (and sometimes, it seems, no two English builders) call the same thing by the same name. And so I set out to avoid anachronisms as far as possible while remaining intelligible. Among my guides were two of Le Camus's architect contemporaries Sir William Chambers and Sir John Soane (who left a rough manuscript translation of about one-fifth of *The Genius of Architecture*).

I set out, in general, to avoid terms first reported after about 1800, a date that soon became stretched to 1815 or so. Among these were some that were hard to do without. "Corridor" (1814) could be used, though it would have been very convenient to have "overmantel" (1882) and "bollard" (1844) as well. But how could I present the modern American or English reader with "toilet"? Nor was the choice of an alternative particularly easy. I have guessed that a contemporary might have used "[looking] glass" (*glace*), "fitness" (*convenance*), "freestone" (in French, more specifically, *pierre de liais*), "press" (*armoire*), "magnate" (*Grand*).

Compromises are necessary, and the result is not wholly consistent, in that for the sake of the modern reader I use terms that a contemporary might have known but would not have chosen. Among these are "genre" and "nuance," which Soane went out of his way to paraphrase, but which seem to have crept into English talk about art in his lifetime. Wherever a choice seemed available, I tended to choose the term that has survived in place of the alternative that has not: "the flat of the dado" and not Chambers's "naked of the dye." Again, I have used "salon" instead of the then established English "saloon," "vapor bath" instead of "stove," and even, for instance, "customs" instead of "manners."

Then there are the names of domestic functionaries. Many of them, it seems, are specific to French culture, if not to the *ancien régime*. The *écuyer* ("squire") seems grander than any head groom; and as for his deputy the *piqueur*, a "huntsman" seems out of place in a town house. The *officier* is a very superior kind of "pantry-man"; and where, in this world of *maîtres d'hôtel* and comic-opera "majordomos," is there room for a butler? On a different plane, it does seem a pity to cut the interesting *petite-maîtresse*, or female dandy, down to size by making her a "lady of fashion."

Le Camus writes in a pale echo of a classic style. Translators are often close enough to their authors to sense their faults and all too often stand accused of making them seem worse than they really are. Le Camus's nodding sentences show a strong tendency to anticlimax. He overuses antithetical and cumulative effects in a very eighteenth-century way; and then he often avoids a heavy emphasis by pulling the final punch:

> *On choisira par préférence la couleur verte pour tenture d'une chambre à coucher: cela tient du feuillage, le sommeil semble y acquérir des douceurs.*
> (By preference, the color green will be chosen for the hangings of a bedchamber; it has something of foliage about it, and sleep seems all the sweeter.)
> *Le Traité que M. Potain nous a donné depuis quelques années pourra servir de modele, il est réfléchi, fait avec goût; on y reconnoît le véritable Artiste.*
> (Some years ago, M. Potain gave us a treatise which may serve as a model; it is thoughtful and composed with taste; in it we recognize the true Artist.)

In an eighteenth-century writer, even one of modest abilities, the instinctive rhythm defies recapture. Is pastiche the answer? The temptation is as dangerous for a modern translator as it is for a postmodern architect.

—D.B.

16

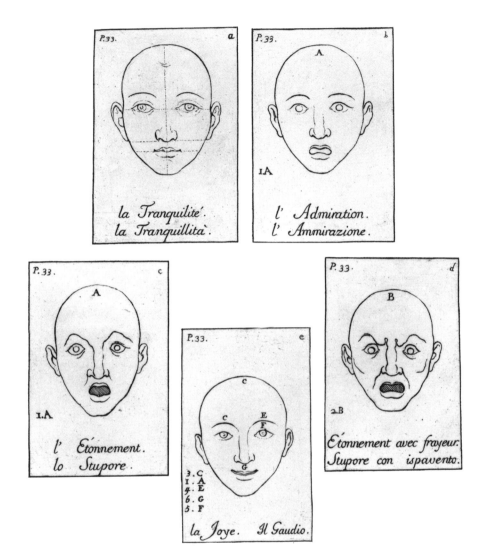

*1a–e. Engravings of heads showing features expressive of tranquility,
admiration, surprise, joy, and surprise and fear. Illustrated in Charles Le Brun,*
Conférence . . . sur l'expression générale et particulière des passions
*(Verona: Agostin Carattoni, 1751), 33ff. (bilingual, French and Italian version
based on the Amsterdam edition of 1713). Santa Monica, The Getty Center
for the History of Art and the Humanities.*

Introduction

Robin Middleton

Nicolas Le Camus de Mézières is usually approached backward, as it were, as the source of some of Etienne-Louis Boullée's more adventurous theories relating to the evocation of architectural character through the effects of light and shade. Boullée greatly enlarged on Le Camus's speculations. Boullée's writings were not published until the twentieth century, but they were no doubt known to his contemporaries and entered the architectural memory long before he died. His fame has thus perhaps robbed Le Camus of the recognition that is his due. Le Camus's most intriguing work, moreover, *Le génie de l'architecture; ou, L'analogie de cet art avec nos sensations* (The genius of architecture; or, The analogy of that art with our sensations), 1780, has seemed only partially concerned with bold conceptual matters. His is not the philosophical stance of Boullée. Le Camus's study is, indeed, essentially a handbook on the planning of the French *hôtel*—the town house, as a rule, of a noble family—though he extended the range of investigation from the merely practical to encompass the whole realm of decorum and the proper manner of stirring ideas and emotions through architectural means. It is a pioneering work; its theory seems at times makeshift and inconclusive.

Le génie de l'architecture has too often been read as an assemblage of tenuously linked parts, enlivened by a handful of brilliant perceptions: an introduction dealing with the way in which feelings are aroused by architectural forms and an exploration of an expressive language to suit; a section on the role of the five orders in

providing a traditional language of architectural expression, followed by a reversion
to the initial theme; and, almost as an adjunct, a detailed analysis, room by room, of
the planning and arrangement of the *hôtel*. This last takes up two-thirds of the book.
And half of this, one might note, is devoted to service spaces, servants' quarters, and
stables. This proliferation of tiny rooms set aside for specific purposes is not to be
equaled in architectural literature until the nineteenth century, and then in England
in such works as Mrs. Beeton's *Book of Household Management*, 1861, or Robert Kerr's
The Gentleman's House; or, How to Plan English Residences, from the Parsonage to the Palace,
1864. There is in Le Camus's work a curious mix of somewhat rarefied theory and
ordinary, commonsensical issues. His special concern, as the word *genius* in the title
makes clear, was with the nature of individual creation—a particular preoccupation
of eighteenth-century architects. By mid-century the phrase "fire and genius" ("*du
feu et du génie*") served as a cant term of praise, though as early as 1652 in *Desseins de
plusieurs palais* (Designs for several palaces) Antoine Le Pautre had described his visionary designs as "children of my genius" ("*enfans de mon génie*").[1]

     Le Camus's theory, as already indicated, is not always fully worked out.
It remains uncertain. But though the parts might not seem at first to relate too well,
they do form a whole. His study is quite coherent, as becomes at once evident when
the pattern of knowledge and the ideas from which it emerges are considered. Some
outline of these ideas is perhaps necessary before beginning Le Camus's book.

The usual means of giving form and expression to a building in classical architecture
was through the use of the orders—in Greek architecture the Doric and Ionic as a
rule (though the Corinthian Order was also a Greek invention) with the addition in
Roman architecture of the Tuscan and the Composite. Variants of all five orders were
used throughout the Renaissance. Their proportions and the whole array of elements
and moldings that related to them were analyzed and classified by architectural theorists, most notably and usefully by Vignola, whose works were published throughout
Europe in many editions.[2] A codified system of classical architecture was thus established. All manner of variations were possible, and nothing was, in fact, fixed; but the
system was sustained by the notion of an ideal that was thought to have emerged first
in Greece and to have attained equal, if not higher, perfection in Rome and in Renaissance Italy. This ideal was, in theory, absolute and scarcely to be affected by historical
change or cultural differences, although for the French of Louis XIV's reign it seemed
that an even higher level of achievement had been attained in France.

     During the second half of the seventeenth century this belief in a universal norm was gradually eroded, in part through an enhanced knowledge of the societies and civilizations of the world and an awakening recognition that the forms of their architecture represented equally valid and coherent systems, but perhaps even more forcefully—certainly more insidiously—through the impact of Cartesian doctrines. For though Cartesians were in no doubt at all that there were universal norms in philosophy and all the arts, they held that these norms were to be established on the basis of reason, not on the basis of precedent. This thesis was, however, of a paradoxical kind, for the standards of good taste were grounded not only in antique precedent but also in custom and usage both in classical times and from the Renaissance onward. Custom and usage represented an expression of the workings of nature, and Nature (*la belle nature*) in its idealized form was itself the seat of reason. The tastes of the Cartesians were thus not very different from those of their predecessors. But the system of classical architecture was nonetheless subject to a profound reassessment.

The most articulate and effective reappraisal of classical doctrine was provided by Claude Perrault, a doctor and scientist rather than an architect. This appeared in 1673 in the footnotes of Perrault's new translation of *De architectura libri decem* (The ten books of architecture) of Vitruvius (which, as the only surviving theoretical text from antiquity, had in fact served to establish the authority of the architecture of Greece, the buildings of Greece being to all intents unknown to the architects of Europe until the second half of the eighteenth century). Perrault's initial reappraisal was later expanded in his *Ordonnance des cinq espèces de colonnes selon la méthode des anciens*, 1683 (translated into English as *A Treatise of the Five Orders of Columns in Architecture* in 1708).

As the title alone of this work makes clear, Perrault was in no way intent upon rejecting the authority of classical architecture or the primacy of the orders as the embodiment of the highest standards of beauty and artistic expression. He aimed rather to subject them to new rules of assessment. His ground was the rule of reason. The orders, he held, should not be regarded as sacrosanct; they should not be upheld as expressions of a universal system of harmony discernible, according to Pythagorean theory, in music in the intervals of the scales, in architecture in the established proportional ratios. Musical harmony was not to be equated with architectural harmony. The ear might indeed register a discord, but the eye was by no means so finely responsive to proportional harmonies. The ear and the eye were instruments of a different kind, and their operations must, on scientific grounds, be considered as distinct. The particular sharpness of this argument was occasioned by the publication in 1679 of René Ouvrard's *Architecture harmonique; ou, Application de la doctrine des proportions de la musique à l'architecture* (Harmonic architecture; or, Application of the doctrine of musical proportions to architecture).

There were, for Perrault, no absolute standards of beauty in architecture. Beauty was of two sorts: positive beauty, which could be readily recognized in the quality of materials, in precision and neatness of execution, in size, in sheer magnificence, and, as might be expected, in symmetry, and arbitrary beauty, which involved arrangements of forms and shapes, proportion, and the articulation of the whole panoply of elements of classical architecture, which had been established by custom. The latter might be subject to rules, indeed in the interest of uniform standards of taste Perrault was determined that it should be subject to rules, but they could not be regarded as fixed. It was precisely in this area of design that the sensibility and imagination of the true artist might be expressed. For Descartes, of course, imagination was a source of error. Perrault aimed therefore at no more than a modicum of expression controlled by reason.

Yet Perrault's reassessment of the classical tradition on the grounds of reason prompted a significant and creative innovation in architecture. The orders, he argued, had become little more than a decorative system applied to wall surfaces, whereas in classical antiquity the column, which was the essential component of the orders, had served instead as a structural element, which had both constituted the architecture, as it were, and decorated it. And this structural articulation he recognized as a vital aspect not only of true classical architecture but also, altogether surprisingly, of French Gothic architecture. He thus struck a note of cultural relativism. But though Perrault might have referred with approval to the French Gothic cathedrals, he was not setting them forth for imitation. He was observing and analyzing their architectural effects so that they might be subsumed in the classical system. He sought to give expression to these notions in the freestanding colonnade that he and a small committee set up by Jean-Baptiste Colbert—consisting of the architect Louis Le Vau and the painter Charles Le Brun—designed for the east front of the Louvre in 1667. This elevation marked a radical change not only in the handling of the forms of architecture in France but in the grounds of aesthetic judgment. The utilitarian aspect of the orders was now seen to have determined not only the original form of the architecture but to provide a new potential for expression.

Michel de Frémin and the Abbé Jean-Louis de Cordemoy took up Perrault's ideas in the early eighteenth century. They thought likewise primarily in terms of the classical tradition, though, like Perrault, they enlarged their understanding of the rational nature of architecture with reference to the Gothic. Their enthusiasm for Gothic extended even to spatial effects. The classical system they sought to reduce to essentials. De Cordemoy aimed to restrict the use of the orders to the three Greek forms; Frémin was intent to deny even these any overt importance. Both men aimed at an architecture of common sense (*le bon sens*), based on sound building practice in which the shape and form of each element would be explained and tested by reason.

The immediate impact of these ideas was limited, for the science of construction was not greatly advanced in the early years of the eighteenth century; building continued to be a traditional operation not yet susceptible to intellectual analysis. The mathematical basis of structural theory was but slowly formulated during the course of the century. Frémin and Cordemoy's chief concern, moreover, was with church architecture and in particular with the role of the freestanding column as a supporting element between nave and aisle. Few new churches were erected in France during the first half of the century, though when the greatest church of the age, the church of Sainte-Geneviève (now known as the Panthéon), was initiated in 1757, their ideals were to be given the fullest possible expression. By then they had been reformulated and presented with far greater clarity and coherence by the Abbé Marc-Antoine Laugier in his *Essai sur l'architecture*, 1753 (translated into English as *An Essay on Architecture* in 1755), the most celebrated and influential of all eighteenth-century architectural texts. The criteria of architectural excellence were reduced there to those subtended by an idealized primitive hut—four upright posts supporting four lintels with a pitched roof above. Architecture became, in essence, no more than a structural framework, albeit a classical one.

Though architecture was to be rigorously tested and purified by reason and reference to origins, architectural understanding was not thereby reduced; rather, it was enlarged. The established classical tradition, rooted in a timeless and fixed ideal, was undermined inexorably, but it would be a mistake to think that it was discredited and cast aside. It was cherished still. And the classical tradition as a whole, not simply that aspect concerned with architecture, could now be explored in terms of the evolving empirical aesthetic. Frenchmen thought in terms of the texts and tropes of antique literature. They still received a classical education. Indeed, when the notion of the absolute authority of the orders was shattered, it was to antique sources that the French turned first to find an alternative form of architectural expression.

The notion of expression in classical aesthetics can perhaps be traced back to Xenophon, who in his *Memorabilia* recounts a discussion between Socrates and the sculptor Cleiton in which they concur that it is the task of the sculptor to give expression to the individual soul in his figures.[3] But in the seventeenth and eighteenth centuries the test of any such ability to give artistic expression to the emotions was usually thought of in terms of a painter's ability to represent with conviction the laughing and weeping philosophers, Democritus and Heraclitus. This was long regarded as the sharpest test of a painter's powers. It was, however, part of a late development—a theme taken up in the fifteenth century by the Platonic philosopher Marsilio Ficino from Sidonius, who refers in a letter to paintings of this sort in the gymnasium at Athens.[4]

The first text of classical antiquity in which the theory of expression was explored at any length was Aristotle's *Poetics*, which was almost entirely taken up with literary forms, with poetry, tragedy, and comedy, as was Horace's later *Ars Poetica* (Art of poetry). But though these works referred only by implication to the arts of painting and sculpture, and to architecture not at all, they offered so compelling an analysis of the art of arousing and expressing emotions—in particular in the theater—that they became the basic texts on notions of expression in all the arts. Even in classical times the implications of these initial ideas were extended with reference to rhetoric, beginning once again with a fundamental text by Aristotle, the *Rhetoric*, and subsequently in Cicero's *De Oratore* (On the making of an orator) and Quintilian's *Institutio oratoria* (The training of an orator).

The aim of these investigations was to establish the style appropriate to a particular character on a particular occasion in relation to a determined aim. It was a matter of propriety or decorum. Cicero summed up the theoretical tenets most succinctly in a late work, *Orator*, in which he set forth decorum as the decisive factor in any consideration of style. There are, he wrote, three styles in oratory,

> the plain style for proof, the middle style for pleasure, the vigorous
> style for persuasion; and in this last is summed up the entire virtue
> of the orator. Now the man who controls and combines these three
> varied styles needs rare judgement and great endowment; for he
> will decide what is needed at any point, and will be able to speak in
> any way which the case requires. For after all the foundation of
> eloquence, as of everything else, is wisdom. In an oration, as in
> life, nothing is harder than to determine what is appropriate. The
> Greeks call it πρέπον; let us call it *decorum* or "propriety."[5]

Cicero was quite clear that propriety, or what is correct, is not necessarily concerned with what is right. It was not a question of morality. The rhetorical modes of expression were thus intimately linked to decorum but not to an absolute good. The relationship between the word *decorum* and *decor* in architecture need scarcely be stressed. But such notions were to be transposed first to the aesthetics of painting before they were taken up by architectural theorists. Leon Battista Alberti and Leonardo da Vinci were the most famous of the Renaissance exponents of the ideals of the proper representation of character through the depiction of appropriate human forms, gestures, and expressions. But though both were architects and though Alberti certainly used rhetorical theory—Cicero's in particular—to underpin his notions of decorum in architecture, they did not explore these themes as fully as might be expected in their architectural writings. They reserved these notions, on the whole, for painting. They continued to rely for expression in architecture on the characteristics of the orders and their proportional systems.

The key to the transfer of such theories into the realm of architectural aesthetics was provided, not altogether surprisingly, by Perrault's contemporary the painter Charles Le Brun. In 1668 Le Brun delivered a lecture on expression to the members of the Académie Royale de Peinture et de Sculpture. He was concerned chiefly with the problems of history painting, with the way in which human emotions might be represented with due decorum so that the event depicted might be convincing. His particular interest was pathognomics, the way in which passing emotions might be expressed in the human body. But the focus of his attention was the human face.

Boldly, Le Brun adapted the scientific aspect of his theory from Descartes's *Les passions de l'âme*, 1649 (translated into English as *The Passions of the Soule* in 1650). Descartes had conceived of the passions as affectations of the soul. The soul, he thought, was seated in the pineal gland in the center of the brain, and it was from there, through the flow of animal spirits, that the human passions were controlled and given expression in the body. Le Brun argued that as the face was closest to the soul, it was the most expressive part of the body, with the eyes and eyebrows the most revealing indices of expression, as they were almost in direct contact with the soul. He isolated four positions of the eyebrows as indicative of particular emotions, concupiscible or irascible, simple or mixed. He sought likewise to demonstrate that the mouth reflected the movement of the heart. The basic modes could, of course, be combined and adjusted, and in a later lecture Le Brun showed how they might be reinforced by the study of physiognomics, the science of the permanent characteristics of the body as affected by the passions.

Le Brun's ideas were circulated in his lifetime in various manuscript versions, but they were not to be published until after his death — *Conférence sur l'expression*, 1698 (translated into English as *The Conference upon Expression* in 1701); many other translations and adaptations followed. Le Brun had aimed at a scientific analysis of the principles governing expression so that painters might work not in imitation of nature but according to its laws, creatively. Instead, his text, and the illustrations accompanying it even more so, came to serve as fixed patterns for expressions, so that particular lines of the eyebrows and mouth were soon recognized throughout Europe as formulae for the representation of such emotions as dejection and joy, astonishment and anger, etc. (figs. 1a–e). Le Brun had also indicated in his drawings how human characteristics might be related to the conventional animal passions — the docile

2. *Charles Le Brun, human and animal heads expressive of common characteristics, drawing. Paris, Musée du Louvre, no. 28.200. Photo: © R.M.N.*

sheep, the brave lion, the cunning fox, etc. (fig. 2)—and these facial types also provided a repertoire of resemblances that were taken up by both painters and connoisseurs. The impact of Le Brun's ideas was immense, for however much his aim might have been distorted and debased, he had demonstrated successfully that character and emotion could be explained and represented in visual terms, that the passions of the soul could be reduced to lines.

Though Le Brun worked on several occasions as an architect, he seems not to have recognized the relevance of such theories to architecture. Indeed, when he attempted to provide expressive forms for each of the twelve pavilions of the Château de Marly, he resorted to the established method of applying the orders or their parts to the facades, together with an array of painted conventional and sculptural symbolical motifs indicative of the designation of each—Hercules, Venus, Jupiter, Abundance, etc. (figs. 3–5). Nothing adventurous by way of a linear interpretation of these characteristic qualities is in evidence in his designs. The pavilions have, in any event, been destroyed.

This long exploration of the proper means of expressing character in artistic terms was set firmly within an architectural context only in 1745 in Germain Boffrand's *Livre d'architecture* (Book of architecture)—the writing of which dates back to 1734. Boffrand was concerned primarily with the presentation of a range of his own designs for *hôtels* and *châteaux*, but his introductory chapters reveal his interest, his obsession one might say, with the issues of expression and decorum in architecture. Like most French theorists, he gracefully acknowledged the merits of the architectural forms of other civilizations, other societies, bestowing special praise on the builders of the French Gothic cathedrals for the finesse of their proportional systems, but he continued to uphold the Greek and Roman example as the most fitting for emulation.

Boffrand relied still on the five orders to provide the basic modes of expression. The orders, he said, ranging in character from the rustic to the sublime, must be regarded as the equivalent of the genres in poetry. It is notable that, good classicist that he was, Boffrand set his text in two parallel columns of Latin and French. It is even more noteworthy that in the most finely argued of his chapters, that dealing with character in architecture, he took up the rhetorical device of transposition; he interleaved his text with quotations from Horace's *Ars Poetica*, a handful of words adjusted or changed in each instance to make explicit the reference to architecture rather than poetry. But though he staunchly upheld the classical tradition, Boffrand aimed to invest architecture with a more complex range of expression borrowed from poetry, the theater, or music so that the purpose of each building should be quite evident in its architecture, both inside and out. The rank of its owner should

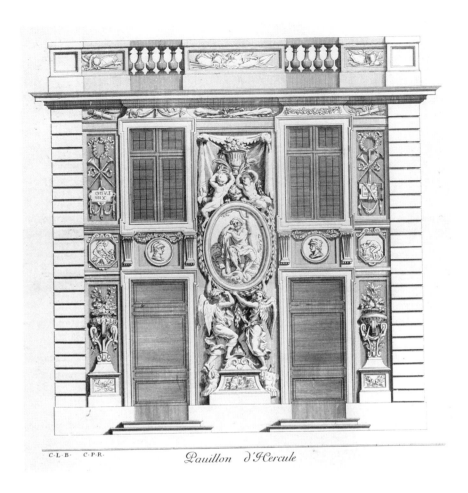

Pauillon d'Hercule

3. *Painted elevation of the Pavilion of Hercules at the Château de Marly,
designed by Charles Le Brun. Illustrated in Charles Le Brun,* Divers desseins
de decorations de pavillons *(Paris: Edelinck, circa 1690). Santa Monica,
The Getty Center for the History of Art and the Humanities.*

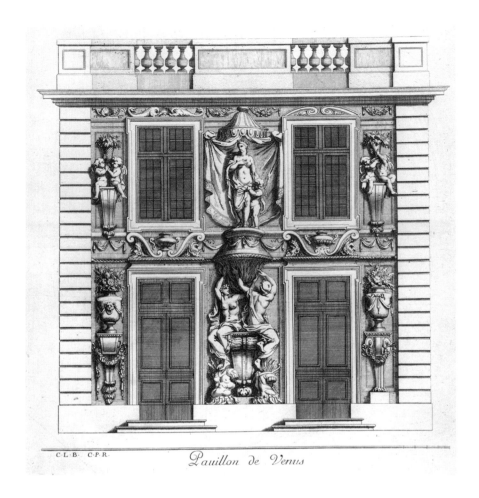

Pauillon de Venus

4. *Painted elevation of the Pavilion of Venus at the Château de Marly,
designed by Charles Le Brun. Illustrated in Charles Le Brun,* Divers desseins
de decorations de pavillons *(Paris: Edelinck, circa 1690). Santa Monica,
The Getty Center for the History of Art and the Humanities.*

likewise be visible, and his intention to evoke a mood of seriousness, gaiety, or joy should at once be effective.

All emotions, Boffrand held, could be expressed in architecture. The added means of expression proposed was that of the line in three basic forms: convex, concave, or straight. He made no mention of Le Brun, but there can be little doubt that he had him in mind when he castigated the architects of the early eighteenth century for designing interiors with lines intertwined to confusion and for evidencing no understanding that such lines were to architecture what tones were to music. By such means the skilled architect might strike chords of sadness or joy, love or hate, grace or terror. The best surviving interiors of the Rococo, it is to be remarked, are those designed by Boffrand himself for the Hôtel de Soubise in Paris, though today they are not often appraised in the terms proposed by Boffrand.

There is a great deal more in Boffrand's book that is pertinent to *Le génie de l'architecture*, in particular his belief that the first principles of architecture rest on the commonsense grounds of health and security and convenience and ease of use and that it is these considerations that should determine the forms and arrangements of *hôtels* and *châteaux* before the decor appropriate to the station and taste of the client is conceived. But consideration of such aspects of theory may, for the moment, be set aside to explore further the emergence of an empirical aesthetics in the early years of the eighteenth century, for this was the conditioning factor of Le Camus de Mézières's novel concept of architecture.

The first clear expression of the ideas that were to shape the empirical aesthetics of the second half of the century is usually thought to be the Abbé Jean-Baptiste Dubos's *Réflexions critiques sur la poésie et sur la peinture*, 1719 (translated into English as *Critical Reflections on Poetry, Painting, and Music* in 1746) in which sentiment is shown to have a more significant role than reason in the formulation of aesthetic judgments. This was, as may be imagined, no more than a relative assessment. The classical tradition and its codes of taste rooted in the notion of *"la belle nature"* were not seriously challenged. The work that was to inflect sensationalist thought to real and disruptive effect, however, was the last of the books of the amateur painter and connoisseur Roger de Piles, the *Cours de peinture par principes*, issued first in 1708 (and again in 1766 and 1791; translated into English as *The Principles of Painting* in 1743)—a book, one might note, that engrossed Dubos.

De Piles was opposed to much that Le Brun represented: the system of rules established by the Académie (though his own *Cours* consisted in lectures on a new set of rules that he had put forward to the Académie when he was finally elected in 1699); the emphasis on design and line rather than color in painting; the notion of the genres, etc. He was particularly scathing about Le Brun's reduction of facial ex-

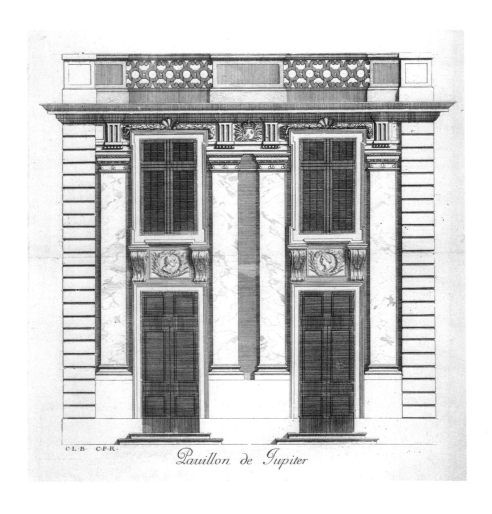

Pauillon de Jupiter

5. *Painted elevation of the Pavilion of Jupiter at the Château de Marly,
designed by Charles Le Brun. Illustrated in Charles Le Brun,* Divers desseins
de decorations de pavillons *(Paris: Edelinck, circa 1690). Santa Monica,
The Getty Center for the History of Art and the Humanities.*

pression to a system of lines—a clever theory, he remarked, but one that could not be applied to the nose. De Piles nonetheless ranked Le Brun surprisingly high in the slightly ludicrous grading system that he devised for the evaluation of painters; Le Brun was set below Raphael and Rubens but above Titian.

In his frequent references to Aristotle and Horace, and especially to Quintilian, de Piles is akin to other eighteenth-century theorists. Like them, he continued to analyze painting in the same terms as poetry and oratory, but he was determined also to free painting from the dominance of literary theory. As we have seen, from Alberti to Le Brun, theorists had thought that the expressive range of painting resided in the representation of the gestures, attitudes, and movements of the human body and in particular in the expressions of the face. The subject matter, so often selected from classical mythology or history, was of paramount importance. But de Piles argued that a painting made an instant and purely visual impact on the spectator that had nothing to do with the subject matter and was in no way related to the conventional modes of expression and that this impact derived instead from the effect of the composition and the manner of execution of the whole—the *tout ensemble*. Furthermore, it was this unity of impact (*unité d'objet*), as opposed to André Félibien's and Le Brun's unity of subject (*unité de sujet*), that gave true value and distinction to a painting. The mere sight of a painting should stir a particular passion. In its ability to evoke a spontaneous mood, painting was similar, at least, to music.

This notion was thought by many to be no more than an extension of the principles of decorum, or *convenance*, from the figures and parts of a painting to composition as a whole, and this was indeed part of de Piles's intent, but he aimed at far more. He thought that the parts should, in fact, be subordinated to the whole and that the power of the work should stem from the arrangement of forms and colors and of light and shade that was determined chiefly by the artist's sense of harmony. This sense he termed the fury or enthusiasm of the painter, and he thought that in its noblest form this enthusiasm comprehended the sublime.

The initial sensuous effect of a picture had, of course, to be sustained thereafter by conventional painterly skills in the representation of an illusion, and this was, inevitably, susceptible still to intellectual analysis. But beauty, after the publication of the *Cours*, could no longer be formulated as a fixed set of rules, "Beauty, say they, is nothing real; every one judges it according to his own taste, and 'tis nothing but what pleases."[6]

The thrust of de Piles's comments was directed at history painting, but his particular interest was landscape painting. He himself collected Dutch and Flemish landscapes, and his propaganda greatly stirred French interest in such works. He liked them, of course, precisely because they did not rely on figures to establish their character. They could be construed as more purely painterly exercises. De Piles in fact introduced the word *pittoresque,* or picturesque, into the French critical vocabulary to denote a view that was painterly. Only later was the term to be taken up by landscape-gardening theorists.

Landscapes, de Piles explained, could be more totally expressive of a particular theme than other categories of painting, because the elements of which they were composed were imbued with intrinsic qualities. Thus cottages might be introduced into a painting to invoke a rustic theme or clear-cut buildings to evoke a heroic mood, but more essentially affective were the elements of nature itself. A distant view, the sky and the clouds, mountains and other irregularities, trees and rocks, each had the power to conjure up a particular image. "Rocks," he wrote, "are of themselves gloomy, and only proper for solitudes."[7] But it was water in its various states from turbulence to calm that stirred passion most deeply; water was to be regarded as the soul of the landscape.

De Piles's small book had a pronounced effect on attitudes toward painting; it influenced patterns of connoisseurship and collecting, and it penetrated the artistic sensibilities of the age of the Rococo in a host of other ways. Primacy of feeling was then in the ascendant, and de Piles had provided a text that justified the instant response, the instant submission to pleasure or other emotion. The complex and fantastical stage sets that the extravagant Jean-Nicolas Servandoni devised for the Académie Royale de Musique between 1726 and 1742 and created on his own account from 1754 to 1758 (in a series of tableaux in the Salle de Spectacles at the Tuileries) may be seen as one particular response to this demand for the striking illusion, the instantaneous stirring of emotion. And though Denis Diderot was to bring such spectacles into disfavor precisely because they offered no further engagement of the mind, his later demands for the fullest expression of emotion in painting and his acclaim for the works of Jean-Baptiste Greuze are yet other reflections of that realm of feeling in art opened up by de Piles.

Attitudes of this sort were given form in architecture in the intimate luxury of *hôtel* interiors, in particular in the intricate network of rooms, all artfully decorated, that made up the fashionable woman's apartment. Although the practicalities of such arrangements were described in some detail by a number of architects in the early years of the eighteenth century, beginning with Sebastien Leblond in 1710, the aesthetics were not much explored beyond the dictates of propriety, or *convenance.* The handling of space, or rather a sequence of spaces, to determined sensual effect was to be analyzed first by Le Camus de Mézières. This was his contribution to architectural theory.

The plan of the French *hôtel* was based on the organization of groups of four or five rooms, though the number was not determined, to form apartments of a distinctive character. Each suite of rooms thus set apart was intended for the use of a particular person. The *hôtel* was made up of many different types of apartments, the chief ones being the state apartment, or *appartement de parade,* and the private apartment, or *appartement de commodité.* The principal rooms were linked by an *enfilade*, a sequence of openings on a single axis that provided both access and a visual link between them. The word *appartement*, it is important to stress, was not known in France before the middle of the sixteenth century. The term and the concept were probably introduced from Italy. The first effective embodiment in France of these planning principles is usually considered to be Cardinal Hippolyte d'Este's *hôtel*, the Grand Ferrare, erected opposite the royal palace of Fontainebleau between 1544 and 1546 by Sebastiano Serlio. This was illustrated in variant forms in Serlio's famous sixth book of architecture, devoted to domestic buildings, which was not to be published until the twentieth century. Manuscript versions, however, were certainly known to contemporaries, and the arrangements of the Grand Ferrare were introduced soon enough into Parisian architecture.[8]

The history of the form is no doubt more complex than this summary suggests. Myra Nan Rosenfeld has argued that the arrangement was in use in France long before Serlio arrived from Italy and has adduced the Hôtel de Cluny (variously dated as 1456–1485 or 1485–1498) as an illustration of the type.[9] This, however, does not have a symmetrical entrance facade, which, as we shall see, is another essential expression of the order of the French *hôtel*. Rosenfeld has, nonetheless, sought to trace the type beyond the medieval manor to the Roman farmsteads of France and thus to interpret it as an Italian import of even earlier vintage. The matter requires exploration still and needs to be considered, moreover, with reference to the way in which rooms were used. For this is another aspect of French planning that is determining.

The sequence of rooms in an apartment was outlined early — once again by Serlio in the description of a royal palace in his sixth book of architecture — as a *salle, antichambre, chambre, arrière chambre,* and *cabinet,* that is, a vestibule or guardroom, an anteroom for people to wait in before being received, a general living space, followed by a bedroom and a study. By the early eighteenth century the classic sequence for a noble apartment had been established as *antichambre, salle de compagnie, chambre à coucher, cabinet,* and *arrière cabinet* or *garderobe,* that is, an anteroom (there might well be more than one), followed by a salon, a bedchamber, a study, and a closet.

The bedchamber was not always used as a sleeping chamber, in particular in an apartment of consequence. The bed to be used would be in the room beyond. For the actual use of rooms was from quite early on, and certainly after the move of the court to Versailles, closely patterned on royal practice. The king's bed with its canopy was identified as the seat of power, even more potent perhaps than his canopied throne. The bed was the real focus of royal ritual. The degree of intimacy with the king was at once made apparent by the manner in which one was received in relation to it—whether in the preceding salon or in the bedchamber itself, whether on the dais of the bed or off it. Even when the bedchamber was empty, those passing through the room had to make a bow to the bed. The royal bed had assumed its purely ceremonial role as a *lit de parade* as early as 1585, when Henri III drew up new regulations for his household management. After disrobing on his bed, the king would retire to sleep with the queen in her bedroom nearby. This arrangement was later in evidence in the royal apartments in the Louvre, though it is to be remarked that the rooms there were still not arranged in *enfilade*. And thus they remained when Louis XIV occupied them.

When work began on the Palais des Tuileries in 1664 to prepare it for royal occupation, the king's and the queen's apartments were set on the same floor, as before, but with their individual rooms axially linked. The king was to sleep in the room beyond his state bedchamber. When, in November 1673, the court moved to Versailles after the completion of the first major reconstruction of the *château*, the queen's apartment was in the south wing, the king's in the north. The main rooms of this suite, the Appartement des Planètes, or Appartement du Soleil, formed a magnificent sequence, in *enfilade*, ending in the king's state bedchamber; his sleeping room was beyond. When Maria Theresa died in 1683, Louis XIV took over the entire first floor of the palace to form his apartment. He then moved his state bedchamber to the center of the palace; inevitably, it could no longer be in *enfilade*, instead it was on the principal axis of both the extensive garden and the building itself, the focal point of all roads leading to it. The *lit de parade* seemed, almost, the center of France. The king's sleeping chamber was alongside. Then, in 1701, he determined that his public persona and his private persona should be as one; he decided to sleep in his state bed. This practice was, in turn, reversed by his great-grandson, Louis XV, who was intent to lead something of a private life and to whom many of the more intimate living arrangements of the eighteenth century were to be attributed. But the bed, in accord with royal precedent, nonetheless continued to be the dominant feature in the classic French apartment, the climax, as it were, to the spatial sequence. The more magnificent the apartment the less likely the bed was to be used, other than on a wedding night or for the birth of children.

Introduction   33

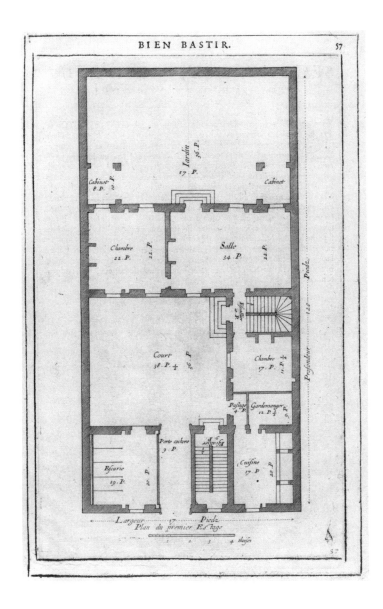

6. *Ground-floor plan of a town house on a 57 × 120 ft site with a* "salle," "chambre," *and* "cabinet" *marked. Illustrated in Pierre Le Muet,* Manière de bien bastir pour toutes sortes de personnes, *2nd ed. (Paris: François Langlois, 1647), 57. Middleton Collection.*

The French manner of setting up tables for eating, almost at will, but usually in one of the anterooms of an apartment, can likewise be traced back to royal custom. As early as 1501 when the Château de Blois was being prepared for an exceptional reception of the Archduke Philippe Le Beau, one of the preliminary rooms in the suite was designated in the description of the arrangements as "the room in which the king eats" (*"la salle où mangeoit le Roy"*). Evidence of such specialization of use, however, appears only in 1637 in the Hôtel d'Arsenal in Paris and not for several years more does it become at all common to set aside a room specially for eating. Even in the eighteenth century, the more flexible arrangement maintained, though it had become more general by then to use the second anteroom for eating. When a separate *salle à manger* was included in a plan, it usually opened off the entrance vestibule, isolated from the *enfilade* of an apartment, for it was thought of as a room of disruptive activity, noisy and smelly.

The placing of furniture in French *hôtels*, the ranging of fixed sofas and chairs around the walls of reception rooms with no more than a handful of movable chairs and stools in the center, can likewise be related to the etiquette of the court. Though far too little is yet known of these patterns of use to judge of their effect on architecture. The earliest surviving decor of a room, the Maréchale de La Meilleraye's rooms in the Arsenal, Paris, dates from 1637.

The literature of French planning begins, perhaps, with books of manners, some of which date back to the fourteenth century; though the first of consequence were Baldassare Castiglione's *Il libro del cortegiano*, 1528 (translated into French by 1537 and into English as *The Covrtyer* in 1561) and Desiderius Erasmus's equally famous *De civilitate morum puerilium* (Good manners for children), 1530 (appearing in French for the first time in 1537 and again and again thereafter). The latter book, as the title makes plain, was directed to the upbringing of children, but this was no more, it would seem, than a tactful device. Other such books followed: another Italian import, Giovanni della Casa's *Il Galateo*, 1558 (translated into French as *Le Galathee; ou, La maniere et fasson comme le gentilhomme se doit gouuerner en toute compagnie* in 1562 and into English as *Galateo . . . ; or rather, A Treatise on the Māners and Behauiours, It Behoueth a Man to Vse and Eschewe* in 1576); Claude Hours de Calviac's *La civile honesteté pour les enfants* (Good manners for children), 1559, modeled in part on Erasmus's work; Nicolas Faret's *L'honnête homme; ou, L'art de plaire à cour*, 1630 (translated into English as *The Honest Man; or, The Art to Please in Court* in 1632). Not until the appearance of Antoine de Courtin's *Nouveau traité de la civilité qui se pratique en France parmi les honnêtes gens*, 1671 (translated into English as *The Rules of Civility* the same year), however, is the relation of manners to architecture tentatively engaged. Behavior in the *antichambre* is defined, as is that in *la chambre où est le lit*; in neither room is one to

wear a hat, in the bedchamber one is not to sit on the bed, etc. The concept of propriety of behavior, or *bienséance,* is linked directly, more than once in the book, to this
same concept in architecture. Later books, Claude Fleury's *Les devoirs des maîtres et des
domestiques* (The duties of masters and servants), 1688, or Audiger's *La maison reglée et
l'art de diriger la maison* (The well-run house and the art of running a house), 1692, in
which the duties of masters and servants are defined in detail, serve even more effectively to indicate the differentiations of usage, and thus of architectural space, that
were gradually emerging in the seventeenth century. But once again these and their
successors—and there was a spate of such publications in the eighteenth century—
have not yet received sufficient careful study with reference to surviving inventories
and plans to provide any real understanding.

    The first book on architecture that offers more—though only marginally
more—than illustrations of the areas enclosed by walls is Pierre Le Muet's *Manière de
bien bastir pour toutes sortes de personnes,* 1623 (issued in enlarged form in 1647; translated
into English as *The Art of Fair Building* in 1670). There, the position of the great bed
(as opposed to the ubiquitous folding beds that were set up anywhere) is indicated in
the main room of each apartment. Labeling of the rooms reveals that the term *salle* is
used for a room of general use, a *chambre* is a room for sleeping (fig. 6), while on the
additional plates of 1647, newly fashionable terms such as *petite salle à manger, antichambre,* and *alcove* are included (fig. 7). This last is sometimes thought to have been an
import from Spain, though one of the first recorded in France was that introduced by
the Marquise de Rambouillet into her house in the rue Saint-Thomas du Louvre between 1619 and 1620. The marquise was born in Rome, the daughter of the Prin-
cipessa Savelli. She is credited with a great deal more in terms of the refinement of
comfort in architecture: the separation of spaces of representation from those used
for private enjoyment, the proper control of heating, the lowering of window sills to
enlarge the view to the garden, etc. But these were all incorporated into a *hôtel* of
somewhat eccentric organization.

    Other books illustrating architectural plans followed Le Muet's, but they
offer no more than the briefest commentary at best. The first full text on the principles of planning appeared only in 1691, when Augustin-Charles Daviler included a
chapter, "De la distribution des plans" ("On planning arrangements") in his *Cours
d'architecture* (Course of architecture). There, he illustrated and described the arrangement of a large town house of his own design (figs. 8, 9). But the form was by
then firmly fixed. It consisted of an entrance court flanked by stables and service
wings, dominated by the main residential block, or *corps de logis,* with a private garden
beyond. Daviler's *corps de logis* is two rooms deep, an arrangement that is thought to
have been adopted first in 1639 in Louis Le Vau's Hôtel Tambonneau, to be taken up a

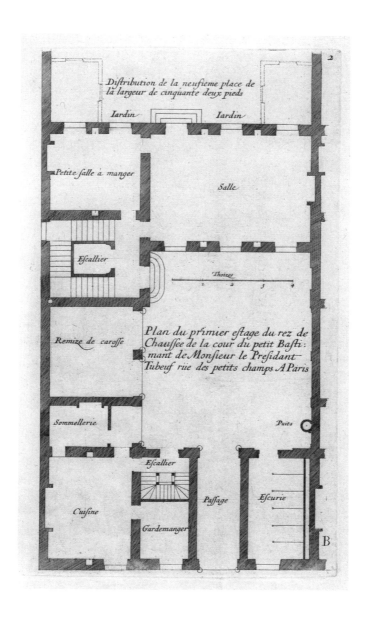

7. Ground-floor plan of a town house on a site 52 ft wide with a "petite salle à manger" marked. Illustrated in Pierre Le Muet, Augmentations de nouveaux bastimens faits en France *(Paris: François Langlois, 1647), 2. Middleton Collection.*

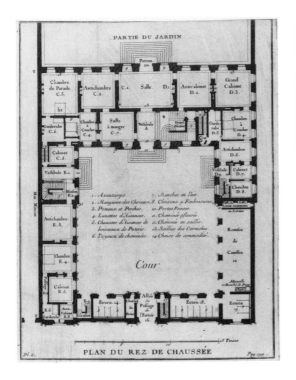

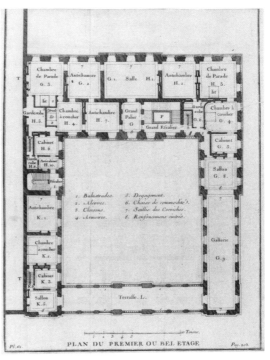

8.   Ground-floor plan of a town house. Illustrated in Augustin-Charles Daviler,
Cours d'architecture *(Paris: Jean Mariette, 1738), 199, pl. 61.*
Santa Monica, The Getty Center for the History of Art and the Humanities.
9.   First-floor plan of a town house. Illustrated in Augustin-Charles Daviler,
Cours d'architecture *(Paris: Jean Mariette, 1738), 203, pl. 62.*
Santa Monica, The Getty Center for the History of Art and the Humanities.

few years later, in 1648, by François Mansart for the Hôtel de Jars, which served thereafter as the model; but though the double range of rooms allowed for far more flexibility of planning than the single range, the latter continued to be used until well into the eighteenth century.

Daviler's *hôtel* is composed, as might be expected, of apartments on both the ground and the first floors—the state apartment, or a*ppartement de parade,* being set on the first floor, still following the Italian usage, which derives from the imperial palaces of antiquity. The dining room, or *salle à manger*, is set off the entrance vestibule, separated from the main *enfilades*. Daviler offered much detailed advice as to the size and finish of the various rooms and technical information of much specificity, indicating that the science of planning was by then an established affair.

When Sebastien Leblond issued a second edition of Daviler's treatise in 1710, however, he thought it necessary to add yet another chapter, "De la nouvelle maniere de distribuer les plans" ("On the new manner of planning") to explain more fully the latest refinements. For in Louis XIV's declining years, a society enriched as a result of his endless campaigns and increasingly independent had established itself in Paris, rather than on the fringe of the court of Versailles, and was there exploring the delights of privacy and intimacy in architecture with an increasing degree of sophistication. Pierre Cailleteau, known as Lassurance, assistant to the king's architect, Jules Hardouin-Mansart, had built a series of *hôtels* that had initiated the new trend, starting with the Hôtel Rothelin in 1700 (figs. 10, 11). Yet, as Leblond's text reveals, the principles of planning had not much changed. The general and even the detailed arrangement of the *hôtel* remained much as described by Daviler. The kitchen and service rooms were now no longer in the basement of the *corps de logis* but in the service wings flanking the entrance court. And the state reception rooms were now on the ground floor, opening directly onto the garden. Leblond's real interest, however, is directed rather to the provision of service stairs and the introduction of numerous small rooms for the storage of clothes or commodes (*chaises percées*) or, preferably, the latest flushing toilets (fig. 12).

This indicates the pattern of change in the planning of the French *hôtel* (and also the French *château*, for they were ordered on the same principles) during the first half of the eighteenth century. These changes were described at length and acclaimed by a succession of theorists—by Jean Courtonne in 1725, by Gilles Tiercelet in 1728, by Jacques-François Blondel in 1737 (and later in 1752 and in 1771), by Charles-Etienne Briseux in 1743, and, as we have seen, by Germain Boffrand in 1745. They confidently asserted that the new art of planning was the greatest of French contributions to architecture; and even that proud Scot Robert Adam recognized the primacy of the French in this respect in his *Works in Architecture*, 1773 onward. Their

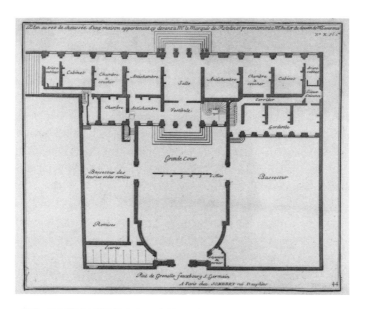

10. *Ground-floor plan of the Hôtel Rothelin, rue de Grenelle, Paris,
designed by Lassurance and erected circa 1700. Illustrated in Jacques-François
Blondel,* Architecture françoise *(Paris: Charles-Antoine Jombert, 1752),
2: pl. 44 (facing p. 232). Santa Monica, The Getty Center for the History
of Art and the Humanities.*

11. *Entrance elevation of the Hôtel Rothelin, rue de Grenelle, Paris,
designed by Lassurance and erected circa 1700. Illustrated in Jacques-François
Blondel,* Architecture françoise *(Paris: Charles-Antoine Jombert, 1752),
2: pl. 45 (following p. 232). Santa Monica, The Getty Center for the History
of Art and the Humanities.*

great achievement was to perfect the apartment as a sequence of spaces of ever-increasing comfort and intimacy, culminating in a warren of small service rooms with bathrooms and toilets supplied with hot and cold water and something of a drainage system. The whole could now be serviced with the utmost discretion.

Even in the grandest of seventeenth-century mansions, rooms had been used indiscriminately by many members of a family and by passing servants. There was an easy promiscuity. But in the eighteenth century, with the opening up of the realm of feeling and especially individual sentiment, privacy took on a new value. Rooms were more often set aside for personal use, which meant, of course, that intimate relationships could be more successfully explored. Masters were increasingly separated from servants. Attitudes toward servants changed noticeably in these years; even personal servants were treated more often as simple employees, less and less as members of an extended family or household.

Not only were service stairs introduced to provide separate access to rooms but whole networks of corridors as well. These had never been part of the planning arrangements on the main floors. The difficulties encountered by architects in integrating these service spaces and corridors into their plans are still in evidence in some of Jacques-François Blondel's designs in *De la distribution des maisons de plaisance* (On the planning of country houses), 1737, and even more so in Charles-Etienne Briseux's *L'art de bâtir des maisons de campagne* (The art of building country houses), 1743 (fig. 13), where they emerge as the crudest of manipulations. Their coherent assimilation was rendered even more difficult by the fact that the new rationalism and the growing concern for expression—clearly articulated by both Jean Courtonne and Blondel—dictated that the interior form of a building should be closely related to its external form. There was to be a neat fit. The outside must not only provide a clear indication of the inside arrangement but must also serve to establish the character of the whole, which was to be sustained throughout a building.

These adjustments in patterns of living and in attitudes led to an increasing specialization in the use of rooms; more were added and the purpose of each determined from the start so that the decor and finishes could more fittingly reflect character and use. Rational criteria, however, were sometimes at odds with one another. The adjustment of rooms to altogether appropriate sizes and the introduction of a wide variety of shapes—hexagons, circles, and ovals (the proliferation of which both Courtonne and Blondel thought somewhat vulgar)—meant that the walls of an apartment on one level might not correspond to those on another level. This led to much manipulation of structure, often rendering the whole quite unstable—as Pierre Patte balefully remarked in *Monuments érigés à la gloire de Louis XV* (Monuments erected to the glory of Louis XV), 1765—and thus served as a curb to the sheer virtuosity

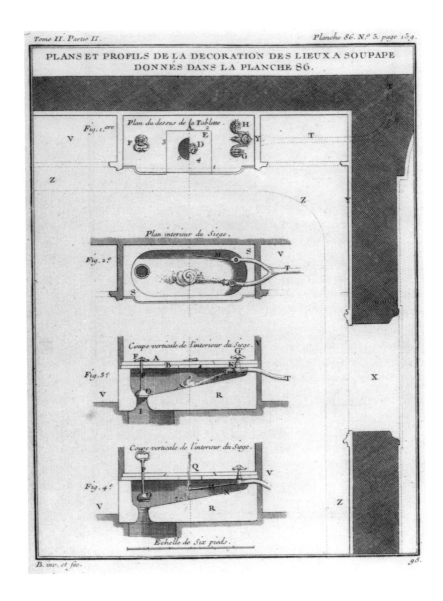

12. *Plans and sections illustrating a flushing toilet. Illustrated in Jacques-François Blondel,* De la distribution des maisons de plaisance *(Paris: Charles-Antoine Jombert: 1738), 2: 139, pl. 86, no. 3. Santa Monica, The Getty Center for the History of Art and the Humanities.*

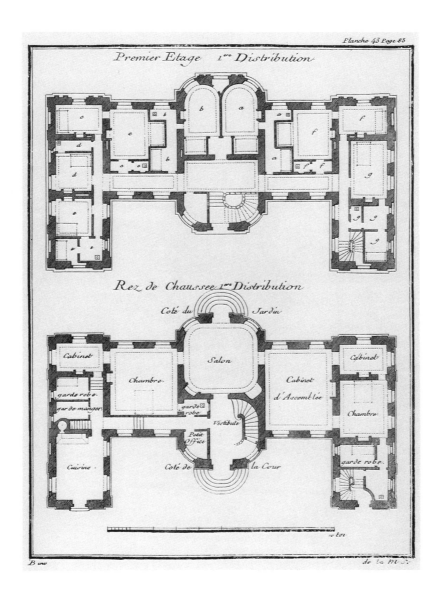

13. *Ground- and first-floor plan of a country house. Illustrated in Charles-Etienne Briseux,* L'art de bâtir des maisons de campagne *(Paris: J. B. Gibert, 1761), 1: 83, pl. 43. Boston, Courtesy of the Trustees of the Boston Public Library.*

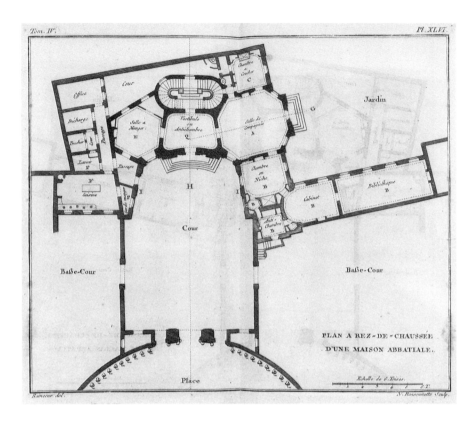

*14.   Ground-floor plan of the abbot's house at Villers-Cotterêts, designed by
Jacques-François Blondel in 1765, showing how symmetries are maintained in
individual rooms and even in their relationship, despite the vagaries of site
conditions. Illustrated in Jacques-François Blondel,* Cours d'architecture
*(Paris: La Veuve Desaint, 1773), 4: pl. 46. Santa Monica, The Getty Center
for the History of Art and the Humanities.*

of Rococo planning. Similarly, the requirements of internal planning, however skill-fully they might be resolved, were not always allowed to determine the external forms of buildings. Both Daviler and Blondel were in no doubt that in the noblest of *hôtels* the magnificence and symmetry of the architecture as presented to the world was of far greater importance than ease of circulation or comfort. These might be sacrificed without qualm when rank and decorum decreed.

Symmetry was of overriding import in establishing the image of the French *hôtel*, and once again, this might often be achieved only through the neglect of comfort or even common sense. When only one service wing flanked an entrance court, the elevation of the *corps de logis* might not lie on the same axis as the garden front, a displacement that was readily enough masked by avoiding a cross axis in the plan. This expedient accorded with the wish to enter each apartment at its extremity, through the first room of the *enfilade* — once again to lay emphasis on the extent of architectural magnificence opened up to the visitor. These *enfilades* were ranged, al-most invariably, through doors set alongside the garden front, which meant that if an appearance of symmetry was to be maintained within rooms, false doors or equiva-lent elements must be provided at the rear of the rooms. The chimneypiece, with a looking glass over, had always to be placed centrally in a wall — usually in the wall facing the door of the *enfilade* so that it should be seen in all its splendor on first entry — and this was balanced on the opposite side of the room with an equivalent projecting console with its looking glass over. Courtonne and Blondel, once again, though they liked reflections, were chary of any too lavish use of the looking glass. The main items of furniture, as one might expect, had to be symmetrically disposed, the bed in particular. Blondel was of the opinion that a bed might be set in a corner position only in a bourgeois establishment.

This deeply felt need for an appearance of symmetry was a spur to the most extraordinarily ingenious feats of planning. Architects learned to dispose even the most awkwardly shaped sites so that the buildings upon them and the rooms within presented an air of the finest order and regularity. Such contrivance, like the provision of false doors, was regarded as no more than a proper expression of ra-tionalist ideals. For though the extreme refinement of *hôtel* design in the early years of the eighteenth century is clearly a reflection of the expansion of individual senti-ment, an essential part of the new empiricist grasp of the world, it is equally an out-come of that earlier affirmation of the rule of reason, an expression of those Carte-sian concerns for sound practice and utility (figs. 14, 15).

This triumph was to be given a further twist of grace in the second half of the century. A succession of architects had learned to look at the architecture of classical antiquity anew and, far from becoming mere imitators of its forms, had ab-

sorbed its lessons with a marked perception and expanded them in fashioning an architecture of a new sharpness and precision of geometry, which was at the same time
responsive to the fullest range of human feelings. Julien-David Leroy, for example,
the first architect to provide a convincing record of the buildings of classical Greece
in his magnificent folio *Les ruines des plus beaux monuments de la Grèce* (The ruins of the
finest monuments of Greece), 1758, was sufficiently dispassionate in his appreciation
of the actual forms and details of those newly revealed monuments to suggest six
years later in his short *Histoire de la disposition et des formes différentes que les chrétiens ont
données à leurs temples* (History of the arrangement and different forms given to their
churches by Christians) that the sensations experienced when walking through or
within even the noblest classical portico might be aroused equally successfully by an
avenue of trees.

This gives a clue to the aesthetics explored soon after by Le Camus de
Mézières. His seminal ideas can be traced to Leroy. Leroy's stance is that of a lover of
nature, a lover perhaps of formal gardens—though this is not certain. For that aesthetics based on a recourse to feeling and individual experience, which Roger de Piles
had revealed, gave a new value at first to landscape painting and then to nature itself,
not so much in its unrefined state as in the contrived form of the landscape garden. It
was the cultivation of the picturesque vision that enabled Leroy and, later, Le Camus
de Mézières to see architecture in a new way. But the process of change was slow, for
in France symmetry was a quality of almost divine import, and it was not readily to be
abandoned. A taste for the overgrown formal garden was cultivated in the years of the
régence and after, no doubt influenced by the Dutch and Flemish landscape paintings
that were then being collected by the more discerning connoisseurs. This was another
response to de Piles. For the pleasure indulged in these gardens was of the painterly
kind. They were seen in picturesque terms, as scenes from the Ruisdaels, Philips
Wouwermans, or Jean-Antoine Watteau.

Another French painter who responded to the wanton neglect of the
formal garden in these years was Jean-Baptiste Oudry, who led outings on Sundays
and public holidays to the Prince de Guise's overgrown park at Arceuil, just south
of Paris, where painters such as Charles-Joseph Natoire, François Boucher, André
Portail, Jean-Georges Wille, and others sketched from nature. One of this group
was Claude-Henri Watelet, a rich amateur, who is usually credited with the making of
the first picturesque garden in France at Moulin-Joli, an estate consisting of an island and the banks of the Seine near Bezons, to the west of Paris. He purchased the
site around 1755 and slowly transformed it into a country retreat, aided by Boucher
and others. The layout of the paths on the island was, perhaps not surprisingly, geometric, though the effect was assiduously wild and unkempt. The fashion for gardens

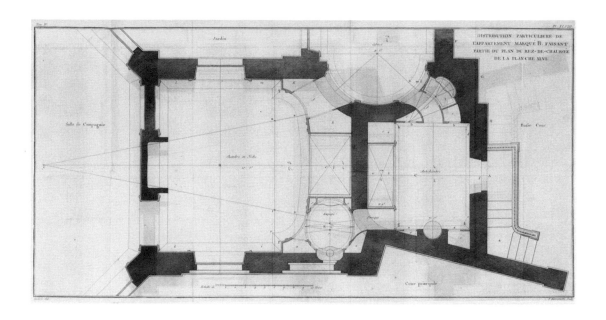

*15. Detail plan of the bedroom and related rooms in the abbot's house at Villers-
Cotterêts, designed by Jacques-François Blondel in 1765, illustrating the
complexity and finesse of geometrical composition. Illustrated in Jacques-Francois
Blondel,* Cours d'architecture *(Paris: La Veuve Desaint, 1773), 4: pl. 48.
Santa Monica, The Getty Center for the History of Art and the Humanities.*

of a sustained picturesque composition, modeled on English examples, did not take
hold in France until about 1770, and then tentatively and awkwardly. It was at about
this time that Watelet wrote his *Essai sur les jardins* (Essay on gardens), 1774, intended
as the first part of a more general study of taste. This was the first French work on the
aims and methods of picturesque gardening. Le Camus de Mézières was to dedicate
his *Le génie de l'architecture* to Watelet and to refer more than once to his example.

But Watelet did not establish the theory of the picturesque in France.
The prime work on this theme, Thomas Whateley's *Observations on Modern Gardening*,
was published in England in 1770 and was translated almost at once into French by
Montesquieu's protégé François de Paule Latapie and issued in Paris the following
year. Whateley used the term *picturesque* often enough and laid down the rules for the
making of gardens in what we still call the picturesque style, but he was determined to
free landscape design from the painterly vision. He considered landscape design, as
an art form, superior to painting. He made no reference to the works of any painter,
and he was careful to note that the word *picturesque* should be used only to describe
natural elements.

For Whateley the configuration of a landscape was essential in establishing the style of a garden. The natural form must provide the character. And this must
be strengthened and extended through design, largely through a stress on line. Landscapes, he remarked, were of three basic kinds: concave, convex, and flat (hinting at a
knowledge of Boffrand's text on character); and these must be reinforced by the manipulation of the four basic elements of landscape design, the ground itself, trees and
shrubs, water, and rocks. Buildings might also be considered as compositional elements, but they were of minor interest. The prime natural elements must be used to
set the mood or sequence of moods; thus, still water might be used to evoke melancholy, bubbling springs to stir gaiety. But line and silhouette and the free play of
forms in all their varieties were the keys to success. Whateley offers all manner of
rules and practical hints as to the way particular characters might be achieved, but he
was sufficiently sanguine to remark that what mattered in the end was the effect and
that when marvelous effects were achieved, the rules might be set at naught.

Watelet, no doubt following Whateley, stressed the difference between
painting and landscape design, and once again, he allowed that the term *picturesque*
might be applied to a landscape composed with natural elements alone. The painter,
moreover, was to be preferred to the architect as a designer of the landscape (the architect having a fatal tendency to turn streams into canals); but best of all, perhaps,
was the sculptor, for the essential enjoyment of a landscape arose from the constantly
changing experiences enjoyed as one moved through it. A painting, however skillful,
was flat; and it offered a single image. A landscape garden provided a sequence of

varied tableaux—akin, in this, to the theater—though the movement through these varying scenes was enhanced even more in the open by the external movements of nature—by the wind and the clouds, by water, and by birds, flying and singing.

Like Whateley, Watelet stressed the use of natural elements in making a garden and indicated how a whole range of tempers and moods might be roused through their composition, ranging from the noble and sublime, through the terrible or voluptuous, to the rustic and pleasant. But the key to the composition of the garden, for Watelet, lay in the handling of changes of level. And it is clear that he thought more fully than Whateley in terms of three dimensions. Watelet compared the architect's ability to compose a moving sequence of forms and shadows, through the use of columns, with the landscape gardener's far wider range of possibilities through the rise and fall of the ground, the contrivance of openings and closings.

Watelet described gardens and parks of several different kinds, but he liked best the *ferme ornée*, or model farm. It was, he thought, the simplest and most rooted in practical concerns. But man, as he stressed, was not alone a creature of practical needs; he was also a creature of feeling, a sentient being. And it was the heightened sensual pleasures of both the body and mind as well as the soul that must be stirred and satisfied by the well-composed landscape. Sensuality, he noted, was "a delicate sentiment that requires a most perfect relation between external objects, the feelings, and the state of the soul."[10] The ideal garden was thus a realm of both utilitarian satisfaction and spiritual illumination. It must respond also to one's whole sense of civility and society. At the end of his essay he appended two descriptions. The first was that of the rural retreat of a studious Chinaman; the second, in the form of a letter to a friend, that of the cultivated Frenchman. Both are designed to practical ends but also for the fullest delectation of their owners and their owners' friends. Each is a consummate creation. They are compared, inevitably; but though the Chinese garden is judged to be perfect, it is not to be imitated in France, for the French rustic garden is the proper background for the cultivation of French sensibilities. The lesson is clear: styles, like civilizations, should not be borrowed or mixed.

Other books on the art of the landscape garden were published in France in these years—Nicolas Duchesne's *Traité de la formation des jardins* (Treatise on the making of gardens), 1775, Jean-Marie Morel's *Théorie des jardins* (Theory of gardens), 1776, the Marquis René de Girardin's *De la composition des paysages*, 1777 (translated into English as *An Essay on Landscape* in 1783)—and these were no doubt known to Le Camus de Mézières, though he makes no mention of them. Morel's text, however, requires consideration, for in it the lessons of landscape design that Le Camus de Mézières was to take up for architectural composition are more sharply defined and more forcefully expressed than in any other publication, including that of Watelet, to which Le Camus paid homage. There is in Morel's work a marked shift to a realm of pure sensation.

Morel too thought landscape design more affective an art than painting. He aimed to instate it as one of the liberal arts. Landscape designers, he felt, should never emulate a painted scene, for a painting was static and fixed. Even in the theater a scene could have only a restricted range of transformations, and Morel mentioned, in particular, the limitation of even Jean-Nicolas Servandoni's astonishing illusions in the Salle de Spectacles at the Tuileries. In contrast, a landscape offered a thrust of sensations in constant flux. Each minute of the day, each step on a path brought a change. Some of the variations of nature, the climate, the weather, the effects of the seasons or the times of the day, were beyond man's control, but their range and their effects were known and could be taken into account. Indeed, the good designer must consider the changing effects of the seasons, the sun, the moon and the stars, the clouds and the mists, the colors and scents of plants and trees. For the aim was the enhancement of nature, the raising of it to an ideal form. Nature was not to be imitated, for that was a puerile approach to design (even Laugier's primitive hut, Morel noted, was not to be regarded as an imitation of nature, rather as a product of reason).

The elements of design were, as in Whateley, clearly defined. Morel offers a chapter on each of the four seasons and one on each of the elements of composition—the earth, water, trees and plants, and rocks. Even rocks, unless natural, were to be eschewed. Buildings were admissible only for utilitarian purposes. There were to be no stylistic architectural conceits. One must compose with nature. Gardening, unlike architecture, was to be conditioned henceforth by the forms of nature and by feeling. Gardens that extended the symmetries and geometries of architecture were permissible only within the city.

Morel's was a rigorous approach, but his methods of design were not that different from those of his contemporaries. He considered that the nature of the site should determine the character developed for it and that character should remain intact however many minor genres were explored. He laid emphasis on line and silhouette and, above all, on movement. To enjoy a garden one must move through it. He was far more explicit, however, when it came to the means of stirring sensations. In one evocative passage he describes the way in which the same elements—trees—can serve to conjure up altogether different sensations. In the deep shade of a forest of ancient oaks thoughts of a heavy sublime are roused, perhaps even something of a religious fervor; whereas, the dappled shadows of a copse of slender trees make for a lively and charming retreat. Morel describes the effects of the sounds, the textures, and the colors, but form and light are the key to the sensations aroused. The first cluster of trees is heavy and enclosed, the light, somber and mysterious ("*sombre et mysté-rieux*");[11] the second is open and spindly, the effect of the light, sharper ("*plus pi-quans*").[12] But perhaps even more various an element with which to conjure up moods was water. Morel provides a litany of conditions of water—still and moving, limpid and turbulent, bubbling and frothing—and notes not only its movements but their sounds. It is, to him, the life force of the landscape. "Water," he writes, "is to the land-scape as the soul is to the body."[13] A sentiment already expressed by Roger de Piles, if only in connection with landscape painting.

The nature of man's response to objects, whether static or moving, the sensations aroused thereby, and the manner in which they might be controlled and manipulated were of the utmost fascination to Morel; but though he touched on the matter in his chapter on the *genres* (characters), he hesitated even to attempt a theory or indicate rules that might relate to it. The matter, he said, partook of philosophy, a philosophy that should sound the depths of metaphysics ("*qui sonde les profondeurs de la métaphysique*").[14] The metaphysics of sensation was, nonetheless, the underlying theme of his book.

By the time Morel wrote his book, the most rigorous text of sensationalist philosophy in France had long been published, the Abbé Etienne Bonnot de Condillac's *Traité des sensations* (Treatise on sensations), 1754. Six years earlier Julien Offray de La Met-trie had published *L'homme machine* (translated into English as *Man a Machine* in 1750) in which he maintained that man was dependent on physical conditions controlled by his senses, and Diderot too had explored the relationship between man's ideas and his individual senses in his *Lettres sur les aveugles*, 1749 (translated into English as *An Essay on Blindness* circa 1750). Condillac, however, went further. What he aimed to prove was that all human understanding, all refinements of emotion and intellect are depen-dent on the five senses alone. Man was born with no innate ideas, no knowledge, no spiritual faculty even. The device Condillac conceived to explain this notion was al-together fantastical: an inert statue, perhaps inspired by that of Pygmalion, in which the senses begin to function one by one. The statue's responses to the sensations it receives are determined by nothing more than the principle of pleasure or pain. He begins his analysis with the sense of smell. A rose is presented to the statue, then a carnation, a jasmine, and a violet. An unpleasant smelling object is proffered next, and the statue learns to distinguish the agreeable from the disagreeable. Comparative abilities are thus enlarged, and memory develops. Intellect, based on sensation, is dis-tinguished from feeling, which is a function of the senses. The statue learns in time to register a whole range of emotions and to reflect on them; it comes to know desire, love and hate, hope and fear; it is able even to extend its imagination and also to dream. All this, and more, is the outcome of activating nothing other than the sense of smell.

The range of experiences opened up by the sense of hearing is next explored (these experiences do not follow the earlier pattern as closely as Condillac would wish—the harmonies of sound arousing emotions unparalleled by those of smell). Smell and hearing are then united. Taste is activated next, then sight, first alone, when no more than color and light can be recorded by the eye, and later in relation to the other senses. Finally, the sense of touch is induced, and for the first time the statue becomes aware of a realm outside itself; all experience up to this point has illuminated no more than the realm of the self. The statue deciphers its own form. Through the use of its fingers, it learns to count and to extend its memory. It learns to explore external objects and to give them shape. A sphere is distinguished from a cube. Such objects are set in relation to each other, and slowly, through an understanding of the effects of light and shade, relative distances are judged. With movement the statue discovers space (a notion based on the coexistence of ideas). The awareness of memory and desire in sequence allow it to comprehend time (a notion based on the succession of ideas). It begins to understand such abstract concepts as past and future, immensity and eternity (though these last, of course, are no more than illusions of the imagination). There is a climactic moment when the animate statue responds with all its senses to the wonders of nature, the variety and brightness of colors, the scents of flowers, the song and flight of the birds, the murmuring and sparkle of water. The figure comprehends itself finally as a sentient, intelligent being, separate from, but partaking wholly of, a world outside itself.

The conceit of the statue, however contrived, was an imaginative tour de force, one that stirred a fashionable interest in Condillac's notions, which were at once widely discussed. He had, in fact, explored them even earlier and at greater length, though far less sharply, in the first of his published books, the *Essai sur l'origine des connoissances humaines*, 1746 (translated into English as *An Essay on the Origin of Human Knowledge* in 1756). There, he made clear his opposition to Cartesian rationalism—not that his view of the universe was any less rational than that of Descartes. Indeed, he wished to imbue philosophy and all language with the precision of mathematics. But Descartes's ideal was an abstract system of philosophy independent, as far as may be, from physical existence. Condillac began rather with the empirical philosophy of John Locke. He assumed though that there was a fundamental system of order behind the observable phenomena of the world and that this order might be grasped in time because it was congenial to reason. Understanding must begin with the study of origins, with the idea of self that emerges from the realm of sensation.

All knowledge, all ideas are acquired through the senses.

In the *Essai*, Condillac begins by asserting that our very first sensations—light and color, pain and pleasure, movement and repose—are in fact our very first thoughts. Reflecting on these, one learns to perceive and to imagine. Slowly, through the analysis of sensations and the stirrings of the soul, knowledge and ideas emerge. The argument, in general terms, is much the same as in the *Traité des sensations*, though it is notable that the soul is more often referred to in the *Essai* than in the later work. More important, and it is related, is the total rejection in the *Traité* of any notion that some knowledge, some ideas might be acquired other than through the senses. Locke had allowed some spiritual faculty other than that stimulated in response to the physical environment. Notable also is the emphasis in the *Traité* on the role of desire in determining the nature of the will. Need, not logic, forms the basis of reason. The *Essai* was concerned rather with understanding.

A real extension of knowledge, Condillac argues in the *Essai*, is possible only with the discovery of a means of communicating information and ideas and recording them. The origins of language are explored at great length, from the first expression of feelings with cries, grunts, and gestures to the evolution of language and the creation of a system of signs to represent emotions and objects. All community, all humanity, almost, relates directly to language. Art arises from language, and here Condillac makes the first of his many references to the Abbé Dubos's *Réflexions critiques sur la poésie et sur la peinture*. From the crudest of gestures the dance emerges, from a succession of cries and grunts comes music, from the rhythms of both arises the communal ritual and the spectacle. Spectacle is vital to the evolution of the other arts. Poetry springs from music, and prose evolves in time as a more prosaic and practical variant. When prose separates from poetry, eloquence, which lies midway between them, evolves. The need to record experience and knowledge—initially for the somewhat humdrum, practical purpose of noting events, rules, and regulations—leads to the development of a system of signs and thus to hieroglyphs and painting. (Condillac had discovered William Warburton's famous work on the subject, *Divine Legation of Moses Demonstrated*, 1737–1741, by the time he wrote this passage, no doubt in Léonard de Malpeine's translation of the section on language, *Essai sur les hiéroglyphes des Egyptiens* [An essay on the hieroglyphics of the Egyptians], 1744.)

Architecture is mentioned only in passing in the *Essai*.[15] Condillac evinced no more interest in it than Dubos. Nor does Condillac include gardening amongst the arts. Though in dealing with the essential need for order, so satisfying to the soul, Condillac concedes that disorder too can please, in particular when in a state of reverie the senses and the intellect are both responsive to haphazard encounters and stimuli. It is here that he refers to the almost irrational delight that might be experienced on occasion in the countryside, as opposed to a garden, and it is clear that he is thinking of a garden of the formal kind.[16] Elsewhere, in dealing with man's capacity—indeed need—to think by association, he conjures up a vision of the countryside with fields and rocks, woods and streams, murmurs and silences, light and shade, the experience of which stirs those emotions and ideas already linked through poetry to the concepts of pastoral bliss—love and constancy, faithfulness and purity. A glimpse alone of the natural objects can stir the deepest of feelings.[17]

But a recognition of the capacity of external phenomena to stir sensations is not to imply that the same sensations or the same associations will be aroused on all occasions by a particular object. Condillac issues a clear warning. Sensations are not intrinsic to objects; an object cannot be relied upon to produce the same emotional response in each of us, nor indeed even in ourselves on different occasions.[18]

Le Camus de Mézières took no heed of this warning. The premise of *Le génie de l'architecture* is that particular sensations are aroused by particular forms and that these can be manipulated and arranged to specific effect—that there is indeed a science of sensations. Le Camus makes no mention of Condillac or of either of his books. It is evident though that he was spurred by Condillac's ideas and, if one is to judge by his vocabulary and range of references, by the *Essai sur l'origine des connoissances humaines* rather than the *Traité des sensations*. The theory that Le Camus advances as to the way the shapes and forms of architecture under different conditions of lighting and shade can stir different sensations and moods is, however, borrowed from the theories of landscape gardeners—and borrowed from Morel, it would seem, more directly than from Watelet, whom Le Camus acknowledges. All three men were in thrall to sensationalist philosophers.

The delectations of architecture, one should note, had been described often enough in literature, but the seductive power of an architectural ensemble was first given full measure in a novella written during the same years in which Condillac, La Mettrie, and Diderot were exploring the relationship between man's ideas and his senses. Jean-François de Bastide's *La petite maison* (The little house) was first published, it has been claimed, in 1753 in the *Journal économique*, though it is not in evidence in that journal. It appeared, however, in 1758 in the *Nouveau spectateur*, and in its final form in 1763 in the *Contes de M. de Bastide* (Stories of M. de Bastide). Bastide was the author of a flurry of lightweight theatrical pieces and stories (disdained incidentally by Diderot). He is not usually associated with architectural theory, though he was to finish off and to publish Jacques-François Blondel's *Les amours rivaux; ou, L'homme du monde éclairé par les arts* (The rival loves; or, The man of the world enlightened by the arts) in 1774—the year of Blondel's death—in which architecture, along with the fine arts, is again used as a means of insinuation.

Bastide offers no theory of architecture as such in *La petite maison*. He tells a story of Mélite, induced to visit the exquisite country abode of the Marquis de Trémicour. It is clear, nonetheless, that Bastide's descriptions of the enchanting rooms and the fragrant formal garden and their overwhelming effect on the senses, and ultimately the mind, of Mélite served as yet another spur to the ideas of Le Camus de Mézières. Mélite is seduced, eventually, more by the wonders of the two boudoirs than by the vows of Trémicour himself. The first of these is lined with mirrors, some of which are screened with gauze; it is decorated to represent a small forest clearing with musicians secreted behind the panels. The second boudoir, in which she finally gives way, is all Chinese lacquer, embroidered Indian stuffs, Japanese porcelains, and crystals. The seduction is, in short, the triumph of architecture over the will.

The language of seduction, which Bastide associates with architecture—words such as desire (*désir*) and possession (*jouissance*), together with its other variants—is taken up also by Le Camus but not by Le Camus alone. These terms appear also in the writings of landscape theorists, even the high-minded Morel.

Enough, I would think, has been written by way of an introduction to Le Camus's text. What I have aimed to sketch is the process of change from the middle of the seventeenth century, when an established classical aesthetic was dominant, to the introduction of a Cartesian structure of thought that discredited the notion of the established ideal and, through dispassionate rational analysis, recognized value in new criteria of artistic expression, such as utility. This reappraisal resulted also in the recognition of value in the artistic expression of other civilizations, other societies. It, in turn, gave way to an empirical aesthetics, based not on an abstract philosophical ideal but on an investigation of the origins of knowledge and thought in the realm of physical sensation. Sentiment and feeling came thus to condition aesthetic responses as never before.

Each of these phases is reflected in Le Camus's work. In tracing this development, I have tried, as far as possible, to restrict my references to those mentioned by Le Camus himself—thus the names of Perrault, Ouvrard, Le Brun, Servandoni, and Watelet all appear in his text. The important exceptions are de Piles, Condillac, and Morel. But there can be little doubt that he was familiar with their ideas, even if only at second hand. Watelet, for instance, though he might make no reference to de Piles in his *Essai sur les jardins*, was himself clearly well versed in his thought, as becomes quite evident in his *Dictionnaire des arts de peinture, sculpture et grav-*

ure (Dictionary of the arts of painting, sculpture, and engraving), completed and published posthumously by P. C. Levesque in 1792. Other examples, other references and turns of phrase shared by some of the forerunners to Le Camus who have been considered here will at once be recognized by the reader. I have offered no summary or analysis of Le Camus's text—that has been done by Rémy Saisselin[19]—nor, other than in a handful of requisite notes following the translation, have I made explicit the connections between Le Camus's writings and those of his contemporaries. I have assumed that Le Camus's text will be read and that readers will respond to it, each in his own way, afresh.

Attention must, nonetheless, be drawn to certain aspects of Le Camus's thought, lest they be underestimated or overlooked. He greatly enlarged architectural understanding. He was concerned for almost the first time in an architectural treatise with movement through a sequence of spaces. One might note that though he took it for granted that the apartment was the basic planning unit for the *hôtel*, he laid no great emphasis on it. He was concerned, rather, with its integration into the total organization. The character prescribed for the exterior architecture should inform the entire interior, down to the smallest part. This was not to suggest that each part should be equally richly decorated but that it should be perfectly appropriate in its own way to its use and to the rank and status of the owner and that the correct decorum should reign throughout. It is tempting to believe that he thought thus in terms of de Piles's *tout ensemble*. Certainly, he went further in this respect than Blondel, whose prime concern was the expression of rank and station.

Another particular feature of Le Camus's thinking that should be noted— and it relates directly to the notion of a *tout ensemble*—is the way in which he sought to stimulate the entire range of the senses through architecture. He is concerned with form and space, light and shade, color and touch. He draws attention more than once to the sensual qualities of materials. He invokes even the sense of smell. He introduces scented shrubs and flowers into his boudoir and bathroom and also into the dining room. These become almost integral to the architecture. The relation to the picturesque vision is made overt. The bathroom of the mistress of the house takes on the aspect of an elaborate grotto, worthy almost of Bernard Palissy or Salomon de Caux. The boudoir, which takes off from Bastide, is decked not only with flowers but with songbirds. And the flowers, whether potted or cut, are freely and informally arranged. Symmetry is discounted here. The harmony Le Camus aimed at is suggested by his reference to Père Louis-Bertrand Castel's famous experimental color organ, in which light and sound effects were to be coordinated. Le Camus also looked back with nostalgia to an even deeper harmony between proportional systems and musical intervals and thus to the notion of a universal harmony that was thought once to pertain. He refers, of course, to the work of Ouvrard and to Perrault's rude rejection of it. Not that Le Camus was the first to attempt to reinstate this article of classical faith. Charles-Etienne Briseux had taken issue with Perrault on the subject in his *Traité du beau essentiel dans les arts* (A treatise on essential beauty in the arts), 1752, and in Rome Antoine Derizet, an architect from Lyons who taught at the Accademia di San Luca from 1728 onward, had tried to elaborate on Ouvrard's ideas in a text of his own. Derizet's work was not to be published, although Bernardo Vittone, who had studied at the Accademia, took up some of his notions. Not until the nineteenth century, once again, when Charles Garnier planned the Paris Opéra, was an architecture so rich and sensuously responsive to be described in a text.

What remains is to offer an outline of Nicolas Le Camus de Mézières's life and activity. Surprisingly little is known. He was born in Paris on 26 May 1721 and is sometimes thought to have died in 1789, though he was still alive in March 1793 when he was forced to sell a property he owned on the quai de Tournelle in Paris. His wife died on 23 June 1809. Until quite recently his career was confused with that of Louis-Denis Le Camus, designer of that short-lived pleasure garden, the Colisée, off the Champs-Elysées, and architect to the Prince de Condé, for whose estate on the Loire he laid out picturesque gardens. Louis-Denis is not known to have been connected with Nicolas. Nicolas had two brothers, Antoine, a doctor, and Louis-Florent, a dealer in iron.

Nicolas Le Camus de Mézières's name appears in print for the first time in 1751, accompanied by the title *"architecte expert bourgeois,"* in the *Almanach Royal* (that is, essentially, a technical expert on architectural matters, able to give advice in courts of law and in other disputes). This status was above that of a mere technician. Antoine-Chrysostome Quatremère de Quincy recognized three classes of architects in his dictionary of architecture contained in the *Encyclopédie méthodique* (Methodical encyclopedia): first, the members of the Académie Royale d'Architecture; second, *"architectes experts bourgeois"*; and third, those that exercised the art as a liberal profession.[20] Not until 1762, however, when he was charged with renewing some timbers at the Ecole Militaire, is there any evidence of Le Camus offering technical advice. He published a *Dissertation de la compagnie des architectes-experts des bâtimens à Paris . . . sur la théorie et la pratique des gros bois de charpente* (Dissertation of the company of expert architects of buildings of Paris . . . on the theory and practice of large timber construction) together with F. A. Babuty-Desgodetz in 1763, possibly a revision of an earlier work. By that time, he had already embarked on the design of the one work of

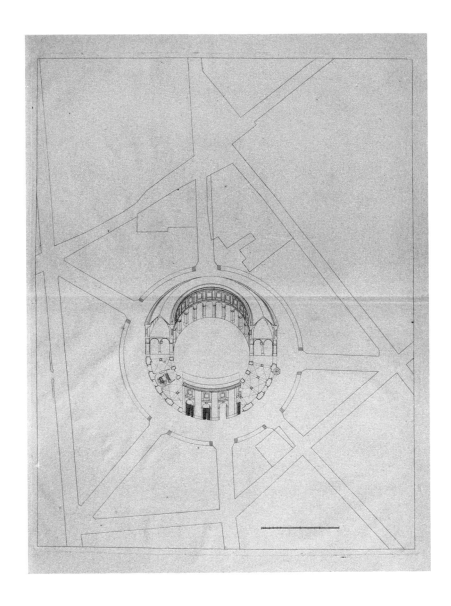

16. *Cutaway diagram of the Halle au Blé. Illustrated in Nicolas Le Camus
de Mézières,* Recueil des différens plans et dessins, concernant la nouvelle
Halle aux grains *(pl. 1 in the ideal copy). Middleton Collection.*

architecture for which he was to become famous, the great Halle au Blé of Paris, erected between 1763 and 1767.

An altogether extraordinary circular building, enclosing an open circular court, the Halle formed the centerpiece of an area of speculative development for some of which Le Camus was responsible (figs. 16, 17). This development was slow to take off, and the Halle could not be used until the building operations were completed two years later. It then became the wonder of Paris, praised as the equivalent, almost, of the Roman Colosseum. Le Camus attempted to record this design in a large folio publication, *Recueil des différens plans et dessins, concernant la nouvelle Halle auz grains, située au lieu et place de l'ancien Hôtel de Soissons* (Collection of various plans and drawings of the new corn exchange situated on the site of the former Hôtel de Soissons). Though copies may have been circulated as early as 1769, it was never to be completed. No text seems to have been intended. Between 1782 and 1783 the circular court was covered over by the architects J.-G. Legrand and J. Molinos with another spectacular structure, a dome of timber construction. The building became then, in popular esteem, the Pantheon of modern Rome (the dome was thirty-nine meters in diameter, almost as large as that of the Pantheon). The timber dome was consumed by fire in 1802, and between 1808 and 1813 it was replaced by the architect F.-J. Belanger with yet another unprecedented structure, a dome of cast iron. This, in turn, together with most of Le Camus's building, was replaced and rebuilt in 1889 as the Bourse de Commerce. The political and social context, together with a detailed history of the building, has been recounted recently, in exemplary fashion, in Mark Deming's *La Halle au Blé de Paris, 1762–1813* (The corn exchange of Paris, 1762–1813), which also contains the fullest and most reliable account of Le Camus's career, the basis of the summary offered here.[21]

There can be no doubt as to the celebrity of Le Camus, yet he built little more. He added a monumental doorway to the Collège Louis-le-Grand in 1764 and began a barracks in the following year for the Gardes Françaises on the rue Mouffetard, but the carpenters commissioned to build it opposed the lightweight structure, and Le Camus withdrew. Between 1768 and 1770 he erected his only other building of consequence, the Hôtel de Beauvau, now the Ministère de l'Intérieur, 96 rue du Faubourg Saint-Honoré (pp. 203–14). This was set on a deep and awkward site at a crossroads, which the architect handled imaginatively and with aplomb—a double screen of columns acting as an entrance and frame to the forecourt so that the *corps de logis* was viewed at the end. This building has been studied only recently by Paul Bouteiller in two articles in *L'administration*.[22] M. Bouteiller has discovered not only the contract document but also the ground-floor plan, both of which are included in Appendix B in this volume. These discoveries allow a detailed comparison of Le Camus

17. *Cross-section through the stair adjacent to the rue de Grenelle at the Halle au Blé. Illustrated in Nicolas Le Camus de Mézières,* Recueil des différens plans et dessins, concernant la nouvelle Halle aux grains *(pl. 19 in the ideal copy). Middleton Collection.*

de Mézières's practice and proscriptions. This is the only large-scale *hôtel* he is known to have erected; it is without the richness of accommodation and the full finesse of arrangement that he was to aim at in his writings, but it is clear that he paid all possible attention to the layout of the dressing rooms, boudoir, and bathrooms. His own house, erected at 5 rue Saint-Blaise in Charonne to the east of Paris, was demolished in 1929, and though photographs of the exterior by Atget exist, no plans are known. These buildings, together with a project of 1770 for a church for the Carmelites in the rue de Grenelle and a handful of alterations dating from 1781 to 1784 constitute the sum total of Le Camus's architectural activity recorded to date.

Information concerning his personal life is even more sparse. Reference is made to him on several occasions, but little is revealed other than that, together with other architects of the period such as J.-F.-T. Chalgrin and Charles de Wailly, he was a Freemason, a member of the Respectable loge des coeurs simples de l'étoile polaire à l'orient de Paris, and that he enjoyed amateur dramatics of another kind; the Société dramatique de Charonne met regularly at his house in Charonne between 1770 and 1781.

Le Camus was the author of a handful of publications in addition to those already mentioned: three severely practical works on building materials and construction—*Le guide de ceux qui veulent bâtir* (Guide for those intending to build), 1781 and 1782 (2nd edition 1786, reprinted 1972), *Mémoire sur la manière de rendre incombustible toute salle de spectacle* (Dissertation on the method of rendering all theaters fireproof), 1781, and *Traité de la force des bois* (Treatise on the strengths of timber), 1782— and two occasional works—*L'esprit des almanachs* (The spirit of almanacs), 1783, a digest of other almanacs, and *Aaba; ou, Le triomphe de l'innocence* (Aaba; or The triumph of innocence), 1784 (2nd edition 1802), a conventional pastoral romance recounting the love of Aaba for the shepherd Hilas. He also wrote a *Description des eaux de Chantilly et du hameau* (Description of the waters of Chantilly and of the hamlet), 1783. It includes an account of the picturesque garden buildings erected in 1774 by Jean-François Leroy, one of which, the *salle à manger*, is decorated internally like a forest glade, somewhat in the manner of the boudoir described earlier by Jean-François de Bastide and implemented in 1764 by Etienne-Louis Boullée in a room at the Hôtel de Monville. The two occasional works form a contrast to the prosaic reality of Le Camus's technical works. Only *Le génie de l'architecture* bears witness to his odd, imaginative energy.

One cannot be sure how widely this last text was read, though, as previously noted, that great visionary Etienne-Louis Boullée seems to have taken it as the point of departure for his excursus into a theory of architecture of light and shade. In the discussion on character included in his *Architecture: Essai sur l'art* (Architecture: Essay on the art) written, it is thought, sometime between 1780 and 1795, though published in full only in 1968, he wrote: "To give character to a work is to use precisely the means needed to arouse those sensations alone that are required for the occasion. To understand what I mean by character or the effects stirred by different objects, look at the great tableaux of nature and consider how we are forced to respond to the impact made on our senses."[23] Again and again, Boullée invokes the lessons to be learned from nature and in particular from nature as revealed in the changing seasons in all their varieties and moods. He describes them in turn, quite lyrically. Each, of course, has a character that is quite specific, but it was winter that moved him most strongly. "I have noticed," he writes, "that in winter the effect of the light is sad and somber, that objects have lost their splendor, their color, that forms are hard and angular, that the barren earth is a common grave."[24] Thus he was led to evolve an architecture of light and shade. The idea came to him, he claimed, while pruning his shrubs in the moonlight. This he regarded as a discovery all his own, but the springs of his thought are evident in the writings of Le Camus.

Outside France Le Camus was evidently appreciated. Most of *Le génie de l'architecture* appeared in translation in 1789 in Gottfried Huth's *Allgemeines Magazin für die bürgerliche Baukunst* (General magazine for civil architecture) issued in Weimar. Significantly, the references to Servandoni's theatrical designs and to French buildings of particular character, together with the section on the orders, were omitted. In England no less an architect and luminary than Sir John Soane painstakingly translated most of the first section of the work (the first fifth, minus that part dealing with the orders) when he was preparing his lectures for the Royal Academy in 1808. What intrigued him especially was that sentence dealing with the effects of light: "A well-lighted and well aired building, when all the rest is well treated becomes agreeable and cheerful. Less open, less sheltered, it offers a serious character: the light still more intercepted it is misterious or gloomy."[25] This passage, in the version of the lectures that was published in 1929 was encapsulated and returned to French as *"la lumière mystérieuse"* and *"la poésie de l'architecture."* These themes had long been at the center of Soane's quest, and there can be little doubt that Le Camus had inspired them. Soane, however, was probably the last architect to be actively moved to such thoughts by Le Camus.

Le Camus's name appears in Adolphe Lance's *Dictionnaire des architectes français* (Dictionary of French architects), 1872, and his doorway for the Collège Louis-le-Grand is described and illustrated by the architect E. Rivoalen in the May 1890 issue of *La Construction Moderne* (Modern building), but his ideas are taken up again only in 1924 in Emil Kaufmann's "Die Architekturtheorie der französischen Klassik und des Klassizismus" ("French classical and Neoclassical architectural theory") in the *Repertorium für Kunstwissenschaft*. That article marks the beginning of Le Camus's twentieth-century reputation; it has been confined to the realm of scholars. Both *Le guide de ceux qui veulent bâtir* and *Le génie de l'architecture* were reprinted in 1972, bearing witness to an awakened interest in the dual aspects of his thought, but even now its special place in the structure of eighteenth-century architectural theory is not fully grasped.

Notes

1. Antoine Le Pautre, *Desseins de plusieurs palais* (Paris: n.p., 1652), Avertissement au lecteur.
2. Giacomo da Vignola (1507–1573), Italian architect.
3. Xenophon, *Memorabilia*, trans. E. C. Marchant, The Loeb Classical Library no. 168 (Cambridge, Mass.: Harvard Univ. Press; London: William Heinemann Ltd., 1959), 3.10.6–8.
4. Apollinaris Sidonius (circa 430–487/88), Roman prelate and writer in Gaul. See Sidonius, *Poems and Letters*, trans. W. B. Anderson, The Loeb Classical Library no. 420 (Cambridge, Mass.: Harvard Univ. Press; London: William Heinemann Ltd. 1965–1980), vol. 2, *Letters, Books III–IX*, bk. 9, ltr. 9.
5. Cicero, *Orator*, trans. H. M. Hubbell, The Loeb Classical Library no. 342 (Cambridge, Mass.: Harvard Univ. Press; London: William Heinemann Ltd., 1971), 21.69–71.
6. Roger de Piles, *Cours de peinture par principes* (Paris: J. Estienne, 1708), 135: "*Le Beau, dit-on, n'est rien de réel, chacun en juge, selon son goût, en un mot, que le Beau n'est autre chose que ce qui plaît.*" Idem, *The Principles of Painting* (London: J. Osborn, 1743), 84.
7. De Piles, 1708 (see note 6), 219: "*Les roches sont d'elles-mêmes mélancoliques & propres aux solitudes.*" Idem, 1743 (see note 6), 134.
8. See Jean-Pierre Babelon, *Demeures parisiennes sous Henri IV et Louis XIII* (Paris: Le Temps, 1977), 2nd ed.; and idem, "Du 'Grand Ferrare' à Carnavalet: Naissance de l'hôtel classique," *Revue de l'art* 40/41 (1978): 83–108.
9. Myra Nan Rosenfeld, "The Hôtel de Cluny and the Sources of the French Renaissance Palace, 1350–1500" (Ph.D. diss., Harvard Univ., 1972).
10. Claude-Henri Watelet, *Essai sur les jardins* (Paris: Prault, 1774), 13: "*ce sentiment délicat qui exige les relations les plus parfaites entre les objets extérieurs, les sens, et l'état de l'ame.*" Unless otherwise indicated, all translations in the text are mine.
11. Jean-Marie Morel, *Théorie des jardins* (Paris: Pissot, 1776), 156.
12. Ibid., 157.
13. Ibid., 116: "*Les eaux sont au paysage ce que l'ame est au corps.*"
14. Ibid., 370.
15. Abbé Etienne Bonnot de Condillac, *Essai sur l'origine des connoissances humaines* (Amsterdam: P. Mortier, 1746), 2: 89. See Isabel F. Knight, *The Geometric Spirit: The Abbé de Condillac and the French Enlightenment* (New Haven: Yale Univ. Press, 1968).
16. Ibid., 2: 285.
17. Ibid., 2: 271.
18. Ibid., 2: 244.

19. Rémy Saisselin, "Architecture and Language: The Sensationalism of Le Camus de Mézières," *The British Journal of Aesthetics* 15, no. 3 (Summer 1975), 239–53.

20. Antoine-Chrysostome Quatremère de Quincy, *Encyclopédie méthodique* (Paris: Panckoucke; Liège: Plomteux, 1788), 1: 108.

21. Mark K. Deming, *La Halle au Blé de Paris, 1762–1813* (Brussels: Archives d'Architecture Moderne, 1984).

22. Paul Bouteiller, "L'hôtel du ministre de l'intérieur et les bâtiments de l'administration centrale de 1790 à nos jours," *L'administration*, no. 150 (15 January 1991): 199–210; and idem, "La construction de l'Hôtel de Beauvau au XVIIIᵉ siècle," *L'administration*, no. 151 (15 April 1991): 122–27.

23. Etienne-Louis Boullée, *Architecture: Essai sur l'art*, ed. Jean-Marie Pérouse de Montclos (Paris: Hermann, 1968), 73–74: "*Mettre du caractère dans un ouvrage, c'est employer avec justesse tous les moyens propres à ne nous faire éprouver d'autres sensations que celles qui doivent résulter du sujet. Pour comprendre ce que j'entends par caractère ou effet subit des différents objets, considérons les grands tableaux de la nature et voyons comment nous sommes forcés de nous exprimer d'après leur action sur nos sens.*"

24. Ibid., 78: "*Nous avons remarqué que, dans la saison de l'hiver, les effets de la lumière étaient tristes et sombres, que les objets avaient perdu leur éclat, leur couleur, que les formes étaient dures et anguleuses, que la terre dépouillée offrait un sépulcre universel.*"

25. Sir John Soane's Museum, London, Ms. 61.

THE GENIUS OF

ARCHITECTURE; OR,

THE ANALOGY OF THAT ART WITH OUR

SENSATIONS

Non satis est placuisse oculis, nisi pectora tangas.

It is not enough to please the eyes;
you must touch the soul.

Poem upon Painting, by Father Marsy.

TO MONSIEUR WATELET,[1]

OF the French Academy, Honorary Member of the Royal Academy of Painting and Sculpture, and of that of Architecture, Associate of the Royal Society of Medicine, Member of the Academies of Vienna, Madrid, Berlin, Rome, Florence, and Parma, and of the Institute of Bologna, etc.

SIR,

IT IS to talent and to merit that I dedicate this Work; you love and cultivate the Arts: you are no stranger to the Crayon and the Burin. You have celebrated in verse the art of painting. Your Essay on Gardens recalls the Golden Age; in the charming places that you describe, you restore it to us. Your Works, Sir, have kindled my zeal; in presenting the fruits of that zeal to you, I pay a tribute that is no more than your due. In craving your indulgence, I beg to remain,

SIR,

Your most humble and
obedient servant,
LE CAMUS DE MEZIERES.

INTRODUCTION

No one has yet written on the analogy of the proportions of Architecture with our sensations; we find only scattered fragments, superficial and, as it were, set down by chance.

These may be regarded as diamonds in their rude covering, which require the aid of Art to assume their full splendor.

This is a new subject; and we offer this study as no more than a sketch, with a view to inciting more fortunate spirits to take up the same point of view and to compose on this topic a finished Work worthy of the enlightened age in which we live.

Hitherto it has been customary to work in accordance with the proportions of the five Orders of Architecture, used in the ancient Buildings of Greece and Italy: this is a priceless model, and we cannot do better. But how many Artists have employed these Orders mechanically, without taking the opportunity to combine them into a whole with a character all its own, capable of producing certain sensations; they have not been inspired by the analogy and relation of those proportions with the affections of the soul.

We sometimes see examples of Architecture that surprise and impress, but leave the judgment uncertain: there remains something to be desired. Why is this so? Because these are the offspring of caprice: good taste may prevail in them, and they may bear the marks of genius; but we find, on inspecting them, that the execution is uncertain, and that the true principles of Art have been mistaken or neglected. At the same time, there are the happy creations of those men of genius who are the wonder of their age: let us take these works as our models. Let us discuss them with reasoned application, distinguish the causes of their effect on our souls, and in this way establish our principles.

Our purpose is to enlarge upon these causes through our Observations on the most remarkable Buildings, those that have most impressed us, in accordance with the sensations that we have ourselves experienced. Nature and art will jointly guide us; theirs is the path that we intend to follow; we shall count ourselves fortunate if this undertaking does not exceed our strength.

Occupied with such observations since my youth, my zeal has sustained itself by fixing my attention upon the works of nature. The more closely I have looked, the more I have found that every object possesses a character, proper to it alone, and that often a single line, a plain contour, will suffice to express it. The faces of the lion, the tiger, and the leopard are composed of lines that make them terrible and strike fear into the boldest hearts. In the face of a cat, we discern the character of treachery; meekness and goodness are written on the features of a lamb; the fox has a mask of cunning and guile: a single feature conveys their character. The celebrated Le Brun,[i] whose talents do honor to his country, has proved the truth of this principle through his characterization of the passions; he has expressed the various affections of the soul, and has rendered joy, sadness, anger, fury, compassion, etc., in a single line.[2]

Similarly, in inanimate objects, it is their form that makes some pleasing to us, others unpleasing. A flower charms the eye: a gentle sympathy attracts us, and the disposition of its parts delights us. Why should not the productions of the Art that forms my theme enjoy the same advantages? A structure catches the eye by virtue of its mass; its general outline attracts or repels us. When we look at some great fabric, our sensations are of contradictory kinds: gaiety in one place, despondency in another. One sensation induces quiet reflection; another inspires awe, or maintains respect, and so on.

What are the causes of these various effects? Let us try to distinguish them. Their existence is in no doubt; and this becomes still more apparent if we combine Painting and Sculpture with Architecture. Who can resist this threefold magic, which addresses almost all the affections and sensations known to us? To

---

i. Charles Le Brun, who died in Paris in 1690, was first Painter to Louis xiv and has left the Public a characterization of the passions, simply drawn in line.

satisfy ourselves on this point, we have only to look at our stage decorations, which use the mere imitation of works of Architecture to govern our affections. Here, we see the enchanted Palace of Armida: all is splendor and delight; we guess that it was built at Love's command. The scene changes: the abode of Pluto strikes horror and dread into our souls. We see the Temple of the Sun, and we respond with admiration. A view of a Prison inspires sadness; Apartments ready for a festival, surrounded by gardens, fountains, and flowers, excite gaiety and prepare us for pleasure. At the sight of the forest of Dodona, the soul is moved; we are seized with the sacred horror of the grove.

The celebrated Servandoni,[ii] whose fertile genius and mastery of the secrets of his Art have so surprised and delighted us in the theater,[iii] once contrived, in a mute Spectacle, to make us feel the burning heat of the Sun.[3] The Camp of Godfrey was seen parched by the fires of the Dog days: almost no shadow, a reddish sky, an arid earth, an effect of light that suggested flames in the air; all this created an illusion to which no Spectator was immune.[4] We supposed that we ourselves were suffering; we were in the power of Art. With equal success, he might have conveyed to our souls the idea of a biting cold, by setting before us an image of those climes in which a few leafless birches are the only signs of vegetation to rise above the rocks covered with eternal snows; a somber air, and a pale and featureless sky, would have betokened the onset of new frosts. Rivers frozen to a standstill, springs caught and arrested in their flight, would have shown us nature devoid of life and movement. That would have been a spectacle to make us shiver. What emotions do we not feel in the contrast between deep shadow and limpid light, or between the delights of calm weather and the confusion of winds and tempests? Every nuance, every gradation, affects us.

The arrangements of forms, their character, and their combination are thus an inexhaustible source of illusion. We must start from this principle whenever we intend to arouse emotion through Architecture, when we set out to address the mind and to stimulate the soul, rather than to build by piling one stone on another, indiscriminately copying arrangements and ornaments that are imposed by convention or borrowed without reflection. Effects and sensations spring from the considered intention that governs the ensemble, the proportions, and the

ii. In France, Servandoni was an Architect, Painter, and Decorator to the King, and a Member of the Academies set up for these various Arts. He served in the same capacities under the Kings of England, Spain, Poland, and the reigning Duke of Württemberg. In Portugal, he was decorated with the Royal Order of Christ. He died in Paris on 19 January 1766.
iii. A performance with stage machinery, given in the Tuileries Theater in 1741.

agreement of the various parts.

Constantly bear in mind and keep as your principal object the harmony of proportions and of the relations between all the parts; this alone forms
the enchantment that delights our souls. Let us seek its causes and examine its
principles, for then we may establish its rules.

The analogy of the proportions of Architecture with our sensations
leads to a string of reflections essential to the interesting Metaphysics on which
the progress of this Art depends. We have sought to avoid all scholastic encum-
brances and all that smacks of oversubtle reasoning, while tempering the aridity
of principles, as far as possible, by presenting them in the agreeable light of simi-
les, descriptions, and examples.

Such are the principles that we have adopted in this Work. We have
gone so far into detail as to discuss the different distributions of the plans of Buildings and the characteristics relative to each room in a House, without neglecting
what is appropriate to the condition of those who are to live in it.

The Building erected for a great Nobleman, the Palace of a Bishop,
the Town House of a Magistrate, and the House of a Military Man, or of a rich
private Citizen, require to be treated differently. The sensations they arouse are
not the same; and consequently, the proportions of the whole and those of the
masses and of the details must be appropriate in character.

Should anyone consider that we have allowed too many rooms for
each part of the fabric, and that he has no desire to live in any such grandeur, he
will find it easy, without blaming us, to keep to his own station in life and live
within his own means. He who can do the greater, can do the less. What is more,
ideas tend to contract; in setting out principles, all must be writ large. It is well to
know how far luxury and comfort can be carried; it will do no good to rail against
the taste of the age.

Our principles concerning the analogy between the proportions of
Architecture and our sensations are founded on those of the majority of the Philosophers. We cannot go astray by following nature; her course is all one, as Py-
thagoras tells us.

Harmony is the prime mover of all great effects; it has the most natural ascendancy over our sensations. Those Arts that have harmony as their foundation inspire, in varying degrees, a feeling of delight.

None of this was lost on Father Castel,[5] that learned Jesuit, the Inven-
tor of the wonderful Harpsichord of colors. By a well-conceived and ingenious
device, he constructed an instrument that gave a concert of colors, while at the
same time producing another in sound. Colors succeeded each other harmonically

and struck the eye with the same enchantment and, to a man of education, a pleasure as great as any that the ears can enjoy in sounds combined by the most able Musician. This masterpiece suffered the fate of all the best projects; it was judged without being known. People want to enjoy, like a ripe fruit in high season, that which is only a forward fruit; and so talent is smothered at birth. Some things cannot be comprehended all at once; the basis of the sciences is to see well, and to see well requires examination and reflection. A Scholar, long closeted in a Library where Books have been his only concern, on finding himself suddenly transported into a magnificent Picture Gallery will not feel the same pleasure, or the same sensations, as one who has made a study of the art of painting. He might even prefer a mediocre Picture that is gay and brilliant in color to the Picture that we prize above all others. Well may we deplore the neglect that has befallen Father Castel's discovery, one which might perhaps have led to others of greater interest; at the least, it would have been one pleasure the more. Our regrets are well founded; a single spark may kindle the greatest fire. But let us leave this digression and say only that a close affinity exists between colors and sounds, that they move the passions to an equal degree, and that they produce the same effects. At the sight of a fine building, the eyes enjoy a pleasure as sweet as any that the ears can receive from the sublime art of sounds. Music, the divine Art that enchants us, bears the closest relation to Architecture. The consonances and the proportions are the same. The City of Thebes, or so legend has it, was built to the strains of Amphion's lyre: a fiction that teaches us, at least, that the Ancients felt how intimately Architecture was allied to harmony, which is none other than the combination of different parts to form a concordant whole.[6]

Architecture is truly harmonic. The ingenious M. Ouvrard,[7] Master of the Music at the Sainte-Chapelle and one of the ablest musicians of the age of Louis XIV, proves it so in the most victorious manner in his Treatise.[iv] To sustain his system, he shows that the dimensions of Solomon's Temple are related by the harmonic numbers; these dimensions conform to those that Scripture has given us and Villalpanda[8] has so finely elucidated.[v] He does not stop at this one Building: he has applied his principles to several ancient Buildings and to all the precepts of

iv. *Architecture harmonique; ou, Application de la doctrine des proportions de la Musique à l'Architecture* [Harmonic architecture; or, Application of the doctrine of musical proportions to architecture].

v. Juan Bautista Villalpanda, an able Jesuit and a native of Cordova, Author of a learned Commentary on Ezekiel, in three volumes *in folio*, which is particularly esteemed for its description of the City and Temple of Solomon. He died in 1608.

Vitruvius;[vi] a number of pleasing works, all marked with the seal of genius, have come from his pen. All cavils against his systems have been in vain. M. Perrault[vii] was in the wrong when he wrote that there should be no fixed proportions and that taste alone must decide; that genius must have its flights; that too many and too strict rules seemed to circumscribe it and, as it were, to make it barren.[9]

Let us say only that there must be some points of departure, and some laws to restrain our imagination, which is generally licentious. Left to itself, it knows no restraint or measure; it would produce monstrous composites, a crude mixture of all the genres; it would not shrink from combining them all within a single scheme of decoration. Gothic Architecture offers a striking example of this.

Fixed and invariable rules govern the formation of taste and the process by which we manipulate, in a manner both distinct and sublime, the mechanism that gratifies the senses and conveys into the soul that delicious emotion that ravishes and charms us. Such are the reflections and such are the models that we have taken as our point of departure.

Those Gardens that we call English, although their true origin is Chinese, have furnished us with expedients drawn from nature herself, whose beauties are always in a just proportion and in a true relation. Their expression is never equivocal; no one is left in doubt by the character that nature presents; she is within everyone's reach. The sensibility that almost all men share is enough to make them feel her influence to the full.

What pictures and agreeable scenes such Gardens present when they are well conceived, when they conform with the genre that is intended, and when they take the beauties of Nature as their model! What an abundance of genres and varieties! The objects of which they are composed, insensate and inanimate though they may be, work upon the faculties of the soul and elevate the mind to the loftiest meditations. Now that we possess a number of treatises on Gardens that do honor to their authors, we have extracted from them a number of ideas: like the bee, we have tried to make them into an agreeable honey; happy if our efforts promote the progress of the Art on which we write.[10]

vi. Vitruvius, a famous Architect of Augustus's time.

vii. Claude Perrault, of whom Boileau speaks so frequently in his Satires, and who died in Paris in 1688, has left us a Translation and a learned Commentary on Vitruvius. His were the Designs for the Porte Saint-Bernard, the Observatory, and the famous Colonnade of the Louvre. This celebrated Artist commenced with the study of Medicine; he was a Doctor of the Paris Faculty.

Such has been the object of our study, and such the sources on which we have drawn; in considering them with reasoned care, we have sought to trace the evolution of the sensations they inspire.

The whole, the masses, the proportions, the shadows, and the lights are the bases of our compositions. We have tried to discern the accords that exist between them, to analyze them, to deduce principles, and to establish rules.

It is for the enlightened Public to decide whether we have succeeded in our undertaking, and this we shall learn from the outcome. At all events, it remains a pleasant thing to have opened a new road with the advantage of being the first to enter upon it.

Finally, may we be permitted to observe that this is the work of an Artist, who, by virtue of his occupation, cannot devote himself entirely to Literature. Provided that it has some order, that the ideas are clear and well marshaled, and that its plan is accomplished, he hopes that he will be granted a measure of indulgence as to the elegance and purity of the style and that, above all, it will be accepted that in Art there are some things that can only be written by those who practice it habitually.

THE GENIUS OF
ARCHITECTURE

Architecture, or the art of building, is divided into a number of branches. It is our purpose to consider this Art relative to decoration, in which true beauty consists in the proportions that relate the various parts of buildings to each other. Their harmony, their accord, produces the whole that gratifies and delights us: from this harmony, and from a real or proportionate beauty, the various sensations spring.

Let us examine, for example, the interior of the Dome of the Invalides:[i] what are our sensations! We are filled with astonishment and admiration; our souls are borne aloft. Caught up in a kind of ecstasy, it seems that we participate in the greatness of the God who is worshiped here.

If we consider the outside of the Dome, its pyramidal composition and the base from which it so majestically rises, we are at once overcome by a sense of grandeur and magnificence.

In the colonnade of the Louvre,[ii] we find an imposing, rich, and noble

i. This part of the fabric was built to the Designs of Jules Hardouin-Mansart, first Architect to the King, the nephew of François Mansart.
ii. The designs are the work of Claude Perrault and were chosen in preference to those of a number of competing Architects, notably the Cavalier Bernini, who had been invited to Paris for this purpose, and at truly royal expense. Claude Perrault was a native of Paris, where he died on 9 October 1688, at the age of seventy-five.

building. The entrance and staircase of the new mint[iii] present the same virtues.

    The interior of the church of Val-de-Grâce,[iv] that of the Sorbonne,[v] and that of the Collège Mazarin or Collège des Quatre Nations,[vi] are such as to inspire quiet meditation. Observe how the openings are arranged: a half-light prevails, our sentiments are fixed, there are no distractions, and the soul concentrates within itself. Cast an eye on our Theaters: the Opera in Paris, made ready for the Ball,[vii] and that of Versailles, above all,[viii] inspire sentiments related to the diversions, the entertainments, the festivities that they promise. The last named unites decorum with grandeur. It is an enchantment, in which there is everything to occupy the mind and nothing to hold it captive.

    The Château de Trianon[ix] was designed to provide for those excursions and pleasures that fill and vary a monarch's hours of leisure; it speaks to us of gaiety. The ensemble of its masses, its openings, the lightness and rhythmic preci-

iii. [Hôtel des Monnaies.] Built to the designs of M. Antoine, Member of the Academy of Architecture, born in Paris, and living at the present time. The first stone was laid on 30 April 1771, and the whole fabric was completed in 1775.

iv. The Val-de-Grâce, whose first stone was laid by Louis xiv, at the age of seven, in April 1645. François Mansart drew up the Designs; and the execution was later entrusted to Jacques Le Mercier, who continued it as far as the entablature, where it was halted for a time. Finally, in 1654, the Queen nominated Pierre Le Muet, in association with Gabriel Le Duc, to complete this fine Building.

v. The Sorbonne, constructed according to the Designs of Jacques Le Mercier, Architect to the King, born at Pontoise. The first stone was laid on 4 June 1629.

vi. The Collège Mazarin, built on the orders of the Cardinal of that name, and to the Designs of Louis Le Vau, First Architect to the King, who died in 1670 at the age of fifty-eight, and carried on under the supervision of François Dorbay, his Pupil, who died in 1697.

vii. By M. Moreau, of the Academy of Architecture, Architect in Chief to the City, and Knight of the Order of Saint-Michel, who has given such happy proof of his talents. The Building was begun in May 1764. The Theater was completed at the end of 1769, and it was inaugurated on 16 January 1770, with the Opera of Zoroaster.

viii. Built for the Wedding of Louis xvi, then Dauphin, on 16 May 1770, to Designs by M. Gabriel, first Architect to the King.

ix. Built in 1670, under the Ministry of M. de Louvois, by Jules Hardouin-Mansart, first Architect to the King. The building of the first Chapel is by Libéral Bruant.

sion of its forms, its variety of marbles, and the character of its ornaments, all concur to the same end.

The Château de Versailles, from the Garden side, inspires a serious and perhaps melancholy feeling. The whole of this grand building, which is stately indeed, but uniform in height throughout its length, forms a simple straight line on the horizon, which seems to circumscribe our soul, to entrap it, and turn it in upon itself.

Today, in the suburbs of the Capital, an endless succession of new buildings seems to promise enjoyment and delight. What is the cause of these sensations? The choice of proportions; the forms that are employed, and the position in which they have been set with taste and deliberation; the ornaments, and their reciprocal relations: all combine to produce this character and to establish the illusions that Architecture creates. Happy is he whose talents show him how to put these means to their right use! This is a precious gift, which is given to few Artists, and few find the happy opportunity of employing it. Let us therefore resist the temptation to digress; let us approach the Art that forms the subject of the present Work by first considering the five Orders that must be regarded as its elements.

From the totality of the buildings known to us and the different sensations that they arouse in us, from their detail and from a description of the fabric and its masses, we shall extract principles that have been passed over, somewhat too lightly, by past writers on Architecture. Our remarks are intended to enable every reader to form conclusions that would not otherwise have occurred to him. If the benefits match our intentions, we shall be amply rewarded for our pains.

The general proportions of Architecture have a striking analogy with those of the human body and seem to be taken from its principal characteristics. Some bodies are stout and robust; others are delicate and elegant. It is in this light that we shall consider the five Orders of Architecture: the Tuscan, the Doric, the Ionic, the Corinthian, and the Composite.

The Tuscan and the Composite are Italian, and the other three are Greek. The Tuscan Order, in its proportions, proclaims strength and solidity; it represents a robust and well-sinewed man. The Doric shows us a man of a noble and well-favored build. The Ionic has the general proportions of a beautiful woman, with a little more bulk than the slender girl who supplies the proportions of the Corinthian Order. As for the fifth Order, the Composite, it is composed of the other four, and this is the source of its name. In the progression of these five Orders, we thus see strength, elegance, grace, majesty, and magnificence.

ORDERS OF ARCHITECTURE

The word Order signifies a regular and proportionate arrangement of masses, moldings, and ornaments, which, when incorporated in a facade or other architectural decoration, make up a beautiful whole. The variety that Artists have introduced into the arrangements and proportions of the various parts is the origin of the different genres or characters that distinguish the Orders of Architecture.

Each Order is composed of three essential parts: a pedestal, a column, and an entablature.

Each of these parts is composed of three others.

The pedestal consists of a base, a dado, and a cornice.

The column consists of a base, a shaft, and a capital.

The entablature consists of an architrave, a frieze, and a cornice.

Such are the essential parts that compose an Order of Architecture; and each of these parts has proportions relative to the various Orders in which it is employed.

In each Order, the column governs all the proportions: its diameter determines the scale or module that serves to assemble and proportion the whole [see appendix A, fig. a].

The Tuscan column, including base and capital, is seven diameters high;

The Doric, eight diameters;

The Ionic, nine;

The Corinthian, ten.

The Composite Order is also ten diameters high.

The pedestal in each Order is one-third of the height of the column.

The entablature is one-quarter.

These major divisions, governed by the height of the column, determine the character of the Orders, just as the Painter takes the height of the head as a guide to the height and all the proportions of the figure.

As for the subdivisions of each member, they vary according to the Orders and to the taste of the Artist concerned; what may be said in general is that the outward projection of each molding must be equal to its height.

It will be seen that the pedestal is divided within itself into a base, a dado, and a cornice; that the same division applies to the base, the shaft, and the capital; and that the entablature has its architrave, frieze, and cornice; we shall come to all these as we put our broad divisions into practice.

To this end, we draw a horizontal line, AA, at about one-third of the height of the sheet of paper on which we intend to draw; on this line we erect a perpendicular, BB. This done, we take any desired width, provided that this width, which will be the diameter of the foot of the shaft of the column, can be repeated upward, seven times for the height of the Tuscan column, eight times for the Doric, nine times for the Ionic, and ten times for the Corinthian and Composite Orders. One-quarter of this height should be allowed, in addition, for the entablature. One-third has already been allowed for the pedestal, by placing the horizontal at one-third of the height of the paper. Such are the main divisions and subdivisions of the principal parts.

Pedestal

The height of the pedestal, which is one-third of the column, is subdivided into seven parts: the base has two, the dado four, the cornice one.

Column

The semidiameter of the column, measured at the bottom of its shaft, gives the height of its base, taking into account that the fillet is part of the bottom of the shaft, and the astragal is part of its top.

The capital of the Tuscan Order, that of the Doric Order, and that of the Ionic are equal in height, namely one semidiameter; in the Corinthian and Composite Orders, the capital is one whole diameter high.

Entablature

The height intended for the entablature is subdivided into four parts: one is for the architrave, and the three others are divided in two to give half for the frieze and half for the cornice.

By this simple operation, all the heights are obtained. It is now necessary to form the masses and projections, remembering that the moldings in general project by a distance equal to their height.

The diameter of the column being decided, as we have said, let us take half of it, which we will call the module, and which we place to the right and left of our perpendicular, DD, above the base; this will be the bottom of the shaft of the column, E. To find the width of the top of the shaft, F, subtract one-sixth of the module, place what remains to the right and left of your axis, B, and you will have the point desired, for this part of the column must be thinner than at the base. This done, divide the height of your shaft into three; on either side of your axis, and parallel to it, draw the lines that will mark the lower part of the shaft, as far as one-third of its height; from this point G, at one-third of the height, draw a line to the points FF, which mark the top of the shaft, and then you will have traced all your shaft.

To form the mass of the projection of the base, take one module and one-fifth, place it on your horizontal line marking the bottom of the base, as K, draw a diagonal from this point to the bottom of the shaft, and you will have the mass of your base.

The same applies to the capital, remembering only to make the projection one module and one-sixth; between this point and the top of the shaft, draw a diagonal L, and you will have the mass of the capital.

To obtain the mass of the entablatures: make sure that the bottom of the architrave, A, and the entire height of the frieze, B, are vertically above the top of the shaft; then, allowing one-fifth of a module to project for the top of the architrave, and drawing a diagonal between the two points 1 and 2, this gives the mass of the architrave.

As for the frieze, we have said that its entire height is vertically above the top of the shaft; consequently, by drawing a line parallel to the axis from this point, the whole frieze is formed.

The cornice must be given a projection equal to its height, and this can easily be determined by further producing the line of the frieze; from this point, measuring outward for a distance equal to the height, you have the entire form of the mass of the frieze.

As for the pedestal, which is, as has been said, one-third of the column, its height is divided into seven parts. The base has two, the dado has four, and the cornice one.

The dado is aligned below the farthest projection of the base of the column, and in consequence two lines are to be drawn from these points, and the outline of the dado is formed. The projections of the base and cornice are measured from that of the dado: by adding one-quarter of a module to the basic line, from the flat of the dado outward, and drawing a diagonal between points 5 and 6, you will have the mass of the base.

Similarly, the cornice is assigned one-third of a module as its projection, and a diagonal is drawn from point 7 to point 8, the surface of the dado.

Such are the masses and such is the ensemble of every Order.

It might seem that we could enter here into the subdivision of each one of these masses; but our elementary operations, once mastered, are sufficient to give a feeling of the ensemble, the relationships, and the harmony of the Orders of Architecture, which must constitute the principles and the basis for the proportions of any building to which we wish to give a decorative form that will not be arbitrary, but will truly please. We may even affirm that true beauty is not to be approached except through observance of these general dimensions.

To learn the subdivisions of the various members, reference may be made to those authors who have written on the subject, and who have provided detailed and complete courses of instruction.

Some years ago, M. Potain gave us a treatise that may serve as a model; it is thoughtful and composed with taste; in it we recognize the true Artist.[11]

TUSCAN ORDER

The Tuscan Order may be studied with advantage in the Work to which I have just referred [see appendix A, fig. b]: the base of the column is simple and fine; the capital is in keeping; the whole entablature is masculine; and the ensemble, although bare of ornament, is pleasing and satisfies the eye. A handsome plainness conveys the strength and solidity that are characteristic of this Order.

DORIC ORDER

The entablature of the Doric Order is a pleasure to behold. Its frieze is decorated with triglyphs and metopes. These last, which are perfect squares filled with ornament, lend elegance and produce a rich and masculine ensemble. The cornice with its mutules [see appendix A, fig. c], which are directly above the triglyphs and are surmounted by a talon, is a great enhancement to this Order, as are the regulae and the guttae, which form part of the architrave directly below the triglyphs. Sometimes, instead of mutules, dentils are used in the cornice [see appendix A, fig. d]; but whether mutules or dentils, they must be positioned directly above the center of the column.

IONIC ORDER

It is a pleasure to contemplate the capital of the Ionic Order [see appendix A, figs. e, f]. There is grace in the furling and unfurling of its volutes; and this characterizes the Order of which we speak. The Attic base is assigned to this Order; this is the most beautiful form of base that we have and is often adopted for the Corinthian and Composite Orders. This base, in the harmony between its parts, may be likened to the intervals of the third and the fifth in music, as M. Ouvrard ingeniously remarks. The first torus, the scotia, and the second torus seem to convey to the eye what the notes G, B, and D convey to the ear. The computation is the same. The fillets are like the passing notes and grace notes. In this Order, the cornice of the entablature includes modillions or dentils, and sometimes both. Various ornaments are often incised into the moldings. This Order allows of enrichment in the frieze, which often includes ornamental rinceaux; some Architects even swell the frieze, a practice that is not always above criticism. When the moldings of the cornice of the entablature are enriched, then so are those of the architrave. But it should be noted that the fillets are never decorated; they must always be smooth, and their arrises must be sharp. It may be taken as a general rule that ornaments and plain elements should alternate; in other words, where ornaments are employed, there must be one plain molding and one carved one. This is restful to the eye and avoids confusion.

Architecture is like a beautiful woman: she should please in herself; she needs few ornaments.

Even so, it should be noted that, where ornaments are employed in the cornice of the entablature, some should also be carved in the various members of the architrave, but in moderation and simply to prevent too sharp a contrast between the cornice and the architrave. A beautiful dress always has its appropriate jewels.

CORINTHIAN ORDER

What beauty, what elegance, in the capital of a Corinthian column [see appendix A, fig. g]! The first row of acanthus leaves unfurls majestically, the second in harmonious relation to the first. The caulicoles fittingly support the abacus. How well their springing is contrived, and how well this capital is crowned! It has justly been admired throughout the ages. The shaft beneath is entirely in keeping: its height proclaims the magnificence of the capital, which is its crown. The base is rich with something of the Attic in it, but less noble; the latter is often used in preference.

The entablature contains modillions and dentils: the modillions must be distributed in such a way that the caissons between them are perfectly square and that there is always a modillion and a dentil directly over each column; the center of the caisson has a rosette, which recalls the nature of the leaf on the capital: sometimes these are acanthus leaves, sometimes parsley leaves, sometimes leaves designed in the form of palms. The underside of each modillion bears one of these leaves; in every case, the leaf employed in the capital determines the kind of leaf used elsewhere. The soffit of the cornice in this entablature creates a fine effect. Harmony prevails; the cornice moldings may be enriched with ornaments, as may the frieze and the architrave, just as we have noted in connection with the Ionic Order and following the same principles. The ornaments of the frieze must be in low relief; their greatest projection must not exceed that of the first molding of the cornice.

COMPOSITE ORDER

The Composite Order is formed, as has been said, from the Ionic and the Co-rinthian [see appendix A, fig. h]. The capital of the column partakes of both these Orders; it has the volutes of the Ionic and the leaves of the Corinthian. The ensemble is a rich one, but markedly inferior to the two others, in respect of that natural nobility that is apparent to the eye. In seeking to embellish his weave, the weaver has overworked it. The base shows traces of effort and artifice and is consequently inferior in beauty to those of the two preceding Orders.

In the cornice of the entablature there are double modillions with dentils between them; caissons appear in the soffit of the corona. This last is an imitation of the Corinthian, or rather a copy in which some liberties have been taken. Too much enrichment impairs the harmony; an excess of finery is rarely becoming. Art must not show itself openly. The Ionic and Corinthian Orders remain models of beauty; they have fixed and decided characters; they are un-disputed originals; whereas, in spite of all the efforts that have been made to date, the nature of this Order remains mixed and resists definition. It inspires sensations that, if not equivocal, are wanting in delicacy. Only the ensemble and disposition of a complete plan can carry them off. All in all, this Order conveys the greatest opulence, but an opulence less considered than that of the Corinthian Order. On occasion, sumptuousness has its triumphs; the prudent Artist will understand the nature of the decoration he needs. The nature of the object, the purpose, and the position must decide.

From all that we have just said, have we reached the last word in Architecture? As emulators of the Greeks and Romans, why should we Frenchmen not aspire to an Order that would characterize our Nation? Let us venture some ideas on the subject.

THE IDEA OF A FRENCH ORDER

Attempts have long been made to invent a French Order.[12] Several Architects have displayed their taste in the efforts that they have made to this end; but they have produced nothing to date but a compound of the known Orders. The ornaments and the forms, rather than the general proportions, must be the source of novelty. For example, to make a column more than ten diameters high is to give it a light-ness that destroys the harmony and makes it seem like a reed, incapable of supporting any weight; and this violates one of the most essential principles of all, namely the idea of solidity that every structure must have.

The aim of Art is to make houses safe to live in, before it is to make them pleasing.

Might it not, nevertheless, be possible to employ proportions that are mixed or that combine two different Orders, just as one employs semitones? This is a moot question, and a delicate one, because, once the overriding harmony of the progression of the Orders by aliquot parts is broken, the result becomes uncertain and the effect doubtful. It is assumed that only the ornaments and the heights can be varied; but why not go further and give free rein to the imagination by breaking the bounds of custom? In this connection, we may expect to see some bold and successful endeavors. Several capitals already proposed seem to promise as much. Perrault's design for the French Order is ingenious in the extreme. The masses are approximately the same as those of the Corinthian Order. But the attributes change the character.

The astragal at the top of the shaft was carved in beads and formed the base of a crown of fleurs-de-lys; instead of leaves, the Architect had used the feathers of a cock, the symbolic bird of the French Nation. The ribands of the various orders of chivalry were draped like garlands from the caulicoles or volutes, and instead of a fleuron in the center of the capital, there was a Sun to recall the motto *nec pluribus impar*.[13]

The idea is ingenious, but the ensemble is nothing but a Composite capital; there is nothing new in the proportions, and consequently no sense of a new Order.

There are barriers that the mind cannot cross when following well-trodden paths. There are times when to stray is to make new discoveries; sometimes the clouds are pierced by rays of light; a subtle genius may receive them, and a noble emulation may perfect their advantages.

ON THE ART OF *PLEASING*

IN ARCHITECTURE

Exact relations in all the parts constitute harmony; and harmony is the sole true means of pleasing in Architecture. We have already likened this Art to that of Painting; and Painting has established this great principle only by following nature, of which it makes an untiring study. What is pleasing in nature charms us by its harmony and attracts us by the fine concord between the parts of every object; true mastery consists in operating by the same means as nature.

It is, therefore (in the Art that concerns us here), the analogy and the concord of the proportions, the happy agreement of plans, of masses, and of elevations, and of each part with the whole, and the characters of grandeur, magnificence, nobility, grace, simplicity, etc., that must gain universal approbation and promote the pleasure, the intellectual enjoyment, which is the most satisfying object of the Fine Arts.

A first proportion, derived from the purpose of a building or of an apartment, establishes all the others.

The site upon which a building is erected largely determines its proportions.

The size and mass of a building must be in accord with the extent of the site. A small building in a large space would make an unpleasing effect, especially if it were to mark an intersection. A large part, set down beside another that is too small, is intolerable; likewise a small one, beside one that is too large.

Take care, for example, not to give a grand elevation and powerful masses to a house where you have no forecourt in proportion to it. Buildings that are too simple, too low, and follow a single line are disagreeable and monotonous. If such faults be joined with any trace of pretension, the building will appear still more absurd. We see this in nature: any woman who hopes to please must herself be suitably proportioned to look well in her dress.

To satisfy the eye, there must be a balance between the dimensions, just as a living body needs a proper distribution of weight to sustain itself.

Each of the parts of which I have spoken has a beauty of its own, and the same is true of every detail. The line, the contour, the profiles, the accessories, the ornaments: all have their own perfection and their own particular character. These beauties, well considered and appropriately employed, produce a sensation analogous to the object in hand, and it is this sensation that we must seek to arouse. Light and shade artfully disposed in an architectural composition reinforce the desired impression and determine the effect.

A building that is well lit and well aired, when all the rest is perfectly treated, becomes agreeable and cheerful. Less open, more sheltered, it offers a serious character; with the light still more intercepted, it becomes mysterious or gloomy. Similarly, in the distribution of the plan, a series of divisions relative to each other confirms the general character. Large rooms must not be preceded by small ones.

The same is true of gardens: without wishing to cramp their size, let us say that the principal walks, the parterres, and the esplanade must be in proportion to the building that commands them. Not length but width is our principal concern. However, if a point of view were required for a principal walk, it would require to be more open and provided with all possible adornments. A general consonance gives pleasure and is the essential basis of the building. Everything must concur to a single end, as in a stage decoration, where all is connected.

The principal rooms in an apartment must be in keeping with the exterior, as we have said; but they must also be in harmony with each other in extent, in the height of the ceilings, and in the decoration. A progression in the richness of the ornament is prescribed; but this is a delicate matter, and it requires great taste and prudence. Always pass from simplicity to opulence: thus, the vestibule is less ornate than the antechambers; the antechambers less so than the salons and cabinets, etc. . . . Each room must have its own particular character. The analogy, the relation of proportions, decides our sensations; each room makes us want the next; and this engages our minds and holds them in suspense. It is a satisfaction in itself.

Too much opulence is burdensome; it flatters the vanity, but we easily tire of it. Gilding tires even by its brightness. Sculpture in quantity lapses into confusion. Looking glasses that are too numerous and ill positioned make a place gloomy and create melancholy. Narcissus exhausted himself by staring into crystal waters.

A fine and delicate taste is needed to use richness with discretion and with that magical art whereby the able Artist conceals his devices. Where he fails, he takes the blame. He alone chooses, places, combines, mixes; he alone prescribes the forms, determines the affinities, decides the correspondences, assigns the proprieties, fixes the degree of expression, and establishes the character of the whole.

The merit of every object lies in its placing, which alone confers grace and value upon it. From the simplest objects, taste alone draws the most delightful effects, as an able Sculptor extracts a masterpiece from the commonest material. Small talents cling to rich materials and suppose that brilliancy adds merit to their work; they deceive themselves. The nobility of the whole and the beauty of the details strike, captivate, and delight our senses. Beauties, to please us, need nothing but themselves; the interest and the pleasure are in them alone. The greatest satisfaction is to find everything in its proper place.

Ornaments, therefore, must be sparingly employed and disposed with taste; one cannot devote too much consideration to their genre, their character, and their necessity.

It is the same with pictures; they are not appropriate everywhere. A superb Michelangelo or a magnificent Raphael would lose some of its beauty if not suitably placed and lit. Moreover, the size and genre of a painting, even its subject, must be relative to the room in which it hangs. It should make us think it had been made for the place.

An apartment is not like a cabinet or gallery of pictures; every room has its own particular purpose, and from its appearance one must be able to deduce its use. The expression, the imprint of character, is decisive; let delicacy hold the scales, taste try the weight, and good sense determine.

These general laws apply to the interior and the exterior alike. For the beauty of an apartment as a whole, it is necessary to give precedence to the long enfilade and the magnificent vista; and one may add greatly to the effect by means of looking glasses, which multiply the objects and extend the views.[14]

Symmetry, or rather the use of repeated and balanced forms, is essential. Where a glass appears on the one side, there must be a glass on the other, of the same dimensions and in a frame of the same shape. The same principle is to be followed in hanging pictures. There must be no more on the one side than on the other; and ensure that they are of the same sizes and similarly framed.

Take great care to fill the central positions with objects of prime importance and kindred nature. Opposite a chimneypiece and beneath a looking glass, it will be quite appropriate to find a marble table; but the design, the character, and the marbles employed must be of the same kind. There is nothing more distasteful than contrasts; they are as unpleasing to the eye as a faulty proportion; they are a defect in the harmony.

In such a case, might one not adopt a contrivance that we have seen succeed? On the chimneypiece, instead of consoles, we have used detached terms, which support the mantel and which are pleasingly reflected in a glass set into the marble of a pilaster; this gives an astonishing play to the ensemble. The marble table opposite is supported by similar terms, and the glass behind extends downward to the floor. The effect is somewhat like a detached altar, adorned with candelabra; one might imagine it consecrated to the Goddess of gardens, to judge by the flowers and the opulence of the vases that contain them.

Let us turn aside for a moment from these ingenious devices, fine though their effect can sometimes be; it will be time to discuss them when we come to examine ways to stir the soul and excite the sensations. Let us first pursue the means by which architecture may be made to give pleasure and seek to determine the most general laws to this end.

Cornices govern the ensemble, wherever they are employed; success depends on them. Interior cornices, above all, are the essential ornaments of the rooms in which they are placed and whose character they determine. Their proportions, the combinations of their moldings, the beauty of their profiles, their pleasing outlines, and their concordance captivate and delight us by their harmony, as does the relation of their height and projection with the size and extent of the place. Their relief, more or less strongly marked in relation to the distance from which they are seen, can make or mar the success of a whole apartment: nothing can remedy the want of harmony between a cornice and the room in which it is placed. Let there be no mistake: often, despite the most artistic arrangement of furniture, glasses, and openings, something seems wanting; we are aware of a deficiency. Glance up at the cornice, and the reason will be evident: the cornice is out of proportion with the size of the room. Either it is too large or too small; it has not enough relief; it has too much or too little ornament; or that ornament is not in keeping with it or not relative to the genre and character of the room. A trifle is enough to disrupt the harmony and suspend the emotion. This is a matter of great weight, therefore, and not by any means to be neglected. The cornice is the frame for the whole; it must have a genre, a character, all its own; it must bear the stamp of good taste. What, then, is this ensemble of mass? What is the fittest proportion? Here is the principle that serves as a point of departure.

The cornice is one-twelfth of the height of the room in which it is placed; take care to give it, according to circumstances, one-fifth or one-quarter more projection than its own height. This observation applies to interiors only, because in exterior work the projection must always be equal to the height. In an interior this excess of projection over height contributes a lightness; the members are elongated, the doucines are more pleasing, and the whole is more harmonious. Add gilding, and the relief is further enhanced; the ensemble is more precious, and its appearance is richer. The reason is a physical one. Internal cornices are seldom or never seen at an angle of forty-five degrees, that is to say from a distance equal to their height; and so the rule given here must be followed in order to compensate the eye and supply the lack of the distance that gives the angle of forty-five degrees, which is the most convenient point from which to see any object in relief. There is another cause; and this is derived from the shadows that every piece of Architecture requires to show itself to advantage. This rule, which is observed in Painting, is determined by perspective. Our celebrated Artists have adopted it in interiors that make an impression at first glance.

No Apartment can please if we deviate from this general law. Ornaments cannot be relied upon to vary the degree of lightness in each member; they would produce no effect, and the result would be absurd. Ornaments are not to be used in profusion; they are like salt in a ragout, to be dispensed with caution.

The taste that is based on *true beauty* is always of a piece; it derives from nature, and nature's course is a constant one. We shall not include under the heading of ornament those indeterminate, baroque masses, which defy description and which we call by the name of *chicory*.[15] Let us dismiss from our minds such Gothic monstrosities, although they were still in use barely ten years ago and they remained regrettably current among us for thirty-five years and more. It is hard to conceive how we ever allowed ourselves to be seduced by a genre that can only be the product of a disordered imagination.[i] Perhaps we were led astray by the spirit of novelty, perhaps also by the ease with which baroque forms could be made. Any form was permissible; if only it rippled, everyone was happy: no harmony, no

---

i. It was Monsieur Pineau, a Sculptor, who first introduced this singular and purely capricious kind of work. And yet he was an Artist possessed of much talent and a great facility for design and who had a busy practice. It was a sorry day for the Arts when he adopted so frivolous and so irrational a manner.

concord, no symmetry. If the moldings contorted themselves into some outland-
ish figure, or if they were set off by some miserable cartouche turned on its head
and plastered with rocaille, all was well; it was a masterpiece. A Chinese plant,
which was the name given to an ornament that no one could define, the result of a
chance configuration of the wood when it was cut, served to combine the moldings and form the centers. The further an ornament appeared to stray from natural
form, the more precious it seemed: such were the follies committed by men like
Watteau and Callot in painting, and such in Literature was the burlesque manner
of Scarron and his imitators.[16] These are the ephemeral diseases, the depravities of
taste, against which we cannot be too much on our guard. There must be no departing from natural beauty merely for the sake of having something new. What
study, what pains, what care are needed to shape a work of beauty in any art! History relates that the Helen of Athens was composed from three hundred of the
most beautiful girls from every part of Greece.[17] To what extremes will Artists not
go, in Painting or in Sculpture, when they feel the noble impulse to compete for
well-earned applause? How many are the different models that they require, for
the head or for the body, which is often subdivided into as many parts as there are
attributes! The leg, the foot, even the outline of the fingers may require a change
of model.

Talent must grasp nature only in what is *beautiful*. All learned Artists
shun exaggerated attitudes; they fly from nature when she is ill-favored. *Beauty* is
all one; this point must be the aim: it will be found only in the purity of proportions and in their harmony; and there, only Genius can be our guide. Genius is a
ray of Divinity, whose faintest glimmer recalls the blaze of its source. Let us endeavor, through constant inquiry and through our own reflections, to form our
own taste. Taste often serves to develop and rectify Genius and often, indeed, governs and determines it.

So much for the general rules of *the art of pleasing* in Architecture: let
us pass on to particulars.

EXTERIOR DECORATION

True harmony in Architecture depends on the consonance between the masses and between the various parts. The style and the tone must be relative to the character of the whole, and the whole must be founded on nature, on the kind of Building that is to be built, and on its purpose.

The part of Architecture that we call by the name of fitness is defined and may be learned not so much by the study of rules as by a perfect understanding of the manners and customs of the age and country in which one lives. Even so, let us essay some general laws, which taste will develop and experience confirm. This will, moreover, be the subject of reflections that will lead us toward perfection by an easier path.

Let us begin with the masses of the building. Their proportion, their mutual relation, gives rise to the sound ensemble, elegant arrangement, and delightful harmony, without which nothing can satisfy.

To this end, all excessively small parts must be avoided; they create confusion, consonance is destroyed, and there is no proportion left; or the proportion is nebulous and doubtful and fails to produce the desired effect. It is an established principle that there can be no proportion between incommensurable quantities and that good proportions in general are founded on correct, immediate, and apprehensible relations. Permit yourself no lapses; for any neglect of the principles of union leads to confusion; it offends the eyes, as the ears are offended by a false note in music. The true Artist pays the closest attention to this; if he be an accurate observer, he will discern in every form the marks that distinguish it from every other; he will understand that if he wishes his building to set a calm and gentle scene, he must combine masses that do not differ too widely; he will see that they must not have too much variety and relief and that the prevailing tone must be one of tranquility and majesty; the contrasts of light and shade must be well regulated, for any excess of either would be harmful. Nothing better conveys the character of mildness than shadows that become less dense as they grow longer.

In a building of a kind in which more harshness is called for, the succession will be less regular, and the transitions more frequent.

If a building is to be marked by simplicity, too many divisions will be avoided. Another, where no pretension to elegance is wanted, may still be rendered notable by the use of numerous masses and divisions to create an effect of richness and profusion. An air of vivacity and gaiety may be imparted by similar means: stringcourses and cornices provide enhancement and variety.

The harsh effects produced by excessive relief, the unduly strong impressions caused by contrasts of light and shade, all, in short, that seems to spring from immoderate effort, disturbs the enjoyment of a scene intended only for amusement and pleasure.

The majestic character, even at its calmest, is never languid. In a building of this sort, a happy mean prevails: harmony must be found in every part; magnificent objects, grand in their dimensions and in their style, suffice to fill and satisfy the soul; it is only where these are too few that recourse may be had to those ornaments that are proper and relative to beautiful Architecture. These are riches that may be employed; but much art is needed, together with great tact and unfailing prudence.

Terror is the effect of magnitude combined with power. The terror inspired by a natural scene may be likened to that which springs from a scene in a play; the soul is powerfully moved, but its sensations are pleasurable only when they partake of terror without repugnance. The resources of Art may be used to render these sensations more lively. The aim is to amplify those objects whose character is in their size and to give added vigor to those distinguished by power; take care to accentuate those that convey terror, while dispensing scattered hints of sadness. Projecting bays may be employed; recessions terminating in a dim obscurity, into which the eye can scarcely penetrate, will be a great resource. Where the occasion arises, afford a glimpse of some distant, vague, and indeterminate vista, in which no object meets the eye. Nothing could be more terrible; the soul stands amazed; it trembles. The stately, bold masses on which the eye first rested have prepared the soul for such a sensation. Even the majesty of the Ocean itself scarcely mitigates its measureless vastness; to become a pleasing prospect, it requires a shore, a cape, or an island in the middle distance. These varied objects give shape and life to the whole.

This genre of the terrible is enhanced by suitable ornaments; but observe that these accessories, though they may serve to designate the character, will do nothing to convey the expression. This bears the stamp of nobler qualities, which nothing can replace.

Great size is indispensable to the genre of the terrible, just as stately and clear-cut masses are the province of majesty.

When we are on the banks of a river, the motion of the water in itself numbs our senses and lulls us to sleep; a quicker motion rouses us and animates us. When carried to excess, this rapidity alarms our senses; it becomes a torrent whose noise, force, and impetuosity inspire terror, a sensation closely allied to the sublime, whether as a cause or as an effect.

Such is the progression of our sensations: the proportion between one part and the whole determines the natural placing of an object, indicates its kind, and supplies the style appropriate to every scene.

It is impossible to pay too much attention to the masses in a building, to their intended effect in elevation, and to the greater or lesser degree of light that may result; the shadows must temper the light, and the light must temper the shadows. In this principle, success resides; here alone *true beauty* is to be found; this is a subject of great importance, which has yet to receive due attention. If only this can be considered and discussed, the truth will come to light, and the greatest benefits will ensue. This observation, we repeat, is essential. Even the most intelligent Architect can hope to succeed only by adapting his design to the exposure of the Sun to the principal parts of his building. Like the skillful Painter, he must learn to take advantage of light and shade, to control his tints, his shadings, his nuances, and to impart a true harmony to the whole. The general tone must be proper and fitting; he must have foreseen the effects and be as careful in considering all the parts as if he had to show a picture of them.

Just as in a play a single action occupies the stage, similarly in a building the unity of character must be observed, and this truth must capture the imagination by presenting itself to the eye.

Never depart from fitness and decorum in relation to the genre to which the intended building belongs.

Infuse the whole with wit, grace, and refinement; these are the qualities that made the masterpieces of the Greeks into the delight of their age. The whole must have an easy, natural air; let the labor not be apparent. When the work of Architecture has been finished with the utmost care, it must seem to have cost little or no effort. The nature of great Art is to conceal itself. But above all let order, propriety of character, and harmony be apparent in every part; let there be a pleasing something in the air; let it appear that the Graces themselves have directed the work. Leave lifeless ornaments to the vulgar: these are weak contrivances, and no more. The grand ensemble alone can draw and hold the attention; it alone can engage both the soul and the eye.

The first glimpse must hold us spellbound; the details, the masses of the decoration, the profiles, the play of light, all conduce to this same end. Large divisions, purity of profiles, a play of light that is neither too bright nor too somber, grand openings, and great harmony will proclaim the grandeur and magnificence to come. These riches will be found in the Corinthian proportion.

Where the martial quality rules, the proportions to be followed are those of the Doric Order; here firmness is wanted, and the plan must be severe.

If you seek to convey the tone appropriate to the Palace of Themis,[18] then the dimensions of the Ionic Order will come to your aid. The solids must be less abrupt than in the previous instance, the openings well managed and less bright.

Sadness and gaiety arise from the greater or lesser compactness of the masses; you must either circumscribe the soul or give it the free rein that nature dictates. We are so constituted that in moments of joy our heart expands and loses itself in space. An open place, abundant daylight, great harmony, great consonance, little shadow, and therefore less contrast, will evoke that spirit of gaiety that accords so well with health.

If you wish to see gaiety unconfined, contrive to have as much daylight as possible and masses that are not too strong, so that nothing seems to engage the mind and that enjoyment may be unreflective. There must be nothing to break the mood. Art must not be evident at any point; all must have an easy, simple, natural form.

To render a place sad, the rules are more or less the opposite: the daylight must be somber and restricted and must create halftones; there must be simple and unified masses, and therefore less liveliness in the whole; impose monotony, that the eye may not stray and be distracted by variety.

An open location, various forms of reflected light, variety in shadow, and an ensemble based on Ionic proportions will be conducive to distraction.

An even, subdued light, which can be created by the use of straight lines, and of masses, and of spaces that are narrow in relation to their height and length, will predispose to thoughtfulness. Lighting from above will enhance the effect; and even a borrowed or reflected daylight may be an advantage. A number of devices may be tried, but these demand the utmost care and thought.

It is important, in any event, to maintain the majestic dimness that ought to mark those buildings consecrated to Religion; here we must look to our Gothic temples and consult them with the most scrupulous attention. The lessons that they have to teach us are judicious; we might even say, sublime.

We have stated that grandeur and magnificence must assert themselves in an ensemble based on the proportions of the Corinthian Order; but if your sources of light become sharp, bright, and numerous, and if you avoid vast, bold masses, then you verge upon the genre of pleasure.

To inspire respect and esteem, grandeur is necessary. Look for masses that are handsome, well proportioned, and pronounced; let the profiles be noble ones; let there not be too much play of light; let the shadows be even, with little reflection.

If you wish to inspire a tender passion, then avoid straight lines in the plan; or, at least, combine them with curves; these forms are sacred to Venus. The light must not be too brilliant, or all her mystery will be lost. Gallantry and delicacy must prevail. Dainty ornaments are fitting here; bestow them with taste.

Such are the principles that can be laid down in general in order to arouse our sensations. They give rise to countless nuances; it is for the true Artist to grasp them and put them into practice.

Let us retrace our steps and say that even the passage through the gateway must announce and bear the imprint of the place to which it leads, in the character proper to it, in its form, and in its dimensions. In general, too great a length, unless its width be in proportion, will make it dismal and gloomy. Its proportions may extend from a perfect square to a rectangle twice as long as it is wide; where the length must exceed this last measure, as often happens, there must be apertures to right and left, even false ones, to interrupt the excessive depth and make it more endurable. The porter's lodge and entries to staircases will offer a pretext for these openings, which must be as large and as well proportioned as possible. At worst, a number of false windows will introduce variety, always provided they are perfectly symmetrical and well proportioned; architraves, stringcourses, cornices, and accessories will contribute some enrichment. A number of niches, tastefully decorated, artfully placed, and adorned with beautiful figures, will have a fine effect; the aptness of their symbols will convey the character of the building and prepare the mind for the sensations to come.

The *forecourt* is another object that merits great attention. It must be neither too large nor too small: the surrounding structures will determine its extent, and their relation to each other provides the first stirrings of the desired sensation. Buildings of differing height around a single space embody the degrees that separate sadness from cheerfulness; and the same applies to other qualities.

To have a forecourt that is well proportioned, at least half of it must always be in sunlight. To this end it will be half as long again as it is wide; this width being double the height of the wings of the building. But what are the proportions of these wings? If they consist only of a single story, an Order of Architecture must be implied, and the proportions must follow from this.

If there are two stories, divide the entire height into six parts: assign three to the lower story, two to the upper story, and one to the entablature.

If you desire three stories, divide the whole into fourteen parts: the lowest story will have five, the next story four, the upper story three, and the entablature two.

Never carry the division further than three stories, for this leads to pettiness, a fault that cannot be too studiously avoided. If forced to it, single out the lowest story, treat it as a basement, give it the same height as the floor above, and then all the other subdivisions will apply to the upper parts.

If convenience demands an entresol, make sure that no sign of it appears on the facade; this would give a weak, impoverished effect, which would mar the beauty of the whole.

So much for the proportion between the buildings and the forecourt; observe also that when the length is greater than twice the width, it seems cramped, unless projecting bays provide contrasting forms of their own.

The wings must not be so high as the building at the far end of the court, which is to be regarded as the principal feature.

The centers of the wings and of the principal building must be decorated with projecting bays; such an arrangement gives a play to the whole plan. The four corners may with advantage be occupied by four projecting pavilions. Sometimes, canted corners with a projecting bay will also make a good effect. Employ varied forms and masses, by all means; but be unsparing in your attention to their affinity and to the harmony of their proportions. These masses and these forms determine the kind and character of the sensation; they modify the play of light and its effect; they govern the shadows; and they delineate the work as a whole.

Furthermore, the relief of the projecting bays should be related to the mass of the buildings and to the extent of the forecourt.

There must be no projections in the entablature, except where there are projecting bays beneath; then, it will form well-shaped masses and lend animation to the design; otherwise, it makes the whole ensemble waver, ruins it, renders it mean and tasteless.

The projecting and receding bays must not be equal in width, or they would become monotonous. The recesses must therefore be double the projecting bays in width, so that for every foot of width in the projection, the recess must have no less than two, and no more than three; this principle must be observed where harmony is to be maintained.

The masses, the recesses, and the projecting bays concur to produce the effect. In plan they give variety; in the masses they supply grace; and in the elevation they break the monotony of the straight line, which would otherwise terminate the building and make it wearisome and dull. Perspective causes the projecting bays to seem higher than those that form the body of the structure; and to our eyes they have the advantage of standing out and tracing the form of their plan against the skies.

In avoiding one fault, however, let us not fall into another; in a plan with too many projecting bays, the whole becomes meager and wearisome to the eye. There is a just mean from which true beauty cannot depart.

Let us also observe that a building of any extent must be relieved and interrupted by inequalities of height. To design a few projections is not enough; it must possess contrast and diversity and must still present an outline when it is seen at a distance from which all the parts seem to coalesce and only the mass remains.

We have the sad proof of this in the Garden front of the Château de Versailles. View its mass and ensemble from any distance, and as we have said, it produces no effect; it has all the sad monotony of a long, high wall. What sensation might not have been produced, on the other hand, had it been designed in accordance with the simple ideas and reflections that we venture to put forward here! Some parts higher than the others and more diversity in the masses and in the plans would have given it play and life; concord and harmony would have made it into a delightful ensemble.

A moment's reflection and a reference to the rules of Art will show that this is so. A projecting bay, in consequence of perspective, will appear higher than the main structure; observation is conclusive, as are the proven principles of optics. From any point, draw two lines forming any angle, and the distance between them will be larger at four feet than at two; and so the more distant of any two bodies will seem smaller, in proportion to its distance.

Let us briefly frame the ideas that govern exterior decoration.

Observe that one cannot be too careful in determining the genre and character of the building that is to be constructed: once this is settled, admit nothing but what is necessary. The finest things, out of place, may displease; they disturb our sensations by leading our thoughts astray.

The ensemble must therefore be well proportioned, both to its own component parts and to the genre and character that it is intended to display. It must be well endowed with rhythm and symmetry, both in plan and in elevation. The right must not be wider than the left, or the latter different from the former.

In a facade where some parts are higher than others, it is generally the central portion that must predominate, forming a pyramid. In a long facade, it is necessary to relieve the straight line that would otherwise mark its upper termination and that would prevent it from cutting an outline against the sky; otherwise, it would be monotonous and devoid of effect. Projecting and retreating bays supply variety to the whole and produce the harmony that is so necessary to the great art of pleasing; in general, the forms of buildings govern the principal effect. A commonplace form, with little regularity in proportion, inevitably produces only sensations of displeasure or disgust.

It is impossible, therefore, to devote too much care to the composition of a plan, the regularity of its proportions, the exactness of its consonances, the beauty of its masses, and the varied play and effects of light. It is light and shade that determine its success and contribute most to its character.

There are a thousand ways to surprise, to please, or to delight; but there is only one true beauty. Our sensations are our guide; they distinguish the nuances.

Let us make nature our study. It is by contemplating her, in all her parts, that we may trace in the general plan of our fabric the manifold series of relations that, like so many links in a chain, form a whole whose component masses generate the true harmony that is ever simple and ever magnificent.

The fecundity of genius, which turns everything to advantage, will always find a way to please through the elegance of the form, the beauty of the ensemble, and the good taste of the ornaments. What obstacles can one not overcome? What effects can one not produce when courage, tireless industry, and a pure and natural taste unite with a judgment sustained by profound study and reflection?

For the rest, I offer my views; it is for those who feel the need of them to heed them, to elaborate them, and to perfect them.

Gardens are a great enhancement to buildings when well related; when the esplanade in front is well proportioned; when the parterres are in proportion, maintaining always the happy disarray, the piquant oddity, that marks the productions of nature; when Art, while seeming neglected, contrives to show us agreeable and charming vistas terminated by delightful points of view that excite the liveliest curiosity.

A celebrated amateur,[i] and one worthy of the position that he holds, has spoken of this so elegantly, in his Book with the modest title of an *Essai sur les jardins* [Essay on gardens], that we can do no better than direct the reader to that work. In it, all is sensed, all is foreseen, all is reasoned and dictated by delicacy.[19] Every part affects us, and every part prompts the appropriate sensation. Such are the delights of a true Philosopher. In reading it, one might be wandering in those Gardens where the Fairies spin their enchantments; and yet, on reflection, there is nothing that is not simple and natural. Such is the hold that truth has over our senses.

A beautiful dream, these ideas may be; but there is no denying that this is a dream that can be made to come true. Analyzed, these same ideas become still more delightful, and to develop them further can only spur our imaginations and place within our reach all the treasures of a mine in whose depths there lies the precious gift of exciting our emotions, gratifying our sensations, and suiting our dwellings to our tastes, to our desires, and to the various needs that luxury creates every day, both for our personal satisfaction and in relation to the customs and manners of the society to which we belong.

i. M. Watelet, of the Académie Française, etc.

ON *DISTRIBUTION* AND *DECORATION*

*T*he principal subject of our dissertation is the distribution of the interior plan. Where a building is pleasing from the outside, we must see to it that the interiors are equally so; these are the parts in which we live, and for that reason they are all the more precious to us. The outer parts are no less interesting: they seem designed to prepare our minds; they convey an initial impression, whether favorable or unfavorable. It is the exterior that must first capture our attention and engage us; it must indicate the nature of the interiors and the use for which they are intended. A temple is not designed like a private building, however splendid. The inner and outer parts must be intimately related. It would be an elementary blunder to make the exterior too magnificent if the interiors were not in keeping; rather keep the outside simple than load it with riches while neglecting the inside. This is a common fault, which one cannot be too careful to avoid. It produces much the same sensation as if we were to see a person in a superbly braided coat but with the rest of his attire poor, rustic, and uncouth.

Before entering into detail, let us briefly survey the buildings of the ancient Romans, those masters of the world. They put everything into the exterior decoration, as did the Greeks, and their interiors were not at all convenient; there was no proportion between successive rooms; the exterior decoration governed their size. Vast galleries were the principal feature of these ancient buildings. Take the descriptions that Pliny gives of his country houses.[20] We find in that of the Laurentine an immense area of land, much sumptuousness, great magnificence; but no private comforts. Their skill extended only so far as to take advantage of the site, of the exposures most favorable to health, and of the delight that wise men feel when enjoying a pure and temperate air in every season, despite the changes in the weather.

Another lesson to be learned is the Art of taking advantage, in Architecture, of all that a climate offers that is pleasing to the eye and to the mind, relative to the site. Among the large and numerous rooms, there were some where one could enjoy the sight and even the sound of the sea; in others, secluded among gardens, that sound was heard only as a distant murmur. In those parts that enjoyed neither sight nor sound of the sea, the profoundest peace and quiet prevailed. In these various situations there were apartments and chambers for day and for night, grand rooms for assemblies and banquets, and others, less large, for gatherings of the family and of a select circle of friends. There were private rooms, where the master could isolate himself from his household, at the end of a long gallery, to work and to rest.

The whole bespeaks great ceremony, much profusion, and a faulty conception of luxury. This is apparent in the size and extent of each room and in its use. If we consider the exterior of the buildings that composed the Laurentine, the length of the principal front appears to have been some hundred and seventy toises;[21] but it may have been as much as two hundred and forty toises,[i] if the lodgings of the slaves and freedmen stretched as far as the corresponding parts on the other side in order to give the whole a perfect symmetry. This was no more than would be needed if we consider that the ordinary banqueting chamber was ten or eleven toises long by a little more than six wide. The great court was thirty toises by twenty-four, and the small, circular court was twelve toises in diameter. The gallery, which Pliny himself likened in size to those of public buildings, was forty-five toises long by five toises wide; a second banqueting chamber was twelve toises by eight; and the adjoining room was twelve toises by about six wide, as was the Tennis court.

Estimate the size of the whole from these measurements; add the gardens, and remember that this was the house of a Consul,[ii] who had several others

---

i. To give a comparative idea of this extent, we shall observe, that the garden front of the Château des Tuileries is one hundred and seventy toises in length. We shall add that the full length of the Château de Versailles, on the garden side, is two hundred and twenty toises.

equally large and equally splendid.[iii]

We might cite the houses of Cicero, as described by Sallust, those of Pompey, or the magnificence of the buildings erected by Lucius Lucullus, Sulla, and many other Romans; but these descriptions, however interesting, would be of little use for the present purpose. They would show us only the way in which the ancients lived, which was very different in internal arrangement from that which we use in France. Our manners are not the same; nor are our customs. We shall therefore confine ourselves to what relates to us and say that the Frenchman alone, spurred by a love of pleasure, has refined upon the comforts of life. Nourished by ambition, inspired by magnificence, he has laid his tribute on the altars of luxury. Because he is industrious, he turns everything to use. A trifle occupies and distracts him, and before long he has endowed it with importance; he has made it useful; fashion then takes a hand, and what was formerly only useful becomes a necessity. He is not seduced by outward size; he knows better how to reconcile his interests and pursue his goal. He likes to concentrate his possessions, but he has no desire to confuse their separate uses. If the rooms appear numerous, this is for the sake of good order and the tone of grandeur.

Ingenious Frenchmen! Our age stands amazed at the breadth of your talents. The man of sensibility admires the apt distributions of plans that you have devised. Such has been your progress in Architecture: one step more, and his soul will take wing; he is transported by the harmony and rapport of architectural proportions wisely employed. You govern the motions of his heart, and by a kind of magic you excite all manner of sensations at will. It is our intention to enlarge upon these various effects, and on them we hope to establish rules and principles. May the happy spirit that gave us the first inspiration now deign to direct our pen. Let us begin with the distribution of the plan, which is a matter of the greatest interest, because it is the source of our well-being.

To avoid confusion, let us take one step at a time. We observe, first, that in general an apartment must consist of no less than five essential rooms: an anteroom, a salon, a bedroom, a cabinet, and a closet. But how many needs has luxury created! A salon must be preceded by several anterooms, and the anterooms themselves must be preceded by a vestibule. A first anteroom for the generality of

ii. Pliny, nephew of Pliny the Historian, who lived under the rule of Trajan, around the hundredth year of our salvation.

iii. His house in Tuscany, another at Frascati, and another at Tivoli, which Pliny designates by the names of Tusculum, Tibur, and Praeneste.

the servants; a second for the valets and for those respectable callers whom it is necessary to announce; the third anteroom is for these same persons to wait in. The dining room must not be far from this first room, and adjacent to it must be a room where the dishes may be placed as they come from the kitchen and stand ready in the order in which they are to appear on the table; there will also be a room to rinse the glasses and to keep the wine and the spirits that may be needed in the course of the meal. All these will, as far as possible, have lobbies to give access to kitchen and offices. There will be no need to pass through the anterooms, and the service of the dining room will be kept away from them. It must be possible to enter the salon undisturbed, without the risk of being jostled and upset by a servant intent on waiting at table.

The third anteroom thus affords entry to the salon and to the closets, which must not be far from the dining room. These must not open upon the salon or the dining room; the second or third antechamber commonly affords access to them.

The bedroom must adjoin the salon. This room entails a quantity of accessories: it requires a closet of its own, a dressing room, a boudoir, and lodging for one or two valets or lady's-maids, and for a footman. Not far away must be the apartment set aside for bathing, which ordinarily comprises a bathroom, a vapor bath, a lobby, and a water closet, and finally a private bedroom.

The apartment I have described, which is normally that of the mistress of the house, is followed by that of the master, whose first and second anterooms are often identical with the foregoing. But two cabinets or studies are needed to take the place of a salon and serve for receiving company. After this comes the bedroom, which must be accompanied by one or two fine, back cabinets and closets with separate lobbies. Not to be forgotten is a library and cabinet at the end: often a gallery is required for pictures and another cabinet for medals and bronzes, even, very often, a cabinet of natural history. It will be seen that all these rooms require others accessory and relative to them, and we shall give an account of these when we enter into more detail. For the time being, suffice it to say that alongside these numerous and extensive apartments there are private apartments in which care must be taken to supply everything that convenience, ease, and luxury may demand. These are more frequented than the state apartments; a preference that has its source in nature. The state apartments, properly speaking, exist purely for display, and this appears inseparable from a degree of unease and discomfort. In rooms that are too large, a man feels out of proportion. Things are too remote from him; we huddle into one part of the room, and the rest becomes useless and irksome.

The lodgings of the domestic servants and of the officers of the household must be within reach.

Often there are summer and winter apartments; salons, in particular, tend to be distinct. One may even have an autumn salon, in addition to those for summer and winter.

It must not be supposed that this description refers to the Palace of a King. A private person, whose wealth inclines him toward splendor, will insist on this superabundance of space in which to live. An Actress or a lady of fashion will often go further.

The kitchens bring with them a larder, a scullery, a roasting chamber, and a buttery.

The offices or pantries require a stove room, an oven, and two store chambers, one for preserves and sweetmeats and the other for fruit; even so, adjoining this, there should be a fruitery. There must also be a room large enough to lay out what is to be served. For the silver there should be a room adjoining the Pantryman's lodging, which will consist of three or four rooms, all the more useful because when guests are entertained, some part of these rooms will be used for the necessary work.

The Secretary, the Steward, and the Majordomo all have their lodgings, positioned in the manner most appropriate to their functions.

The Head Groom and the Undergroom will be lodged within reach of the stable yard; and close to the stables there must be places to keep the saddles and bridles.

The carriage houses will face North; mostly open, but there must also be some that are closed for the best carriages, which it is expedient to protect; and there must also be a place to store the cushions, tassels, ribbons, and the horses' cockades.

Make the stable yards large enough to turn the carriages when harnessed as they are intended to be; there must additionally be a yard for manure with access to the street outside; it is here that the latrines for the servants are generally placed.

It is highly inconvenient to alight from a carriage without being under shelter.

The Porter must be within reach of the principal entrance, and he must have at least a lodge, a bedroom, a little woodshed, and a cellar.

Such is the ensemble of that which we call a Town House, or Hôtel; such, also, is that of most of the country houses in the vicinity of our Capital.

This summary will convey an idea of the whole, but at the same time it does not sufficiently describe the relations between all the parts, and consequently the analogy between the proportions and our sensations: we shall therefore discuss all these parts separately, describing the qualities of convenience and pleasantness appropriate to each.

To this end, let us determine the general rules that govern the distribution of the plan and observe that one cannot be too careful to maintain long enfilades;[22] the aim should be to create as many as possible and to prolong them by means of looking glasses.

The spaces between the corners and the reveals of the windows must be equal in any given room, as must the intervening piers; the window openings too must be of the same size; all the doors must be of equal height and width, or at the very least they must be disguised or hidden when it happens that they are not of the same dimensions, or not in the center of a wall, or when they are not placed symmetrically. They will be located in such a way that no one is forced to brush past the furniture in order to turn into a room or to pass from one room to another. In parading, one should trace, as it were, a segment of a circle; we are like those carriages that are driven in a wide sweep in order to avoid snagging.

The chimneypieces and stoves will be so placed as not to impede persons walking from one room to another, especially in the anterooms. The Domestic Servant is gross and uneducated, in general; it is pointless to lay him open to the consequences of his own carelessness.

It is essential to embed the flues of the chimneys in the thickness of the walls; otherwise, the returns of the cornices, or rather the projections that will be necessary, are unpleasing and occasion great difficulty with the ornaments, especially in cornices with modillions, the caissons of which must always be perfectly square.

The width of the fireplace recess between the flanking piers will be relative to the room where it is situated; in general, it is one-sixth of the room. As for the width of the piers, this is one-sixth of the width of the opening. The height below the mantel should be two-thirds of the width of the opening.

Have no fear of making mantels too low: a pressing argument is the resultant ease of seeing oneself in the glass above; the less high, the less the exposure to smoke.

In many cabinets, I have seen chimneypieces no higher than a tabletop, and the effect was excellent; this proportion, being in keeping with the room itself, was pleasing and seemed to give satisfaction. There are prejudices, or rather habits, of which it is best to rid oneself. Besides, all must be in proportion. This principle, drawn from nature, is among the most important in the Arts.

The parquet must be laid symmetrically about the centers of the chimneypieces and the enfilade of the principal doors.

The passages and lobbies will be convenient, easy, and well lit and will contain stairs to the entresols commonly situated above closets or other small rooms, which cannot be as high as the grand and principal rooms. It would be useful if the Master of the House could pass from one end of it to the other without being seen; it is easy to arrange a device whereby, while seeming to pass through the thickness of the walls, he may traverse them lengthwise. For this purpose all that is required is a passage constructed between the two rooms of any fabric that is two rooms deep. In such a case, this passage may be concealed by either leaf of the principal door when this stands open: it would otherwise be apparent that the wall is a hollow structure. Some Architects have made a second, entresol, passage at the height of the doors, so that its floor forms the ceiling of the door embrasures; this is a resource additional to the one we have mentioned. One can pass through and see the various parts of one's house at any time without being seen, but only after first mounting a little hidden stair. I have put this into practice, but in my experience only the passage at ground level has been used. Nevertheless, this second passage is extremely serviceable: one observes through a little concealed opening at the top of each room. It is a way of keeping one's servants in check. It is used when the need arises, and the knowledge of its existence inspires respect. Any unwelcome curiosity can be obviated by closing off the opening with a locked flap, to which the Master alone has the key.

The rooms within the apartments vary in their shapes: some will be square, others rectangular, others will be round, oval, or octagonal; in fact they can be made in all kinds of regular figures. The rectangle, or oblong, is the form most generally adopted. The octagon is convenient for entrances and for reflections in glasses. Often the corners of a rectangle are canted; often, also, a room will end in one or more segments of circles. The forms may be varied in endless ways. In rooms where a serious character is desired, square forms will be chosen; round ones are more cheerful, and curves are more voluptuous. We shall give the reasons for this.

For the moment, let us examine each room in detail, its purpose, and all the related considerations. These things once understood, it will become easier to apprehend the harmony and the proportion of the parts to one another and to the whole.

Vestibule

The vestibule is the entry, or rather the room, that leads to the grand staircase and the other lobbies: it is therefore decorated in accord with the genre of the whole building of which it forms part. It is frequently open at both ends. The stairs must be on the right,[23] thus affording the facility of entering or leaving a carriage under cover. This principle must never be neglected, although unfortunately we have many examples to the contrary. Most of our Royal Residences are deficient in this respect, and the defect is a fundamental one; you cannot be too careful to avoid it. What handsomeness and what convenience there is in the porch of the Palais-Royal![iv] [24] There is every facility for the duties that fall to Servants whenever their Masters enter or leave their carriages. In most other buildings, on the contrary, whether Châteaux, Palaces, or Hôtels, when it rains, it is the Masters themselves who feel the inconvenience. Observe that in any building the vestibule, being the first room that is encountered, must set the tone for the whole. It is for the skill of the Artist to capture the purpose of each room by employing the character proper to it, as we have already noted; and this will emerge as we describe the character of each room in relation to its purpose.

First Anteroom

The first anteroom is the common room that is entered from the vestibule, or from the landing, and in which the Servants are. It must consequently be proportioned in relation to the numbers intended to occupy it. Its decoration is to be simple: its walls are to be plainly wainscoted to their full height; its ceiling is often without a cornice; or the cornice will have very few moldings. The floor is normally paved with freestone in octagonal slabs of lias with black marble dressings. This room is most often heated by a stove in a niche, and the heat from this will be communicated, if desired, to the second anteroom, the niche being within the thickness of the wall. Care must be taken, as has been observed, to keep this stove away from the areas through which persons pass. It is essential to place the doors in such a way that no one, in passing from one room to another, may be in danger of knocking against the furniture. In this room there will be large wardrobes to keep the hats and greatcoats of the Servants, also candlesticks and lanterns. One of these may contain a bed, which can be let down for the Servant on night watch. There will be a fireproof location for the torches; on another side

iv. By M. Contant d'Ivry, Architect to the King and a member of his Academy, who designed the Church of the Madeleine, and who died in 1777.

there will be a recess for the day's firewood. It is not convenient to leave this exposed, because of the dirt that it creates; and at the same time it is best not left to the discretion of the first Servant who happens to come in. Not only would the consumption of timber be immense, but accidents might ensue.

Second Anteroom

The second anteroom must be more ornate; it serves for the valets de chambre. This room is commonly parqueted or boarded in a herringbone pattern for greater solidity. It has a chimneypiece with a plain marble mantel, and the fireplace will be formed by cast-iron backplates and covings. There must be a looking glass and frame over the mantel. This room is also to be wainscoted to its full height. It even suffers decoration, of a kind: some sculptural ornaments may be employed, but always in the genre and in the character appropriate to the condition of the Master, as we shall explain. The cornice may be enriched with dentils and ornamentally carved. Opposite the chimneypiece there may be a glass of the same width, and in a frame of the same design, as that to which it corresponds; ensure, however, that the lower member of the frame descends further, because this glass must spring from the marble table beneath it, which is ordinarily thirty-two inches high.

In this room, once again, one must become aware of the sensations to be expected in the rooms that follow; it is, so to speak, a proscenium, and the utmost care must be lavished upon it to announce the character of the performers in the play.

Third Anteroom

This third anteroom is a kind of lesser salon or preliminary cabinet in which persons of a certain distinction wait for the salon, or else the grand cabinet, to admit them.

This room is parqueted and ceiled, with a sculptured cornice; the chimneypiece must be in fine marble; the fireplace with an iron backplate and covings; a glass above of ample width and height, its frame carved and sometimes gilt. The moldings of the doors and doorcases will be ornamentally carved, and their architraves may even be crowned with a cornice supported by consoles; above this, if desired, there will be bas-reliefs or pictures. Of whatever kind, these objects must form a pleasing culmination to the door by means of a pyramidal form artfully imposed upon the principal subject: this group must always be in the middle, and its subject must be in keeping with the general character.

Here the Artist must begin to harmonize masses and details with his general intention. He must be at pains to produce impressions that are relative one to another, and to the purpose of each successive room. Here, too, he may employ painting, gilding, and sculpture. Looking glasses here become essential; but he must observe that this is a form of ornament that is not to be abused. Too much of anything is prejudicial to the end in view; where ornament is too profuse, it becomes impossible to enrich progressively, as one must, the successive rooms that remain to be decorated. In this room damask or tapestry may be used, enclosed in frames that exactly conform, in size, in kind, and in extent, to those that correspond to them, either symmetrically or across the room. Above all, let the Artist set a curb on his imagination; the genius that is his guide must remind him of the beauties and the splendors that are to be kept in reserve for his salon, his bedchamber, his cabinets, and other rooms no less interesting.

Salon

The salon is the assembly room, used for festive occasions. It is here that the greatest formality prevails; in this room, magnificence must unfold; wealth must be lavished; and the Artist must deploy his taste and his genius. Marbles, bronzes, gilding, sculpture, painting, and glasses will come to his aid; tapestries, which we have raised to such a degree of beauty, may enrich the effect. Rock crystal for the lusters, girandoles, and candelabra; precious statues; the richest of vases; the rarest of porcelains: all may combine to improve the room. In elegance and convenience alike, it will be enhanced still more by its furnishings; such is the perfection to which we have carried that art. All must proclaim the Master's magnificence; a studied care must prevail. Art, without obtruding itself, must unfold freely; let the centers be well sustained, the cadences pleasing, the openings symmetrical; looking glasses will serve as an effective accessory, although never in excess. Sculpture will be arranged with taste; its forms must be beautiful, noble, and majestic, as must the parts that they enrich. The length of the room must be in proportion to its breadth and height; and these measurements must not be left to chance. The cornice and the entablature, if any, are to be proportioned in relation to the rest; the principal moldings are to be enriched, but let the ornaments be in good taste and well designed. The profiles must project with grace. In part, the arrangement of the modillions governs the harmony of the whole; the modillion is the source of those large masses that determine character; its alignments are the source of concord, and it alone sets the tone and regulates the distribution of the whole. Where there are no modillions and it is desired to employ cornices, the principal ornament performs the same function, and its center must form the governing line. Where no ornaments are wanted in the cornice, taste alone must be the guide, but a balance must be maintained, lest the right outweigh the left; symmetry is essential. If the openings chance to be inconvenient for the arrangement of the remainder of the room, then genius must be called upon; art must supply the deficiency. Even so, care must be taken to conceal the art that is used: we have already said, and we repeat, that art is not to make itself felt, and that things must be so disposed that it seems unthinkable to do otherwise.[v] [25]

Ceilings are sometimes painted. A beautiful sky, well executed and not unduly vaporous, imparts much grace and lightness; the cornice stands out more clearly, and its effect is fully architectural. Where figures are desired in the ceiling, the subjects must be allegorical; and here the Artist must be on his guard. Too many figures or too lively and brilliant a coloring would entirely destroy the harmony of the Architecture. And so the painting of a ceiling must always have an airy tone; the objects must seem remote, as if lost in immensity.

Where this room is intended to proclaim the Master's opulence, it may convey a character of gaiety; or in some instances it may be sober and even serious. In any case, the general tone must produce its effect; and whatever character may be chosen, it is essential to make it felt. We shall endeavor to make this clear through descriptions adapted to the various sensations; such, at least, is our purpose. But let us repeat that this principal room is capable of all sorts of forms; and it is in these forms themselves that we find, in part, the characters that form the subject of the present Work. For the moment, let us simply observe that the Ancients distinguished salons by their construction: they called them *Tetrastyle, Corinthian*, and *Egyptian*. A salon was *Tetrastyle* when the soffit was supported by four columns. They called it *Corinthian* when it was decorated all around with columns engaged in the walls; and they called it *Egyptian* when it was surrounded by detached Corinthian columns, crowned by a simple architrave and supporting a second Order with a soffit.

We call a *Salon à l'Italienne* any that runs up through two stories; it is usually lit only by the windows on the upper story.

v. Read Voltaire, in his description of the *Temple du goût* [Temple of taste]:
  "Noble and plain, its Architecture rose;
  "Each ornament in due position shows,
  "As if necessity had set it there:
  "There art deceives by stealing nature's air;
  "The eye with pleasure all its structure seized,
  "Never astonished, and yet always pleased."

A salon may be built in any shape: there are square ones, such as that of the old Château de Clagny,[26] whose demolition we so much deplore, but of which, fortunately, we possess all the drawings in great detail; others of the same shape are at the extremities of the Gallery at Versailles.[27]

Some are round or oval, such as those of Vaux and Raincy; some are octagons, such as that of Marly.[28] We cite these as examples; such precious and important works can but stir and rouse the imagination, which cannot be too plentifully furnished with fine objects and grand conceptions; the time always comes when one rediscovers such treasures. We might review many other buildings, above all those built in the past ten years: in these, opulence and elegance reign supreme; the beauties of Art are fully revealed; the most exquisite taste is manifest; the soul receives pleasing and varied impressions; and France perhaps possesses a larger number of these beauties than any other country, because the genius of this nation inclines toward inventiveness. In any wealthy State, where luxury and pleasure prevail, new needs are constantly born, and these new needs are a spur to industry. Artists are inspired to mutual emulation; understanding evolves; fine discriminations are made; and even the simplest building receives the enrichments natural to it. Self-esteem and emulation combine to render Artists inventive and to lead clients to take advantage of their talents. Never has there been so much building as there is today. We see buildings rising on every side, each more sumptuous than the last. Rome may have built larger, but never with more elegance. Our interiors, above all, are elaborately contrived in decoration, in arrangement, and in convenience. Every need has been anticipated; although we often miss the gradation in opulence from one room to the next, which would be necessary for absolute perfection and for the total satisfaction of the soul. One single salon, decorated as some now are, would formerly have sufficed to make an Artist immortal. This is not enough; nowadays, the call is for ensembles in which all is in harmony. Let us therefore apply our talents; let us summon reflection and genius to our aid; let us look to the impression that every object ought to make. Let us study and pursue the precious nuance that can but delight and surprise our senses.

Bedchamber

The bedchamber that completes the state apartments will often serve only for show.[29] It is too large. There is a preference for a room with a lower ceiling, in which one feels better enclosed and in which one can be oneself. But a bedchamber there must be, for propriety's and custom's sake, and it must be in keeping with the rest of the apartment. It will be meant for ostentation, if you will; all the more reason to give it a character that inspires repose and proclaims tranquility. Avoid, therefore, the noise from the courtyards, and anything that might distract. This is the palace of Sleep, and all must be simple and uniform. The light is to be dim and faint, as it is painted at the moment of the waking of Venus, when the Graces inform her of the coming of dawn. Gauze curtains, drawn across the windows at two-thirds of their height, will admit only so much light as is appropriate to the place. The shadows, however, must not be too heavy. The Artist who concerns himself with decoration must adopt as a principle that the brighter and stronger the light, the harder the shadows become. Light and shadows influence the character of a room, and the effects that flow from it. The arrangement and the choice of furnishings contribute to the same ends. The bed will accordingly be placed at the end of the room, in the center of its width, and generally facing the windows. The chimneypiece will be halfway along the side wall, beyond the bed; otherwise, it would be too close, and symmetry would be lost; a setback or a segment of a circle will indicate the depth to be occupied by the bed. All will then be in due order, and the decoration will be in keeping.

The glass over the mantel will be the same both in dimensions and ornament as the one opposite to it, beneath which will stand one of those commodes that are called *Régence*. The room may be hung with tapestry or damask, all framed with gilt borders. The panels to left and right are to be the same. A tranquil and sedate ensemble must give a sense of the nature of the room, as we have said. Its proportions will be Ionic: this Order represents a proportional mean between the others and is well suited to such an effect. Furnishings contribute to the character more than is thought: their design and arrangement will be determined by the Artist who has devised the ensemble and not by the Upholsterer, whose task is only to execute. The proportions, the forms, and the choice of colors will thus be in the province of the Architect. All too often, the Upholsterer decides on the entire furnishing and does so without any regard to the principles enunciated here; self-interest is his only guide, and the consonant effect of the whole is lost. It is therefore the Artist's duty to attend to these details and to direct the work; only he knows what he intends, and only he can employ all the necessary means to a single end, namely, the ensemble that establishes the desired character and inspires the proper sensations.

By preference, the color green will be chosen for the hangings of a bedchamber; it has something of foliage about it, and sleep seems all the sweeter. Green is to be favored for its uniformity, and the evenness of its shades contributes to the mild and tranquil impression that is conducive to repose. The panels will be framed with gilt moldings, but these will have simple profiles; they will show little relief and almost no ornament. A few pictures may be admitted if tastefully arranged; too many would disturb repose.

The bedchamber, as we have said, is the sanctuary of sleep. Beds may take on pleasing shapes, and those called *à la Polonaise*[30] convey the idea through their elegance, their pyramidal forms, and their domed canopies; their plumed tops have a pleasing effect, but one must have the wit to keep these ornaments in proportion with the rest of the room and to compose them to suit the condition and the age of the persons for whom they are intended.

Alcoves are out of favor at the present time; not only are they inconvenient for service, in case of sickness above all, but they fail to provide for a sufficient circulation of air. It is difficult to find room in them for beds of any elegance or ornateness; and taste, luxury, and health have united to dispense with them.

Beds in niches had fewer disadvantages; but still they did not offer all the necessary convenience. The closets that were commonly placed to left and right of them were not easily reconciled with the magnificence of a state bedchamber, and such arrangements are now proscribed and relegated to subsidiary apartments of little importance.

In general, therefore, a detached bed is to be preferred, placed, as we have observed, at the back of the room, as if it were in the sanctuary of the temple. For the rest, opulence and even magnificence will set the tone for the whole room. But, once more, beware of that excess of ornament that seems to depart from the character proper to a bedchamber.

The room that follows is similar and no less interesting; this is the boudoir.

Boudoir[31]

The boudoir is regarded as the abode of delight; here she seems to reflect on her designs and to yield to her inclinations. With such thoughts in mind, dictated as they are by the manners of our age, spare no pains to make the room as pleasing as you can. All is to be subordinate to luxury, comfort, and taste. The proportions of the Corinthian Order are elegant, and here they are appropriate. Impart a tone of dignity and self-regard; this room is a lady of fashion to be adorned. The air of delicate gallantry from which there is no departing demands that the masses be light and rhythmical, the forms not pronounced. Take care to avoid the harsh shadows cast by undue brightness. A dim, mysterious light will be obtained by the use of gauze artfully disposed over part of the windows.

This is a room where there must be no lack of openings and reflections; looking glasses will produce the necessary effect. Take care, however, that they do not form the principal part of the furnishings. When used to excess, they create a sad and monotonous effect. Place them so as to leave, between each one and the next, at least twice as much space without a glass as with a glass: these intervals of repose may be adorned with fine, rich hangings. Against each panel a picture will be artfully hung with heavy tassels and silk cords braided with gold. The subjects will derive from the pleasing and amorous themes of mythology. The triumph of Amphitrite, Psyche and Cupid, or Venus and Mars, all suggest compositions apposite to the character of the room.[32] Here, all must be convenient and all must please. In keeping with the dimensions of the room, those details made to be seen close must satisfy by their harmony. The burden of the whole is this: that enjoyment is close at hand.

To the boudoir let us add private closets that are made with artistry and apt in their design.

Where the windows are to the East, the light will be softer; the prospect must be a pleasing one, as far as possible. In the absence of natural beauty, have recourse to Art: here, taste and genius must come to the fore. The magic of painting and perspective must be applied to create illusions. If a view of a private garden can be procured, then arbors, trellises, and aviaries will have a fine effect. Birdsong and an artful cascade, whose waters charm the eye and the ear alike, will seem to summon Love. Often, too, such sounds cause a sweet slumber to overcome our senses, and airy dreams set our souls adrift. Varied statues divert us with the subjects that they represent. Orange trees and myrtles, planted in choice vessels, enchant the eye and the nostrils. Honeysuckle and jasmine twine like garlands around the Deity who is worshiped at Paphos.[33] A well-contrived variety affords the interesting spectacle of the beauties of nature. Here the soul rejoices; its sensations are akin to ecstasy. This is the retreat of Flora; here, decked in her liveliest hues, she waits in secret for the caress of Zephyrus.[34] Here, the beauty and mildness of spring will always prevail. Maintain, therefore, the freshness of the shrubs and flowers; renew them as the seasons progress; it requires no more than care. The principal garden and the greenhouse will come to your aid.

The boudoir would be still more delightful if the recess in which the bed is placed were to be lined with looking glasses, their joints concealed by carved tree trunks artfully arranged and leafed and painted to resemble nature. This would repeat to form a quincunx, which would be multiplied by the glasses. Candles, their light softened by gauzes in various degrees of tautness, would improve the effect. One might believe oneself to be in a grove; statues painted and suitably placed would enhance the pleasure and the illusion.

Let us continue to survey the details. The chimneypiece may be adorned with ormolu in a delicate design on veined white marble. All the other marbles must be of the same color to sustain the cool, ornamental, and magnificent air that must prevail in this place.

Opposite the window or the chimneypiece, a niche is required for a daybed, or an ottoman; this niche must be decorated with looking glasses all around, even on its ceiling.

An alcove or rather recess ten or twelve feet deep, if discreetly lit, will gain in effect by enhancing the air of mystery. Glasses all around; a well-proportioned dome in the center of the ceiling; and a bed placed directly beneath, detached on every side and decked *à la Polonaise*, would create a pleasing effect.

The colors of the furniture and hangings are not without influence on the desired character of the room. Red is too harsh; yellow would create unpleasing reflections; green would appear too serious. White and blue are the only admissible colors.

The furniture and the frames of the glasses and of the hangings must be gilt and carved; the cornice that crowns the room may be similarly enriched; but the carving must be delicate; as for the gilding, let it not be used in excess. It must be applied only to the ornaments and some of the fillets, and the whole must be no more than heightened and picked out in gold on a fine white ground. Levity is the whole charm of this room, which is frivolous by nature.

It follows from these principles that the moldings in general must not be too pronounced, nor must they be too weak; never fall into a vice through seeking to avoid a fault.

The ceiling may represent an azure sky with few clouds; it need be enlivened only by a pair of doves taking wing to join Venus's chariot.

The paneled dado will be white and the moldings gilt and carved, as in the rest of the room.

The parquet will be laid in compartments or in marquetry, and in the winter a fine carpet will cover it.

One cannot devote too much care to a decoration of this kind; the masses may vary, but take care to keep to a circular plan. This form is appropriate to the character of the room; it is sacred to Venus. Consider a beautiful woman. Her outlines are gentle and well rounded; the muscles are not pronounced; the whole is governed by a simple, natural sweetness, whose effect we recognize better than we can express it; this stems from a tender quality that is already apparent in the cradle. We can give no better example. Such are the notions that may serve as guides; add only lightness in the ensemble and grace in every part.

Take care to avoid looking glasses that are curved in plan; they create reflections that are distorted and elongated in relation to the degree of curvature.

We must also observe that all possible attention is to be given to the purity, the color, and the setting of glasses. The least flaw, the least scratch, the slightest fault, and they must be rejected.

It would be absurd if a nymph desirous of contemplating her own charms were to find, instead of a regular form, a crabbed and crooked figure. The fixing of glasses in itself may sometimes occasion such mishaps, which arise in any that are out of alignment, out of square, or out of plumb. They are easily remedied, unless the glasses in a single frame fail to match in thickness or in color. These faults are of the essence; they must never be tolerated. Change the glasses, or the eye will be fatigued or, as our ladies of fashion themselves would put it, "teased." For then the face, or any object reflected in the glass, seems fractured and divided between two complexions, which occasions the most disagreeable disparity: one does not expect to be vexed in such a manner in one's own boudoir.

This delightful retreat must arouse none but the sweetest emotions; it must confer serenity upon the soul and delight upon all the senses. It must aim for the ultimate perfection: let desire be satisfied without impairing enjoyment.

Looking Glasses

Since we are on the subject of the quality of glasses, it should be noted that few of them are perfect; their selection is a matter deserving of the closest attention. The purest and clearest are to be placed level with the eye; they must be large enough to show the figure at full length. If a second glass be added above, it must, as I say, be of the same color and the same thickness as the glass that it surmounts; but in this piece, which must be one-third as large as the one beneath, a few flaws may be tolerated if necessary. Glasses enclosed in a single frame must never differ in these two qualities of color and thickness. The fault is too obvious and becomes intolerable. There is a great art in their fixing. A glass that is inclined a little more or a little less often conceals its flaws, so that they can be detected only with difficulty, and then only from the side; often, indeed, they are effaced altogether. The flaws in glasses placed against the light between two windows are very hard to detect, and it is here that the worst are placed; the Glaziers take care to set up their faulty glasses here in the hope that they will not be rejected. Without close attention to this point, one will be cheated: the Merchants, apart from their ordinary discount of one inch in height and in breadth, enjoy additional discounts in respect of flaws in the glass; and there are some glasses for which the price is reduced by more than one-third. Most Merchants accept them, and their great art is then to pass them off as unflawed. But take care: in disposing of them or in exchanging them for others, one would lose more than half their cost. An attentive Architect cannot therefore be too careful or too strict in his examination. His duty demands it; and if there are some positions in an apartment where flawed glasses might pass, it is not the Merchant who should have the profit, but the client, since every glass has its intrinsic value and the makers have a tariff of discounts according to the number of flaws.

May I be excused this digression, which is a matter of economy and not of decoration.

Let us proceed to the dressing room. To lovely women, every moment is precious, and they know how to dispose of their time; they count the minutes, and every one bears the hallmark of pleasure.

Dressing Room

The dressing room is the place where the Graces hold counsel: they are simple and unaffected; their greatest charm springs from nature. This idea and the character of the Graces themselves must preside at the making of their chamber. They are slight and delicate of person, neither too tall nor too small. Their abode must be in keeping. Its proportions will be Ionic, the proportional mean between the Doric and Corinthian Orders.

The dressing room belongs by its nature to the private apartments.

In general, twelve feet wide by fifteen or sixteen feet long and nine feet high are the most suitable proportions. This room must be parqueted; the ceiling is to have a cornice; but if the cornice be ornamented, this must be done with restraint, lightness, and taste.

The whole chamber will be wainscoted to its full height; the panels will be handsome in shape, well framed, and symmetrically placed.

All ostentation is to be avoided: magnificence offends the Graces and puts them to flight; they take pleasure only in noble simplicity.

Eliminate sharp angles in the form of this room; it is highly advisable to have canted corners in which looking glasses will be mounted. Segments of circles make a very fine effect, and the wainscoting, in such cases, can take on this form instead of a flat panel; but then the corner glasses are inset in a recess, which is rectilinear in plan; as, in general, the canted panels are not wide, such recesses are not unpleasing, and they have the advantage of softening the effect of the room as a whole. If the reflections of the reveals in the glass give rise to complaint, have them painted to represent half a mosaic, which together with its reflection will appear whole and produce a fine effect. You will be glad of this when you cast your eyes upward and see how the angles of the ceiling have become less pronounced. The doors and fireplaces must be so placed that they do not interfere with the position of the dressing table, which must be lit from the East. It would be inconvenient to have the dressing table in line with the doors. To be in its natural place, it must have a favorable light. This need for light must not cause it to be placed too close to the chimneypiece; the fire might cause discomfort and is incompatible with the scents and pomades. The entrance must therefore be at the far end of the room, but not opposite the window. A glass is best in the latter position, especially as objects are reflected in the glass above the dressing table; and it is not without interest to observe the arrival of those who come to pay homage. The door must therefore be in one of the side walls.

The chimneypiece will be in veined white marble; its consoles will be rounded in plan, and the mantel will follow their contour. The top of the opening cannot be placed too low; and the view afforded by the glass over the mantel will be all the better if another is placed on the opposite wall. These repetitions are necessary, so that one may see oneself from every side.

This room will be parqueted and wainscoted to its full height and painted white or two very pale shades of gray; the same will apply to the frames and borders of the glasses, with the exception that the molding nearest to the glass itself will be gilt. This trace of gilding will counter the excessive sameness, which might otherwise bring in a touch of melancholy. The dressing table sets up a kind of constraint, which must be softened. To this end, place in each panel of the wainscoting a print of some agreeable subject, enclosed in a gilt frame with flat, plain moldings to avoid dust. These prints will give variety to the room and enliven it. The cornice will be of a simple, light, and low profile, and that of the wainscoting will be similar.

Flowers must be placed in a number of vases around the room; have no fear of overloading the mantel with them. It would be pleasing to set in the corners little stands bearing finely designed vases. These would contain flowers, which would be all the fresher if their stalks were to stand in water. These vases may be of copper, enameled in lapis lazuli and with gilt trimmings.

The hardware of the doors and windows will produce a finer effect polished and varnished than gilt; the braided bell ropes will form swags, with white and blue as their basic colors.

Such is the aspect of a dressing room, always remembering that cleanliness and grace must be its principal ornaments; let the whole room proclaim the exquisite freshness enjoyed by those who emerge from it.

Closet for Clothing

The closet for clothing and accessories will adjoin the dressing room, or at least must not be far from it. This chamber will be furnished with large wardrobes with well-fitting doors, in which there will be shelves and hangers. Its most advantageous aspect is Northerly: the light is even; the fabrics will be less exposed; feathers and furs will keep better; and insects dislike this aspect. There must be no fire; smoke might penetrate the doors of the wardrobes, however well closed. This room will be paved with freestone; parquet is less suitable, because it harbors vermin. This will not be a high room; nine feet will suffice. It will have a ceiling; where there is a cornice, this will serve as a crown for the presses. In the center of the room will be a large cloth-covered table, where the dresses and other articles that are needed may be spread out. Any chairs that may be placed here must not have cloth seats, because of the insects; use straw or cane. Straw is best, especially in frames of acacia wood.

The linen room will be discussed when we come to the lodgings set aside for the lady's-maids.

Closet of Ease

This must not be far from the bedchamber and the dressing room; it is paved with freestone and ceiled, with a cornice if desired. Shelves will be placed in the corners to hold various vessels, potpourris, and scented waters. There must also be small cabinets, made to the height of benches or sunk into the walls, to hold the various accessory objects that this place requires.

As for the closestool, it is placed in a niche contrived for the purpose, usually in the center of one of the lateral walls.

This place may be heated by flues from a stove in the adjacent room. The light should come from the North; a fanlight above a door may serve, but only as a last resort. This closet must have a second door leading to a lobby so that the servants may attend to it without passing through the principal rooms of the apartment. The whole is painted in white or grisaille. Although of little consequence, these rooms demand some thought if they are to be arranged to best advantage. Nothing must be neglected: the least corner must have its use, either for the napkins or for a little fountain with a marble scallop shell or a basin to receive the water that falls when one washes one's hands, and which is ordinarily carried off by a little discharge, which leads to a sink or to the outside. Arrange this room artistically, but always bear in mind that it must be in keeping with the rest of the apartment. When a closet is pretty, one does not suppose the other rooms neglected.

Water Closet

This room closely resembles the foregoing; it serves much the same purpose, except that it is not in such general use. It is called *cabinet à l'Anglaise*, because it came to us from the English. The bowls are marble troughs to receive the matter, and this is soon washed away when one lifts the plug with its valve and turns the faucet, which gives water in abundance and carries away whatever is in the bowl; the plug closes hermetically, so that the odors cannot pass; it is even covered by a little water, so that no vapors may escape. There are also little conduits from which water springs when one desires to wash oneself, a custom that combines cleanliness and health. A cistern is usually placed in the mezzanine above. Delicacy suggests the attachment of a cylinder of hot coals, so that the water shall not be too cold in winter. Water is drawn from this same cistern to supply a little fountain for washing the hands, which is emptied by an overflow pipe. It is easy to give an artful arrangement to this room. The seat must never be placed facing the door, but to the right or left. It most commonly occupies a niche, square in plan, and to either side there are shelves for white napkins. At the height of the seat there is a little press in which to drop the day's soiled linen. The frames that support the little shelves for linen and scented waters normally taper to serve as a base for a vase full of perfumes and scents. This room is paved with freestone or with marble; it has a ceiling and a cornice. It is pointless to lavish ornaments upon it. The wainscoting must be simple and massive, with the look of architecture rather than of woodwork, and with panels that are either in relief or recessed in the walls; for it is generally to be painted to resemble marble, well polished, and varnished. The effect is more solid than stucco but lacks its brilliance. The same decoration may be made in plaster; but observe that the arrises are never sharp enough, which is a great disadvantage. To remedy this, you may leave your walls quite smooth and paint them to look like marble. Shadow and perspective will create whatever masses you may desire. The windows in this room will face North, so that the odors may be less in evidence; the fermentation of the matter is less promoted by cold than by heat.

But, once again, this room must not offer an elegance that would be out of keeping with the rest; without a just relation between the parts and the whole, there is no architecture.

Baths

The baths demand several rooms; they require an anteroom, a room for the bathtubs, a vapor bath, a small bedroom, and a number of private closets.

Anteroom to the Baths

This anteroom is at the end of a passage; it leads to the bathroom, to the water closet, to a number of cabinets, which serve as lobbies, and to the stair to the mezzanine above, where the cistern is and where the lady's-maids have their lodging.

This room is paved with freestone, has a ceiling with a cornice, and is generally wainscoted to its full height. It should be painted in grisaille: its aspect is of no consequence.

There will be a stove, and it is ordinarily from here that all the flues convey heat to the closets, water closet, and baths.

Bathroom

Diana descends to her bath. It is here that you must strive to divert her in the form of the room, in its arrangement, and in its ensemble. The proportions are to be Corinthian; this room demands elegance and lightness, and there must be some play in its plan. The light should be full, without being multiplied by too many windows; one will suffice, and this will face the bath. The aspect, where possible, will be to the East and will look out along a walk that ends in a grove, where Art will weave its most elegant spells. The sense of idleness that accompanies the bath calls for objects of distraction. Melancholy thoughts intrude; the mind must be diverted.

The bath itself, as we have said, will be so placed as to enjoy a pleasing outlook. If gauzes seem to banish an indiscreet daylight, it is for Art and taste to draw them aside.

The bath is not to stand on the floor, for it could not then be entered without too much effort. It must be sunk, so that its rim stands, at most, eight or nine inches above the floor. This makes access more convenient and obviates the dangers attendant on stepping into the bath. One might desire to have the bath in the center of the room rather than in a niche; it would be more easily attended by the servants, and one would have the advantage of a clear view all around. There must be at least three looking glasses, one opposite the window, another over the mantel, and the third opposite the second. These glasses will extend as low as possible, so that one may see oneself from every angle. The mantel must be fifteen inches at most above the fireplace opening, which should be two and one-quarter feet wide. Veined white marble is the most appropriate material for the chimneypiece and for the floor.

The entire room should be finished in the same marble: it might also be painted with trelliswork, so that in the bath one would see jasmine and honeysuckle all around; it would be an easy matter to contrive in the walls a few little waterfalls, which would be reflected in the glasses and which, by their murmur, would make the room more agreeable.

The shape of this room may be octagonal, and the ceiling painted to represent the sky, which would form an azure dome above the arbor just described; a few birds, seeming to swoop through the air, might add animation to the scene. For greater animation, bring in a birdcage, standing low and to the full width of the window. The movements of the birds and their singing would help to dispel the ennui of the bath. For absolute tranquility, a canopy, or rather a bed *à la Polonaise*, might be placed over the bath to support curtains whiter than snow. But Diana sometimes ranges through the forests, and her skin may be marred by the heat of the Sun. In such a case, blue curtains will have a better effect. Foresight is all. What is proper for a blonde has not the same advantages for a brunette.

The entry must have two doors, so arranged that one is closed when the other opens. Diana is in her bath; let no Actaeon surprise her.[35]

In the matter of decoration, it would be possible to go further, and give the whole its proper character. Why not represent it as a grotto, worthy of Amphitrite, sparkling with all the riches of the deep? Why not create a chamber from Neptune's palace? How many interesting objects might be gathered there! Looking glasses, suitably placed, would reflect groups of columns; and these would form the basis of the decorative scheme. The resulting splendor of openings and perspectives would have the finest possible effect, inclining the soul toward a sensation of delight.

The chariot of the Sovereign of the Deep might serve as the bath itself, harnessed to sea horses whose nostrils would spout jets of water and lace the rocks with rivulets of silver to delight the eye; one might be in the midst of the seas. The bath itself would nevertheless be served by faucets dispensing hot and cold water, as is the custom.

Shall we enrich this composition? Let us add birdsong, as we have suggested, to animate it and give it life. Before and behind some of the openings we place birdcages. We plant trees; with winter in mind, let us add some that are artificial; let illusion reign supreme. Let us set the foreground with terracing, with aquatic herbs, and with various seashells scattered on the shore. In default of nature, silver gauze may replace the crystal waters; their sound may be imitated by some further device. Let us set all the magic of optics to work; this is the moment for the Artist to display all his talents, and make known the extent of his Art. He may give his fancy free rein, but, above all, he must divert. His invention may be prompted by pictures and prints or by stage decorations.

Let us take every opportunity that arises to improve the ease of service; neglect nothing that may tend to greater convenience.

Baths such as these must far exceed the advantages of bathing in a river, for here the soul enjoys a healthful tranquility, which is beyond price. A bath is never a matter of indifference; its advantages derive from the manner of taking it. Let us try to make it pleasurable as well as healthful.

We may regret that no public baths have been established in France; such baths would have a twofold advantage in that they would serve as schools of swimming, a useful and, one might even say, an essential accomplishment. In many circumstances, this might be a means of saving life; and it would be one more occasion for the Artist to produce an Architecture that would bring us closer to the taste of the Ancients, both in the distribution of the plan and in the decoration, and would allow our Arts to compete with those of Greece and Rome.

If it were our intention to imitate the bath of Diana, other, and no less agreeable, compositions would suggest themselves. We might counterfeit a kind of boscage formed by various trees, some evergreen and some aromatic, mingled with groups of rose, honeysuckle, myrtle, and orange bushes standing in tubs, which might be partly concealed from view by other plants in low pots.

In compositions of this kind, what an abundance of ideas mythology can yield if only we set our minds to it and if we give free rein to a sound and rational imagination! This is the palace of the Gods; these apartments that we have to decorate are theirs, and it is for us to impose our customs upon them.

We shall not speak of the baths of the ancients in any spirit of comparison with our own: they were magnificent, but they were public; and their character is not to be reconciled with the manners of our time, which combine the utmost sensuous refinement with the utmost delicacy.

We shall say nothing of the manner of the Turks: to supplement the use of water for bathing, they have sweat rooms to provoke perspiration; such a method could do nothing but harm in climates such as ours. We have other ways of making ourselves perspire.

There are also vapor baths; such matters belong to the province of Medicine. We speak of the decoration of baths; this is our sole concern.

Vapor Bath

The entrance to this will adjoin that of the bathroom. Like the bathroom itself, it will have an inner and an outer door and will be enclosed on every side. The space will not be a large one, and it must be floored with a single flagstone, scooped out so that the falling water may flow out through a pipe fitted with a valve. There should be no window but a borrowed light. At the end of the room, there must be a small basin, into which water will fall from two faucets, one of hot water and one of cold. Marble shelves will be situated in the corners for linen, perfumes, and scented waters. There will also be a small table for the servant's use, which will be in a niche to avoid encroaching on the room itself. Square in plan, this niche will face the window; it may be backed by a glass with an ungilt frame, with a light molding but without carved ornament. The walls all around are to be painted to resemble marble, with architectural panels and compartments. The dado, faced with real marble, must cover the edge of the slab that forms the floor; otherwise the whole would be destroyed in a very short time by the water that descends on it in quantity. This room is to be heated by flue pipes, which will be easily contrived from the stove in the adjoining room. Observe, in this connection, that the heat conveyed by a flue pipe never flows downward; a dip, even of less than one inch, would frustrate its entire operation. The heating pipes must therefore be positioned in such a way as to slope upward; it is essential to have a rise of at least two inches in every toise, and the more the better. It is common to lack heat for want of attention to this principle, or else from ignorance of it, as it runs clean counter to that of fluids.

Bedroom Adjacent to the Bath

This room will be very simple, small in size, and very sparingly lit. A Westerly exposure is appropriate; it is here that gauze curtains are necessary; their effect is to form a half-light, propitious to sleep.

In this room, neatness is the only requirement; nothing frivolous, and no ornaments. It will suffice to have wainscoting to the full height of the room, painted a very light gray, the chimneypiece in white marble, the bed in the same color with a little border in which blue predominates; this will convey a fitting air of simplicity and freshness to the whole. An alcove, fashioned as a niche, is appropriate to this room; it seems more conducive to repose. On either side of this will be a closet, unless other special ones exist; these are essential for the sake of good order; repose will be the less disturbed, and the servants will work more conveniently.

This chamber will be parqueted and ceiled, with a cornice adorned with few and simple moldings, so that everything seems expressly made to avoid catching the attention. A labored pretension, or too much opulence, or too much contrivance might dispel the gentle vapors of Morpheus. Remove all distractions, respect the rights of sleep, and endeavor to preserve it for a few precious moments. Give the room Tuscan proportions, as its serious character demands. Do not hesitate to place a number of looking glasses in it; they will imitate a lovely pool, whose tranquility seems to summon and detain the presence of sleep. Let monotony prevail; it numbs the senses and binds them captive; one yawns and falls asleep.

Closet for the Bath

Closets of this kind serve expressly to hold all the accessories that relate to the bathroom; dresses and linen are placed here during the bath, and the servants in attendance withdraw here when they are not required.

Here, in particular, everything must have its place; it would be displeasing to see clothes strewn here and there. Neglect nothing that would tend to establish order and cleanliness. These closets must convey an impression of perfect arrangement.

There must be a fire to warm the linen, paneled doors with shelves and hangers behind, a table covered with a cloth, and a few chairs. The room will have a ceiling and a freestone floor; all around the walls will be a wainscoting to the full height, painted in a light gray, as will be the doors, presses, and windows.

Closet of Ease

There must be a closet of ease; we have said enough on the subject in speaking of the bedchamber, and reference may be made to this.

Such are the dependencies of the apartment of a lady, always remembering that above these rooms, which should not in general be too high, there is an entresol, with lodgings for the lady's-maids; each will require two rooms with fireplaces, and they will share a third, large enough for their usual work, where there must be a stove. Two other rooms may be added, one for a seamstress and the other for the wardrobe maid. Provide a staircase to communicate with the closets and the bedchamber.

Linen Room

The linen room must not be far away; this is a large room, lined all around with presses that contain shelves. In the center is a large table on which to place the linen that is to be used or repaired.

The housekeeper's lodging will be adjacent. She will require three rooms with fireplaces and one for her usual work, in which there will be a stove.

Let us set aside these rooms, which we discuss, for the moment, only as a group, related to the distribution of our plan only in that each part must bear a relation to the whole. We shall say only that they must have an easy, neat appearance, ample light, easy communications, and ready access.

The interior of the apartments must be free of the noise and bustle of these places; however, their closeness to the principal rooms is a practical necessity, as a lady's-maid must always be within reach.

The whole of such an apartment is usually set aside for the Mistress of the house. That of the Master demands a different style and a different character; the profiles and the masses must be more severe, and the forms must be square.

For a Military Man, the ornaments differ entirely from those employed in the apartment of a Magistrate: in one, the attributes are those of Mars; in the other, they are those of Themis.[36]

The projection of the moldings must differ entirely from one apartment to the other. In that of the Military Man, all must be abrupt and nothing mannered, with many square forms and few round ones. We hesitate to entwine a frond of myrtle with the laurels on the proud brow of a warrior. For the Magistrate, on the contrary, the whole must be more connected, more harmonious; its character must breathe a noble simplicity. Such a tone serves to predispose and to calm the anxious minds of his clients. Following a principle that cannot be too highly commended, the harmony of the whole must convey to the client the probity of the man before whom he has come to lay his case; he must believe that this is a man who can bring order out of a chaos of chicanery and reduce matters to their true principles. The purity of the moldings contributes much to this impression, as does the lighting; the whole must be well lit, but not too bright.

This is no vague system; it is founded on firm foundations. There are few persons who fail to experience, on entering certain dwellings, a sudden emotion quite contrary to that with which they came. This is inspired by the place itself; the whole aspect of an apartment may inspire confidence, just as a prison arouses horror.

Let us survey a variety of decorative genres as they relate to social position.

The apartment of a rich man admits of prodigality and sumptuousness of ornament and gilding. This is the palace of Plutus,[37] and its character is magnificence; but there must be a calculated progression, so that the most important rooms excel the others. The gradation of opulence, as one progresses further into the interior, casts the spell and stimulates the senses. It follows that the ensemble of such an apartment must very largely follow the scheme that we have outlined for the Mistress of a house; the character is much the same, and the difference lies in the degree of opulence.

The apartment of a Magnate must be treated with nobility and majesty; the fineness of the masses predisposes the response, profiles stimulate it, and ornaments determine it. Magnificent openings and vistas, and glasses repeated but not too numerous, contribute to the solemn magnificence that may prevail; for such, in our state of society, is the prerogative of title and rank.

An apartment for a Courtier or a man in high office demands large rooms, grandeur in the dimensions, plans simply disposed, and breadth of effect above all. Minor details must be sacrificed, mean objects banished, and excessive elaboration studiously avoided.

The apartment of a Prelate must be in very much the same style as that of a Magistrate; only the attributes in the ornaments must differ. It is hardly necessary to say that there is no need for a dressing room or a boudoir, but that there must be a private cabinet and oratories: these rooms manifest the owner's modesty and invite meditation. Lighting well disposed and great harmony in the masses and the profiles will reinforce such sensations. Adjacent to the apse of the Church of Saint-Roch there is a fine example of this genre, which supplies an invaluable model.[38] In general, every room in the apartment of a Prelate must inspire respect and piety. This, the visitor must say, is the apartment of a true Pastor; and its air breathes the beauty, the purity, and the simplicity of our religion. In such a palace, if any concession be made to ornament (for one has a position to maintain), there must be nothing sumptuous, in the furnishings above all. This would infringe upon a basic principle, that of character; it would be a sin against charity, which requires a more commendable use of revenue.

The apartment of a Minister corresponds entirely to that of a Magnate: he must represent his master, while conveying an impression of authority, power, goodwill, affability, even the desire to capture men's hearts: noble sentiments worthy of humanity. This sensation will be derived from the high relief of the moldings, from their fine proportions, from their harmony, from the masses as a whole, and from careful lighting. Different exposures to the Sun have propensities of their own to excite and express sensations. The times of day will produce many others, which will derive their character from masses carefully disposed. It is for the able Architect to put them to the best use: if he is ambitious and feels the spur of fame, then he must study, grasp, contemplate, and explore those grand and beautiful effects that are the gift of nature.

Composition, variety, development, and the relation between the whole and its parts are the principal sources of such qualities. Remember that forms satisfy us only in as much as Art presents them to us in the guise of truth; where the illusion is not carried through, nothing is achieved beyond a certain initial surprise, swiftly followed by ennui and disgust. Great effects come from the thing itself; they do not depend on those petty ornaments to which too much importance is often attached. Even the most elegant forms, the happiest inventions, leave us unmoved if their choice and arrangement express nothing; they please only when they are used appositely. The ensemble must first strike the mind with an air of magnificence or simplicity, of gaiety or of tranquility: in short, by some general character. Any objects that conflict with such a character, however pleasing in themselves, must be excluded.

Character, in relation to the persons for whom one may build, is something, but it is not enough; there exist both general laws and particular means of expressing them. These we shall now review; these are the images that we must now bear in mind.

Cabinets

We have set out the considerations that relate to the apartment of a Mistress of a house; we have spoken of the anterooms and have said that the husband's apartment might share the first of them. We shall note for the moment that after the first these rooms now take on the name of cabinets and that two are needed to precede the principal cabinet or study. These are customarily parqueted and ceiled, with a cornice; there should be a progression in their enrichment. These cabinets most often have a wainscoted dado, the walls above being hung with cloth, in a plain color, ornamented with a few good pictures. Sometimes they are hung with fine Beauvais tapestries, but then, as far as possible, care should be taken as to the subjects depicted; these become interesting only when they bear some relation to the character of the owner. This is a consideration that is too often neglected.

The chimneypieces are in marble, each with a glass above; but the frames of the glasses should be decorated in keeping with the situation and with the rules that we have already set down. In addition, a writing table should be placed in each of these two rooms, the second of which may be adorned with a chandelier.

Frequently the grand salon may take the place of the grand cabinet or study, but then it must be arranged in accordance with our observations concerning genre and character. It is always better to make this into a separate room; let us see what is appropriate.

Grand Cabinet or Study

The light must be good, and to this end it will be taken from the East. It must not be made excessively bright by an excess of windows; better too few than too many. This room will be parqueted; if richness be desired and no expense spared, precious inlays and marquetry might be suitable. During the winter the floor will be entirely covered by a splendid carpet. The ceiling is to have a carved and gilt cornice, but let everything be prudently arranged with a circumspection that admits only appropriate objects. A fine wainscoting, to the full height, designed with large masses, will be appropriate to the general character; in well-proportioned panels, fine pictures will be artfully placed and hung with grace. The chimneypiece of veined white marble will be mounted with ormolu, as will the andirons. The candelabra that may be placed in the corners of the room will be so designed as to be in harmony with the furnishings; they may be gilt. A glass will adorn the chimneypiece.

The doors will be in a line with those in the anterooms; but in this room, as the persons within must not be too much in view when the doors are opened, the doors must be at one of the ends; they must be double doors, so arranged that on leaving the room, one does not find oneself imprisoned between the inner and outer doors, as often happens. They must in any case be well proportioned, designed with large panels, and the doorcase ornamentally carved; taste must govern the form of the overdoors, into which pictures or bas-reliefs are to be inserted; but these ornaments must tend to a pyramidal form and crown the whole. Sometimes the upper architraves will bear friezes and cornices, supported by consoles embellished with acanthus leaves. The frieze itself may be enriched, in which case scrolls will serve very well. The cornice and the architraves will always be finely profiled; their proportions will be Corinthian, as will those of the room itself, which will be painted in a fine royal white. The moldings, carved with taste, will be gilt, as will the other ornaments. But, once again, to maintain the character of the room, all must be so arranged that it seems that it could not have been otherwise. Give it opulence but nothing superfluous; never depart from this principle, for without it there is no attaining to beauty.

In this room there will be a writing table with its accessories and a number of presses, recessed in the wainscoting, to hold those precious papers that cannot be left on the writing table; this is a special place of safekeeping, which cannot be made too secure.

This room must have a back cabinet and a storeroom for papers; it must also have a closet and a lobby.

Back Cabinet or Private Study

The private cabinet or study is a miniature of the grand cabinet. It must not be too large, and in consequence the height should be in proportion: this may be turned to double advantage. Within the height of the story, an intermediate floor may be inserted, and this makes room for a repository for papers; it is reached by a small staircase at the end of the private study, and the entrance, concealed in the wainscoting, will be from the lobby or else from the study itself. This cabinet is sacred to the Master's tranquility and to his work, and no one may enter. It must be parqueted and ceiled, the cornice lightly enriched with carved ornament. The chimneypiece will be in veined white marble with a glass above; the wainscoting, to full height, will be painted white, as will all the rest, including the upright members of the furniture. No gilding; a rosewood writing table with a morocco leather top, a deed box on the writing table, a few chairs, and two armchairs, will complete the furnishing.

Repository for Papers

This is a room in which the Secretary places the papers that are needed from day to day; it may be assumed that there is also a muniment room where the deeds and other vital documents of the household are kept. We shall discuss this when we come to the details of the lodgings of the various Officers. As for the repository, the room will have a floor of freestone to banish insects. All around there will be presses glazed with large panes of Bohemian glass, all locked by the same key. The ceiling will have a little cornice that will continue along the fronts of the presses; no chimneypiece, for fire is dangerous; a morocco-covered table; and a few chairs: that is all.

Closet of Ease

We have said enough on the subject of closets of ease; this one requires less art. The architect will dispose according to his own lights.

Lobby

This lobby must open onto some passageway, such as that outside the bathroom, or to some other room with direct access to the bedchamber. Such lobbies are essential in the plan of apartments, most notably for the greater tranquility of those persons who have some state to maintain by means of these lobbies. It is known that in most houses there are concealed doors; they are used to give the impression that you have gone out, when all the time you are at work inside. The bedchamber will not be far off, and the whole will be in keeping with the position of the Master who is to occupy it, while having regard always to the character and nature of the room itself.

It is in such an apartment, most especially if it be that of a Prelate, a

Minister, or a Magistrate, that a library is called for. Such a room is essential. It is not convenient to have one's books scattered, as often happens, in bookcases standing in the anterooms; disorder of this kind is to be avoided. It is unseemly to transform one's anterooms into a place of work; the necessary tranquility cannot be established. Books behind simple grilles are not safe enough; they are too much exposed to dust, to the smoke of stoves, and even to fire. It ought to be a general rule, as it is in some communities, never to carry a naked light into places where there are many books.

Library

The library is a room that deserves attention; its character must be noble and serious. The Doric proportion is proper to it; the rest depends on the masses and on the natural sequence of light and shade. Not all exposures are equally suitable: a North light is the most propitious; the light from that quarter may be dreary, but it is even, and the air is inimical to insects, which might prey upon the books. However, to have windows on one side alone detracts from the symmetry; to make false ones on the other side is a waste of space and a superfluous expense. To remedy this, would it not be appropriate to light this room from the ceiling, either through glazed skylights or by erecting lanterns or cupolas artistically arranged and distributed? These may be square or round, like our rooms *à l'Italienne*. Square lanterns, or clerestories, seem the best choice. Take care to arrange the height of their sills so that the sun does not strike the bookcases directly. This will constitute a kind of attic story supported by a graceful coving, which will spring from the cornice above the bookcases; the whole cannot fail of a fine effect if the vault be continued in the intervening bays by transverse arches and caissons. It may be said that this kind of decoration demands a very high ceiling, and so it does; but at the same time there is no reason why there should not be, at a height of eight or nine feet, an artfully suspended gallery, reached by little staircases within the depth of the bookcases and the walls, for which, as if for windows, openings will have been left in the masonry. This gallery will make it possible to reach all the books without any of the risks attendant on the use of tall and dangerous ladders; little library steps, four feet at most in height, will suffice for the lower part. In the gallery itself, the cases must not exceed six feet in height. With such proportions and such an ensemble, the whole will be noble and majestic; it will also be convenient to use; the light will be conducive to tranquility and study. Between the bookcases, there will be busts of great men, set on decorated plinths inscribed with their names. This provision will satisfy the visitor, avoid injury to self-esteem, and forestall questions that are often irksome.

The length of the library, there must be tables covered with cloths; the cases themselves will mark the divisions between the tables. Between them will be spaces of no less than three feet. Perhaps it would be no bad thing to fashion small private cabinets for those persons who love quiet and who, as it seems, can give free rein to their ideas only when they know that they are not overlooked. Each would need no more than a little table and a chair; it would be useful to have a shelf at elbow height to hold books and to keep the table clear.

We consider that good terrestrial and celestial globes are fitting and useful ornaments of a Library; they afford a noble and interesting variety of decoration.

I would rather see a freestone than a parquet floor. If cold be complained of, carpets could be placed beneath the tables at little expense. Stone has the double advantage that it collects less dust and that it harbors no rats and mice. The slight chill for which it is blamed will serve to discourage those insects that destroy books and their bindings.

A refinement of perfection would be to have the entrance toward the South, but preceded by an anteroom; and opposite, at the Northern end, a wide window embrasure. These two parts could be decorated with the greatest symmetry, and there would be the advantage of a through draft of air, which could be renewed at will. The doors at the entrance might be of iron, clad with thick iron plates, and the window frames would also be in iron with shutters to match the doors; there would thus be no fear of fire from either end.[39] The frames for the skylights would be of the same kind, as would the carcasses of the bookcases and the shelves. But this forms no part of our plan. Harmony and proportions are our guides, and our object is to describe the sensations that they may evoke; to these we hasten to return.

Cabinet Adjacent to the Library

This is a small library in which are placed the rarest books, special manuscripts, and objects that are not to be left within everybody's reach. Here, also, new books are placed before they are arranged. In general, all that we have said of the library will hold good here. Light from above is more suitable than from a window at elbow height; we accordingly advise that this room be furnished with cases all around, six feet or so in height, crowned with a small cornice and a plinth on which to place, at regular intervals, bronze vases or other precious ornaments. It is for genius and taste to dispose, while keeping the whole in character. The necessary light may be derived from above, very much as a Painter does in his workshop; it is gentler, and such an arrangement conduces to reflection and prevents distraction.

The ceiling will be all white; unless it be painted with *Apollo and the Muses* against a clear sky.

In the center of this room will be a table on iron legs, draped with a green cloth. This color is restful to the eyes. Some chairs, and pens, ink, and paper are all the further furnishings that are needed.

There might be a need for still another back cabinet; but this is no more than an ordinary room to serve as a depository for the parcels of books when they are delivered. It need have only a number of shelves around the walls. This room will be vaulted, the doors with iron frames clad in heavy iron plates, the shutters likewise, and the windows will have iron frames. Such measures cannot be too earnestly recommended in any place where papers are kept.

Cabinet of Medals and Antiquities

The cabinet of medals and antiquities will have a rectangular plan, half as long again as it is wide. It must be parqueted and ceiled; it cannot be too austerely lit, and an Eastern aspect is the best. It will contain several handsome cases, artistically arranged, filled with little drawers lined with cotton on which the medals will lie. Around the walls will be marble tables on which the bronzes and other pieces will stand. The room as a whole will embody the Doric Order. The windows, the doors, the lintels, the masses, must all have Doric proportions, as must the profiles. The effect must be severe; all the forms must be foursquare, very much as we have described them for the cabinet of a Military Man.

Cabinet of Natural History

The cabinet of natural history is to be in the form of a fine gallery; one might wish to have light from above, or at least from above the cases, which should line the walls all around. Each case may be given the kind of ornament that is appropriate to the objects it contains, although all of them will be equal in their masses and in the sizes of their compartments, for fear of destroying the symmetry. By this means, the contents of each will be known at first sight. The heights of the shelves will be determined by the objects that they hold. It is for the keeper to decide. All the doors must close tightly and be glazed with large panes, to avoid dust and to increase enjoyment.

The lower part of each case, up to elbow height, will consist of something like a sideboard, perhaps seven or eight inches deeper than the parts above. The shelf that covers the projection will be of white marble and will have the advantage that objects may be placed on it, either when awaiting their final arrangement or when it is desired to take them out and see them at close quarters. This also serves to make more room for large objects, which require space.

This whole room will be paved with freestone and ceiled; the proportions of the whole should be those of the Ionic Order. The riches of nature are collected here, but those riches are still raw and in their primitive state. This is a place for nature herself; its character is simple, but noble; its beauty is pure and without artifice.

The proportions will therefore be Ionic. Next to this room there will be another, less large and furnished only with shelves, to serve as a depository and also as a workroom when repairs are in hand.

Cabinet of Machines

This room will be treated in the same way as that of natural history, but its character will be different. Its proportions will be those of the Doric Order, which is severe; for severity springs from reflection, and this is the sensation best suited to this place.

Such is the full complement of rooms necessary for a library and for the various collections of objects whose value resides in the branch of science that they enshrine. But the mind cannot always be at work; let us pass to other forms of distribution, such as that which concerns the dining room.

Dining Room

In the grand and numerous suites of rooms that the Ancients gave to their buildings, they incorporated several banqueting chambers. These were large rooms, their walls broken only by doors and windows, but devoid of all decoration; they were incapable of inspiring any sensation whatever; the idea of a good feast was enough in itself to inspire joy.

Lucullus, that opulent Roman, was visited unbidden by friends who desired him to give them dinner. Without specifying the magnificent repast that he wished to have served, he told his Majordomo only that he would entertain his guests in the Hall of Apollo. This sufficed to bring forth, without delay, the most complete and sumptuous banquet.[40] What could be better? But then, the feast was the principal object. We are more sensuously inclined, though nonetheless gourmands for all that; and so we are more inclined to analyze our pleasures and to include among them the beauty of the surroundings. Let us therefore dispose the room that we are about to describe so that the fair Hebe may long to adorn it with her presence; let her freely dispense the nectar of the Gods; let gaiety, freshness, lively colors, and the character of youth and beauty set the tone of the decoration. Let Comus become a god of delicacy, and Bacchus a god of grace.[41]

The doors will be to the West, preceded by a grand room in which tables will stand, bearing the successive courses in symmetrical array. The light will be taken from the East; the prospects on this side will be the pleasantest that can be arranged. Parterres, groves, fountains, waterfalls, will embellish the room at dinnertime; in the evening, the decoration will change, and chandeliers and candelabra will replace the beauties and splendors of nature. Reflections in the glasses will heighten the enchantment. Cloris well knows the effect of lights; and Cloris seizes her opportunity.[42] It is her triumph to equal the beauty and the youth of Hebe. Her mood becomes gayer, she adds to the magic of the whole and inspires the most delicate enjoyments.

The dining room will have the proportions of the Ionic Order. Its dimensions will depend on the number of persons who are to be received there; make it too large rather than too small. At table, one must be at one's ease, and convenience of service is essential. The length of the room will be in proportion to its width. In general, to achieve good proportions, the length of the long side is to be determined by the diagonal of the square on the shorter side; that is to say, the length of the longer side of the rectangle will be greater by a third, more or less, than that of the shorter side. This is not a strict mathematical proportion; our aim is to speak to the eyes in the least complicated form.

The corners may be canted and fitted with looking glasses; the resultant reflections are a pleasing touch if disposed according to the rules of Art. Beneath these glasses will be basins of veined white marble to rinse the drinking glasses and to receive in summer a wide jet or a cascade of pure and limpid water, playing in a thousand variations and filling the room with a delightful coolness. In winter this must be avoided as a source of unpleasing damp, and a small quantity of water will have to suffice, issuing from the beaks of aquatic birds. It is for the Artist to comply with the constraints of the place and the season. What happy repetitions are created by looking glasses! What animation in the ensemble! The Ancients had no such advantages; they seem, indeed, to have felt the lack of them, for there was no end to the expedients they tried. If we consult Petronius, we find the vault of a banqueting chamber imitating the motions of the heavens and scattering the most delicious perfumes like a gentle dew.[43] No resource must be spared; all must combine to give satisfaction, with simplicity and without pretension.

Windows placed along the longer sides can never fail of success, having a prospect to the South and North. This would have the double advantage that they could be opened or closed on either side, according to circumstance. On fine summer days, the North would be preferred; and in winter there would be the South. With a little care, it would be possible to maintain a constant temperature at all times. Art has great resources to combat the rigor of the seasons. In summer there are movable blinds or windows shuttered to keep out the heat of the South. In winter, on the North, there are closely fitted, padded shutters. If you desire to draw heat from neighboring fires, without robbing the other rooms in any way, then use flues to conduct hot air.

At one end of the room there is a well-designed stove standing in a finely decorated niche suitable for its location. At the opposite end, there is a corresponding niche with a sideboard to serve, as does the stove, as a pedestal for the statues that adorn both niches: Hebe at the one end, Flora at the other. Statues of men would not succeed; the preference must be given to pleasing objects, nothing severe, nothing that might overawe. Constraint is foreign to pleasures; ease and freedom are to prevail.

We have sometimes seen detached stoves in the form of pedestals and, above them, columns rising to the full height of the room that they adorn and serving to carry off the smoke. In such a case, the appropriate Order of Architecture is made to dominate the whole room, and what began as a rule becomes an ornament of the greatest opulence. Between the columns there are statues or bas-reliefs and medallions above the impost. This room, in short, is capable of the most delightful decoration. It might be inlaid with the finest marbles, but this would be so costly as to be almost impracticable; let us rest content with stucco, with fielded panels, and with architectural frames. In default of stucco, the whole may be painted and varnished to resemble polished marble. Take care that the colors harmonize; white-veined marbles and Sienna marbles assort well together. Those of a lively coloring should be preferred. As for the figures, if any, they will be in statuary white. The color of the furniture will be matched to that of the marbles; the whole must be ruled by a harmony that will satisfy the eye and content the soul.

Marble decoration is one of the finest that can be employed; its effect is extremely rich. The whole must please through variety and aptness of assortment, and the way to succeed is to use only two or three kinds.

The Order most appropriate for a dining room, as we have said, is the Ionic; this is the character that best fits such a room, and it is not to be departed from in the general arrangement.

This room can, moreover, be decorated in a thousand different ways; it may be wainscoted to its full height with large panels framed in a finely profiled molding; sometimes pictures will be substituted. Taste will determine the choice of subjects; they must always be in keeping with the room. Never anything serious: gaiety, which is so appropriate in a feast and which is the character proper to the French nation, might be disturbed. Quarrels arise, at times, from causes of which we are unaware.

Alexander, inflamed by the overpassionate strains of music,[vi] slew Clytus, one of his favorites.[44] There is, in Switzerland, a very common air called the *danse des vaches*, which no soldier is permitted to sing when he is out of his own country on pain of imprisonment, for otherwise the malady comes upon him, and he deserts. Aristotle mentions a custom, prevalent among the Greeks, of softening the horrors of an execution with music.[45] The celebrated Tyrtaeus, by passing from the Lydian to the Phrygian mode, gave Sparta its victory over the Messenians.[46] Why, then, should Architecture not have the same qualities and the same powers to influence the soul? If we have remained unaware of them until now, it is because we have not given them our attention. I shall be glad if these reflections lead others to new thoughts on the perfecting of the art of building and of decoration.

It is said, and it has become proverbial, that for a pleasant repast those present must number no fewer than the Graces and no more than the Muses;[47] this being so, one might wish to have a small and private dining room. A room too large for a small company seems deserted; the space must relate to its occupants. Our individual selves are lost in immensity, and such an idea is oppressive to our self-esteem.

A small, octagonal salon may thus become a necessity; it may be arranged in the most interesting way. The bathroom may serve as a model, the attributes being changed. A round table is pleasant and well suited to such a room; it seems, moreover, that such a form is more convenient. No one is incommoded by sitting at a corner, and all are equal in enjoyment. The guests face each other; communication is easier and more prompt; and the elegance of the service is not impaired. We will go so far as to say that this is a room suited to every refinement of luxury and delight. Let the stem of an orange tree grow through the center of the table to shade the guests and surround them with its pleasing scent; would not such an adornment be finer than the most magnificent centerpiece? From the depths of its foliage would emerge the alabaster of its blossoms and the brilliant gold of its fruits. Ideas drawn from nature are always pleasing; beautiful vases of flowers might adorn the window embrasures; keep myrtle in mind, for it is a gift of the gods. The goddess of Paphos herself planted it in the shaded vales of Mount Ida, and cupids frolic beneath its delicate leaves. In the Elysian Fields, happy lovers roam in silence through a forest of young myrtles. All this let invention supply; such is the time for its fullest exercise. Let it take wing.

vi. Plutarch, in his *Treatise on Anger*.

Charming in summer, this room would be no less so in winter, when heated by a stove placed within the thickness of the wall and stoked from an adjoining room. Various flues can be used to convey heat and to allow the temperatures of spring to prevail in the season of ice and snow.

The floor must be of marble, and under the table there must be a carpet on which to rest the feet.

If you have the ceiling painted, insist on a calm and serene sky, with few clouds, to cheer the soul and incline it to the sweetest and most tranquil enjoyment. Such are the sensations appropriate to this room, and such is the aim to which it should tend.

If any subjects be painted in the sky, then let them be entirely in keeping with the situation: those of Flora, Pomona, and Bacchus.[48] Avoid confusion and multiplicity of figures; the eye must not be too much distracted. The feast and the room as a whole are the main concerns.

Above all, endow the room with a sense of gaiety; but this is a quality that must be artfully bestowed.

It must be founded on qualities of liveliness and neatness, combined with delicacy and taste.

To evoke a sweet sensation, fitting to the room, a little amphitheater of two or three steps might be set along the wall, constantly furnished with fresh flowers in vases of a pleasing and well-designed form. Their bright colors, their variety, and their scent will convey pleasing sensations to the soul. Flowers have always adorned the choicest feasts: when fruit is served, flowers are set upon the table to grace the dessert and to instill new life into a languishing repast. In country parties, where joy reigns supreme, flowers and garlands are everywhere. A young bride, though magnificently adorned on her wedding day, would feel her state to be impaired if she had no bouquet. A Queen in all her glory, though laden with jewels, will not disdain this rustic adornment. To celebrate someone's name day, our first thought is to give a flower; if winter forbids it, then art must supply the lack. Let us not be sparing in the use of this simple and natural ornament; let us set flowers in all the places where we want gaiety; let us array them on our tables and place them at random and without symmetry. Too much art and a contrived arrangement detract from the effect.

A charming actress, known for her qualities of heart and mind and skilled in the analysis of true pleasure, has well understood the value of such a notion. She has made a conservatory the most delightful part of her house, which is a Fairy's palace.[49]

The decoration of a dining room could not but succeed if it were to be painted with flowers in finely framed panels and with garlands playfully entwined all around the cornice; I have seen ornaments of this kind, artfully carved and colored, which have created an entirely delightful effect. Taste and genius together can work miracles: instead of panels, it would be possible to make shallow glazed cabinets containing splendid arrangements of those artificial flowers that seem to vie with those produced by nature, that fruitful mother, in her happiest moments.

Serving Room

The dining room is customarily preceded by an anteroom, which contains a sideboard to hold the requisite utensils for the service, and a stove, which not only heats the room in which it stands but also, by means of flues, conveys to the dining room that gentle warmth so necessary when one is at table. This stove also serves to warm certain dishes, or at least the stacks of plates are placed on it lest they be cold when set before the guests. There is nothing more disagreeable than to see a dish grow cold almost as soon as it is served.

This room may be paved with freestone; it will have a ceiling and cornice, and its proportions will be Doric. It will be decorated in the same style as the dining room. When the latter is in stucco or painted to simulate marble, then so must this room be; but in such a case the variety of marble must be a more common one. There must always be a gradation of opulence; this principle we repeat, and it admits of no exception. At one of the ends, or on one of the sides, opposite to the way that leads through, there must be large tables on which the dishes will be placed in due order before they are carried into the dining room; here the Majordomo can see at a glance that nothing is lacking from the list that he holds and all is fittingly arranged. When the service is in progress in the dining room, it is too late to notice an omission; intelligent though the person in charge may be, he still needs time to make good a deficiency.

In this room, a shelf is needed below the sideboard to hold the napkins for those who wait at table and a host of other small articles. There must be a place set aside for all that is cleared away. By this means, the table will be set in no more time than it takes to change a scene at the Opera. The dishes must not be carried through the main rooms of an apartment; it is barely permissible for them to pass through the first anteroom. From the serving room, there must be a private passage to the Kitchens and the Pantries. There will also be a place to keep the wines and spirits that will be needed during the meal. This room must be preceded by another in which the tubs for the ices will stand; as water tends to be spilt in such a room, it will be paved with flagstones, which will have a slight slope, so that the water may run to a lead conduit and so to the outside.

There must also be a place to keep the wood for the stove; and perhaps it might be as well to have yet another little room containing an oven with hot plates to heat the dishes and to maintain the warmth of certain dishes when the stove is not lit.

The dining room naturally leads us to the kitchens, and to the pantries and offices; although these are not to be decorated, they have a proportional relation and a character that is proper to them, and so they form part of our plan. For the true object of our remarks is good order and general harmony.

KITCHENS AND OFFICES

Kitchen

The kitchen has its own requirements. Cleanliness is its prime attribute, which seems to betoken the excellence of the dishes; this demands constant attention, and the arrangement of the room has much to contribute. The walls, well whitewashed, will be true and in a straight line, to avoid projections which are mostly repositories of filth. This is a room that must be well lit; let the fire and the ovens directly receive the light; lamplight is good for night work only, and then because it cannot be dispensed with.

The Tuscan proportion is the most appropriate; it betokens, by its forcefulness, the idea of a kitchen that is soundly based.

Every kitchen should be spacious, and a Northerly aspect is appropriate. It is to be paved and vaulted, as far as possible. The ranges beneath the windows will be twenty-eight inches high at most; otherwise the Cooks are put to inconvenience. The number of hot plates and fish kettles depends on the size of the household. For some feasts, there may be several kitchens. The chimney hood must be large and wide and must overhang the walls between the ranges. There will be cast-iron plates in the hearth and the fireback; those in the fireback will be held by heavy iron bars, which will cover the joints and seem to unite the plates into one.

Usually, only the upper parts of the windows can be opened. There are several reasons for this: the first is that heat always rises, and in this manner the steam is more easily dispersed; the second is that if the windows were to open at the bottom, they might spoil the dishes that are cooking on the ranges, fan the dust, and raise the litter on the floor.

It might perhaps be appropriate to make all the window frames of iron to avoid fire, and even to make the table legs of the same material. There would be a twofold advantage in this, for ease of cleaning and for the avoidance of fire.

The walls are to be lined with shelves with hooks at regular intervals on which some of the kitchen utensils may be suspended.

At one end there will be a faucet with a trough beneath it to receive the water and also to wash the fish; this water must not be discharged through the kitchen but pass directly out-of-doors; otherwise, the damp and the smell would be unpleasant and contrary to the need for cleanliness.

In the center of the room, there is to be a long beech table; most of the other tables will be built into the walls or so placed as to be easily moved, so that the floor may be frequently washed. To this end, lay the paving with a slight slope and a corresponding channel, so that all the water may flow outside and the whole may dry quickly. It is better to pave a kitchen with good split setts, in mortar, lime, and cement, than to use flagstones, which involve a danger of falls; it is easy to slip should there be greasy patches or even a little water. The most lamentable accidents are apt to ensue; setts have not the same disadvantages.

Larder

Adjacent to the kitchen, but with a separate entrance, there must be a larder. It must face North, and the windows must be made like grilles, with louvers, in such a way that no ray of sunlight can ever enter. There must be at least two openings of this kind, so that the air may circulate all round the walls. Set up two tiers of shelves and stout tables beneath them; the room would be best vaulted, and in the highest part there should be pulleys from which to hang meat or game on wooden rails or on hoops furnished with hooks. This room may be flagged. All the walls must be well plastered, and there must be no holes; all the window frames must close tightly, as must the door, to exclude rats and mice. Across the windows there must be iron bars and a mesh of brass wire; the sashes must have cloth in place of glazed panes, so that the air may be constantly renewed.

Fish Larder

There are times when for greater convenience and for better conservation there must be a second larder for fish. This will have windows, flagstones, tables, and shelves like the foregoing. There will be a faucet for the water that serves to wash the fish, and below it a trough, which will discharge out-of-doors.

These rooms, like the kitchen, are to be fronted with a kind of porch to shelter their doors from the heat of the South. Their light, as we have said, is to come from the North.

Wood Cellar

The entrance to the wood cellar, where several days' supply of firewood is placed, must not be far away.

There must also be a separate place for charcoal. The place for firewood being in the cellars, there must be hatches or holes large enough to unload it. Otherwise, if it were to be tossed down the steps, the treads would suffer; they would break, and it would very soon be impossible to descend.

Roasting Chamber

It is common to have such a room next to the kitchen. It is to be paved and vaulted, as far as may be, in the same way as the kitchen and the larders. The hearth will be wide, and its hood will occupy the full length of one side. The back wall of the hearth will be covered with sheets of cast iron; the window frames and table legs will also be of iron, as has been noted in speaking of the kitchens.

Pastry Kitchen

The same will apply to the pastry kitchen, which is nearby. This room must be flagged and vaulted; there must be a kneading trough beneath the windows and a table in the center with iron legs. On one side wall will be a hearth; its hood will also serve to take the steam from a stove with a fixed boiler, which will provide hot water at need. The water will be drawn off by a little faucet. For the rest, this boiler will be replenished from a cold-water faucet placed above it. On the other side, there will be an oven facing the windows, or rather diagonal to them, in such a way that one may see inside when putting the pastries into it.

Hooks or iron supports must be attached to the mantel, or rather along the chimney hood, to hang the pokers and other utensils.

Scullery

The scullery is the place to which all the silver, the dishes, and the plates are carried after use; as for the porcelain, this is taken to the pantry or to a special room, which is often a subsidiary scullery.

This room will be paved and vaulted, if possible; there should be a sink, a boiler, and a chimney hood. The water is taken by a faucet from the pipe that supplies the kitchen and adjacent rooms. The discharge is out-of-doors.

The windows will be glazed, and outside there will be iron bars and brass wire mesh. It is advisable, where this room is at ground level, to raise the sills to five and a half or six feet above the ground, because of the silver that is kept there. The door cannot be too stout or too securely locked. Tables are required all round the walls, and the room must be frequently washed down. To this end, the paving must be on a slope, and channels must be provided so that the water may flow easily out-of-doors and the whole floor dry promptly. We have given reasons for using setts instead of flagstones; the most serious accidents are avoided in this way.

Servants' Hall

The servants' hall is the place where the principal Officers of the household and the people entitled to maintenance forgather. It is a large room, which must be well lit, with a board floor and a ceiling. To render it more complete, there must be a faucet for water and a basin beneath from which the water will drain out-of-doors. A stove is required here, unless the kitchen fire can furnish warmth through its backplate; this will be masked from the servants' hall during the summer by iron doors at a distance of three inches from it with a vent to carry away the heat and renew the air. Place a valve on this vent to enclose and concentrate the heat during the winter. If this device cannot be used, then have flues that will issue from the fireback in the kitchen and rise in a gentle slope, as already described, to whatever place is desired. Should this room not have a boarded floor, which might be the best and which I would prefer for the sake of cleanliness, then it will at least have large quarry tiles: for, once again, never trust flagstones; they are treacherous. There must be a press, or else a recess with doors, containing shelves to keep the everyday linen: that is to say, the napkins that are given to servants when they wait at table. Along the middle of the room there will be a large, stout table on iron legs, fastened to the tiles with a neat joint; otherwise, this room would be liable to smells, such as are found in certain refectories. This is to be avoided with care; there must be no hiding place for dirt; this room is best washed down at least once in every week, and to this end it is wise to give it a slight slope, so that the water may flow outside or otherwise find its way to a convenient place where it may be mopped up. In such a case, a floor tiled in freestone would be preferable to any other.

Kitchen Yard

The kitchen yard must be large enough to turn two carts at least. On one of its sides there will be a porch in which to load and unload in bad weather any supplies that might be spoiled by damp. This will also be a shelter for the porters, who might otherwise crowd the kitchen or the passageways. Take care to place a trough in this yard to receive water from a faucet above. Furthermore, water from the kitchen must never run through the principal forecourt of the house; it is most often greasy, dirty, and malodorous. It is therefore wise to distribute the mass of the building in such a way that the yard adjacent to the kitchen and offices has a gate to the street that is quite separate and distinct from the principal entry; the same applies to the stables and carriage houses, of which we shall speak later. Let us first examine the offices or pantries in detail.

Offices or Pantries

The pantry brings with it a large number of rooms. First there must be one that serves as a vestibule, and from which the others open: (1) a workroom, where the confections and candies are made; (2) another, where the desserts are prepared; a third, a storeroom for candies; a fourth for fruit; a fifth for trays and for porcelain; a sixth for all the silver; and four more to lodge the Pantryman or Officer. This will make ten or twelve rooms essentially attached to the pantry, all of which must communicate with each other and lead back to the first; as we shall now see in detail.

First Pantry Room

This first room must be very large, well lit, floored with large quarry tiles and ceiled; it generally serves as a lobby for all the other rooms dependent on it, and it is useful also for porters and for baskets. Along the walls there must be a number of fairly stout tables; opposite the windows there must be tables supported by iron frames built into the walls; there should also be three or four stout blocks. It is here that the mortars are kept, for pounding and making pastes; here all the rough work is done; everything is distributed from here.

Second Room, Workroom for Confectionery

This room must be well lit, tiled with large tiles and ceiled; opposite the windows there will be ovens with hot plates, as many as the size of the household demands. These ovens must be twenty-eight inches high at most, otherwise the work is too hard. The chimney hood is large, and the oven facing the windows is placed as in the pastry kitchen, so that it is possible to see inside. In the center of the room will be a table on iron legs, as we have already prescribed; around the walls, tables and shelves: in a corner, or rather in a recess, will be a stove to dry the candies.

Third Room, for Preparing the Desserts

This room must be very large, longer than it is wide, and well lit; it will be floored with large tiles and ceiled; in the center must be a long table on which to lay the trays and assemble the desserts. There should also be tables along the walls and facing the windows; in general they must be fairly stout, for some activities require this. A row of shelves above; one or two sideboards with locks; and a dozen straw-bottomed stools: this is all that is needed in this room.

Fourth Room, Storeroom for Confectionery

This room need not be very large; it is to be tiled, ceiled, lit by a single window facing East. All around, there will be presses with well-fitting doors, shelved within. Often, the only access is through the Pantryman's lodging, and this is best. There can be another door, leading to the room where the desserts are prepared, but this must be kept locked and opened only on days when the work to be done is extensive and demands speed. A stove is incorporated in one of the presses in this room; there are times when this is needed.

Fifth Room, Used as a Fruitery

This room must be enclosed by four stout, thick walls; entry must be by way of the Pantryman's apartment. It must be closed very tightly by inner and outer doors. The windows face South. Where it is not possible to have a direct Southern aspect, then it should be to the East; any other aspect is harmful. There must be double window frames and double curtains; outside there must be gratings and brass wire mesh, especially when this room is at ground level, as it should be. A fruitery cannot be in a loft, where the air is too cold, nor in a cellar, where it is too damp; for the fruit would be tainted. It might well be eighteen inches lower than ground level. It must be dry, for damp would rot some of the fruit and cold would blight the rest. For safety's sake, furnish this room with large presses, tightly closed; they serve best if lined with stout and well-glued matchboards, so that no damp air from outside can reach the interior. The shelves are ordinarily given a rail, to prevent the fruit from rolling off. The shelves slope forward, so that, on periodically inspecting the fruit, one can detect any that are spoilt and remove them to save the rest. A bare board is bad for fruits as they roll against each other, and their own weight is sufficient to bruise them at the point where they touch the wood. A bed of straw or bracken may give them a displeasing taint; sand will rot them, through the moisture that it attracts when kept in the dark. Nothing better has been found for this purpose than moss from the bases of tree trunks, well dried in the sun and well beaten. The fruit rests in a soft little hollow that it forms for itself in the moss; it can be inspected or touched without risk.

A well-appointed fruitery is the best means to provide each of the winter months with its appropriate fruit. As is known, fruits ripen better in a hot-house, because they are protected from the outside air. Experience tells us that such air brings them on too quickly, sours them, or robs them of their savor.

This observation leads me to describe an economical means of conserving fruit and having it ripen in due time, but in successive stages.

First take the bottom out of a freshly emptied barrel, and have tiers of shelves placed in it; on these, arrange on moss, as described, as much fruit as one can eat in a fortnight. For best results, the fruit must be freshly gathered in the best weather, so that it has all its bloom. Bunches of grapes should be hung upside down. All must be disposed in a careful and orderly manner, and according to the various kinds that are to be eaten at the same time. The barrel is then sealed to exclude the air, just as if it contained a liquid, and careful note is taken of the date on which it is to be opened. It is deposited in the fruitery, with great care, for fear of disturbing the contents. One can thus can be sure of finding, when required, a fruit as fine as if it had just been plucked from the tree, and with the advantage that it will be seasoned and will have acquired a degree of flavor that is neither tart nor insipid but is that pleasant combination of sweet and sharp that constitutes the perfection of fruit.

Sixth Room, for Trays and Porcelain

This room must be large, tiled and ceiled; the aspect is of no importance. In the center and around the walls there must be large tables, and above those that range along the walls there must be two rows of shelves. It would be convenient to have nearby a scullery similar, but inferior in size, to that of the kitchen. The room for trays and porcelain is to have its entrance through the Pantryman's lodging and the scullery to have another, through the lobby or the servants' hall.

Seventh Room, for the Silver

The entrance to this room must necessarily be through the Pantry-
man's room, for he is responsible for the silver; he is its treasurer. This room will be
tiled like the rest and will have a ceiling. Along the walls there will be tables and
above them a row of shelves, in such a way that all the plate can be placed in order,
on blue cloths made for the purpose, so that one may tell at a glance what pieces
may be missing, and select those that are needed. Such an arrangement cannot fail
to be pleasing to the eye; here taste will accord with wealth. For the rest, this room
will be securely locked; the doors will be good and stout; the windows, although
they will have shutters, will also be closed on the outside with good iron transoms
and crossbars. One cannot take too many precautions.

Eighth Room, for the Pantryman's Lodging

The Pantryman's lodging will require five rooms. The first is a kind of
anteroom, which will serve as a lobby and entrance to the sweet room, the fruitery, the plate room, and finally those rooms that are set aside for his private use.
These comprise a room that will on occasion be useful for the service of the household, a bedroom, a cabinet to keep the registers and to write in, and a little pantry
for his experiments.

Ninth Room, for the Under Pantryman

The Under Pantryman must also have a room of his own, but this will
be a garret, a long way off, furnished with a bed, a table, and a chair.

Lodging for the Majordomo

This lodging comprises seven rooms: an anteroom, a room to lock
away a number of things of which he has charge, a cabinet, a bedroom, a room to
receive the persons and Merchants with whom it is his business to deal, and two
others for his private use.

This apartment must be very close to the kitchens, for it is the Majordomo's duty to watch over them at all times.

Lodging for the Head Cook

The head cook is to have two rooms, and as far as possible they will be
close to his work.

For the under cook, one room will suffice, and it may even be a garret.

This arrangement must not be regarded as a fixed distribution; it is
practiced in a number of great town houses. It is more or less customary nowa-

days; it seems impossible to do without it.

Let us pass on to the lodgings of the Secretaries, the Steward, the other Officers and Domestics; we shall then discuss the stable yards and carriage yards, including the lodgings for the Head Groom, the Under Groom, and the others whom it is customary to lodge beneath one's roof.

If we were to discourse at length on those Country Houses, some of whose dependent farms are worked by their Masters, we should have to add many other details: the Custodian would have his lodging, as would the Carters and the Gamekeepers; there would be various barns and granaries, stables, byres, etc., etc.; nor would the Gardener's lodging or his hothouses be forgotten. But let us leave these matters aside, to speak of the lodgings of the Officers necessary for the good order of town houses and to examine the details of the stable yards, stables, carriage houses, and their appurtenances.

LODGINGS OF THE VARIOUS OFFICERS

Secretary's Apartment

The Secretary's apartment is to be composed of an anteroom, three cabinets, a parlor, a bedroom, a closet, a kitchen, and rooms for two Servants, namely a Cook and a Footman.

The anteroom is ordinarily tiled and ceiled, wainscoted to a dado all around. The two cabinets are furnished with presses with Bohemian glass fronts and shelves, on which are laid the title deeds of the household, in boxes and files, labeled and arranged with neatness and taste. The eye is satisfied, and we see all at once the useful and the agreeable; the mind is engaged by the idea of great possessions and of the good order in which they are kept.

The third cabinet may also be furnished with presses, with papers secured similarly to those in the preceding rooms; it would be best wainscoted to its full height; there should in any case be no fireplace, because of the hazards created by a fire too close to the papers. The wainscot will be painted white; the chimneypiece will have a marble architrave, and there will be a glass in a frame over the mantel; a writing table with a morocco top, a few chairs, some armchairs covered with Utrecht velvet; that will be the main furnishing.

The parlor will also be wainscoted to its full height, as is customary; but, if desired, the wainscot may be to the height of a dado, with paper hangings above, a chimneypiece of common marble, a glass in a frame above, cabrioles in

Utrecht velvet, and ordinary chairs with straw bottoms. This, in general, is the decoration of such a room.

In the bedroom there is often an alcove, which naturally forms a closet. Around the room a wainscoted dado, with paper hangings above, a chimneypiece, a glass above, chairs, and armchairs. At either side of the chimneypiece, recesses with paneled doors; shelves for clothes are placed in one, and hangers in the other.

We shall say nothing of the kitchen; it will be clear that it requires little. As for the Servants' rooms: a bed, a table, and chairs are all the furnishing that they require.

Under Secretary's Lodging

The second Secretary is to have two rooms: one will serve as his cabinet, and the other, as his bedroom. Sometimes the former contains a sleeping alcove closed by a screen, in which case this serves as his cabinet, and the other as a parlor; a wainscoted dado all around both rooms, paper hangings above, a few chairs and a writing table, and the apartment is furnished. Where there is a glass over the mantel, wardrobe doors may flank the fireplace; in this case they will not be glazed and will be hung with the same paper that covers the walls. One will conceal shelves, and the other, hangers.

Librarian

Sometimes the second Secretary has charge of the books; but sometimes a man of some education is employed expressly for the purpose. He will require three rooms, an anteroom, a parlor, and a cabinet, at the end of which there will be a sleeping alcove shut off by a pair of doors with grilles; at one end of the anteroom there may be a section, walled off and lit by a borrowed light, to accommodate a Servant. This lodging will be furnished like the foregoing, with a wainscoted dado, paper above, and a mantelpiece with a glass; a stove will be placed in the anteroom, and the two other rooms will have fireplaces.

Lodging of the Children of the House

We shall distinguish two apartments, that of the boys and that of the young ladies.

Until they reach the age of five, all the children are kept together, with a Governess and a Maidservant. They require five rooms: an anteroom, a large room for exercise, a bedroom large enough to contain the necessary beds, and notably that of the Governess; another for wardrobes and linen; the fifth for the Maidservant. It would also be an advantage to have a closet, well lit and well aired, to hold the closestools and a press for the soiled linen.

These rooms have no particular decoration: a simple dado rail all around, and walls otherwise hung with paper. The anteroom is to be heated by the same stove as the large room; these stoves are ordinarily made of earthenware; they produce no smells and are stoked from the anteroom, lest the children play with fire and fall victims to the accidents that may ensue.

The other two rooms have fireplaces with mantels and glasses. Beds, tables, and chairs are generally all the furnishing; there must be a grille and brass wire mesh in front of the fire and in front of all the windows. This apartment is ordinarily on the second story, and its exposure is to the East; this is essential for health; its influence on the temperament cannot be exaggerated. We are like plants and must keep ourselves safe from intemperate weather and unwholesome exposures.

Lodging of the Sons of the House

When the children reach the age at which they must take up a new form of education, they are given a Governor, sometimes also a Tutor, and a Footman.

The apartment of the Governor and the children must consist of five rooms, an anteroom, a large room, a bedroom containing several beds, and a cabinet for the Governor.

This is approximately the same arrangement as the foregoing. The exposure must be to the East, both for the large room and for the bedroom; and all that we have said of the apartment for the children in general must be observed here.

Young Ladies' Lodging

This lodging is the same for both sexes, until a certain age; the boys leave it when they are given a Governor. The apartment should be similar to that of the second Secretary or the Librarian, to which we refer the reader; it should be adjacent to that occupied by the young gentlemen, and to another room for a Footman.

What we must observe in general, on a matter to which insufficient attention is paid, is that the children's apartment cannot be too cheerful; the colors must be pleasing. Such things affect the disposition more than is commonly thought: a favorable aspect, good air, much cleanliness, are necessary for health and often determine the character of the young by developing cheerful ideas and by inspiring the vivacity that becomes one of the charms of social life.

Steward's Lodging

The Steward has everything in his charge; he is responsible for the whole household economy, and it is to him, in general, that the other Officers render their accounts. His apartment must therefore be situated in such a way that nothing escapes his eye. He should be given seven rooms: an anteroom, a parlor, a cabinet, a bedroom, a kitchen, and two other rooms in which to secure a number of articles that are in his care. The furnishing must be neat and simple. At either side of the chimneypieces there must be recesses with paneled doors; there cannot be too many places that can be locked. There will be a wainscoted dado in most of the rooms, or otherwise a simple dado rail; the whole painted in grisaille, as are the doors and windows. All the walls are to be hung with paper or light cloth. The parlor, the cabinet, and the bedroom will have common marble mantels and glasses above. The other fireplaces will have architraves of freestone. As for the anteroom, this will be heated by flues and by the backplate of one of the fireplaces; a niche may be made for the stove, if desired, in which to place a shelf at the height of thirty-two inches, which is that of a table. The flues will pass beneath this, as will the backplate; the latter, if well placed, can supply sufficient heat in itself.

This whole apartment must be austere; it must inspire reflection and convey a sense of order and economy.

Lodgings of the Valets de Chambre

The lodgings of the valets de chambre must not be far removed from the apartment of their Master. They are often located in entresols above the closets.

First Valet

The first valet is to have four rooms at his disposal, an anteroom, a bedroom, a cabinet, and a large room with presses to hold his Master's linen and suits of clothes. The anteroom, the bedroom, and the cabinet will have a wainscoted dado or a rail, and paper hangings above. The fireplace of the bedroom, or that of the cabinet, will heat the anteroom and will be made with freestone architraves, a common marble mantel, and a frame above with a glass. As for the large room for the clothes, it requires all that we have spoken of in reference to the ladies' clothes: the same care; the same consideration as to the exposure and the floor; the same care as to the wardrobes, the tables, and the other furnishings.

Second Valet

The second valet is to have two rooms in much the same quarter of the house, one of them a common anteroom, in which there will be presses to secure whatever is in his care. This room will be tiled underfoot and ceiled, as will the adjoining room, which is his bedroom. In this last, the bed will be in an alcove, with closets lit by glazed doors on either side of the alcove; one of these closets requires access to the anteroom, and with a double partition it would be possible to pass round the head of the bed, always supposing that the size of the room would permit it. This bedroom will have a wainscoted dado or a rail. Paper hangings, a chimneypiece with a freestone architrave, a marble mantel, and a framed glass above, straw-bottomed chairs, and a table; such, as a rule, is the appropriate furnishing.

First Lady's-Maid

The lodging of the first lady's-maid will contain three rooms: namely, an anteroom, a bedroom, and a room for lace making and needlework.

The first room will be tiled and ceiled, the walls papered, and a dado at the base; at the end, wardrobe doors.

The bedroom will also be tiled and ceiled; there will be an alcove with closets at either side, a freestone chimneypiece with a common marble mantel and a frame above with a glass. The whole room will be hung with paper, and there will be a dado rail or a wainscot, which will be painted a light gray, as will the anteroom, the doors, the windows, and the paneled doors of the recesses on either side of the chimneypiece.

The third room will as a rule be furnished in the same way; but it will be lined, on one side at least, with wardrobes, with shelves and some hangers; in the center of the room there will be a table; there must be straw-bottomed chairs, as in the other rooms, and a chest of drawers in the bedroom.

Second Lady's-Maid

The second lady's-maid will have a lodging similar to that of the second valet, except that in her bedroom she will also need a chest of drawers.

The lodgings of both lady's-maids will be in the entresols above the Lady's closets, where there will also be another little room for the wardrobe maid; but this last will require only a bed, a table, and some chairs. No fireplace is necessary; this room is hung with ordinary paper, and for cleanliness' sake it is to be tiled and ceiled.

Linen Room

The linen room must not be far from the lady's-maids. It will be a large room with an Easterly aspect, if possible. Make sure that it is well lit; work is done here, and daylight is necessary. All around this room there will stand presses with shelves. Perhaps one might wish to have these faced with large panes of glass, as an inducement to the persons in charge of them to maintain order and cleanliness. We have had them made thus, and experience has confirmed our reasoning.

This room will be tiled and ceiled. If there be a cornice, it will run along the tops of the presses; the whole will be painted in gray. In the center of the room will be a table covered with a green cloth, to lay out the linen. A few straw-bottomed chairs and two little tables will make up the rest of the furnishings.

Housekeeper's Lodging

If such there be, her lodging will be like that of the first lady's-maid, and the third room will serve as a workroom for the women who mend the linen.

Cleanliness, good order, and neatness of arrangement constitute the character of these rooms; for these are the symbols of true opulence. There is one other place that demands these qualities to no less a degree; and this is the infirmary. Let us examine it.

Infirmary

The infirmary is necessary in order to seclude the Servant who falls ill. It is the mark of a respectable household to have such a place, and humanity demands it. It is commonly made up of five rooms, namely an anteroom, two other rooms, one for ordinary patients, and one for those near death; for there is nothing more cruel for a person who is sick than to see another die at his side.

Near to the sickroom there must be two others for the Surgeon Valet, who in this case is the nurse.

In the three first rooms, the greatest cleanliness must be observed; they will consequently be tiled, ceiled, and painted all in white, including the walls; there will be a chimneypiece with a freestone architrave in each of the two rooms that flank the anteroom. In the sickroom, there must be three or four beds, and in the other, one only. These beds are to be white, to be washed frequently and thus prevent foul air. The aspect is properly an Eastern one, and the door facing the fireplace will serve as a ventilator. In an infirmary, this arrangement becomes indispensable. The two other rooms will serve as a lodging for the Surgeon Valet. The first will be a kind of apothecary's room, where the medicines and other remedies necessary for the sick will be made up. To this end there will be a fireplace, a stove with several hot plates, and a press to secure the drugs and medicaments that must be kept constantly within reach; the slightest accident might make us regret the omission of such a precaution; they may be needed from one moment to the next.

The fifth room will be a bedroom for the Surgeon; it will be arranged and furnished in the same style as that of the second valet de chambre.

Most commonly, the infirmary is at the top of the house; the air is healthier, and especially so in Paris. Take care to suffer no bad odors there, and it will be best to make at the top of one of the windows, in place of one light, a *ventilator* in the form of a bellows that can be opened and closed more or less, according to need. The air is renewed by this means, and the patient is not incommoded in the slightest. This is an expedient frequently employed against smoke; and if the advantage of this kind of ventilator were once understood, there is hardly an inhabited room but should have one. One might also desire to add to all this a cabinet in which a bath might be placed; but it ought not to be far away. By the means of a boiler above the stove and a lead conduit, it would be an easy matter to have hot water. There might be a tank in which cold water from the roof would collect; and, indeed, such a tank is necessary. In all houses of any size, it is essential to have water in reserve in a high part of the house in case of fire; let us take twofold advantage of this for the infirmary, for rainwater is highly beneficial.

Close to the sickrooms, there should also be a closet of ease; it might even be appropriate to construct a small closet adjoining the large sickroom, which could be served by way of the anteroom. This would contain a closestool; and a second for the soiled linen would be equally useful, except that it is better to take such linen to a well-sealed loft and hang it out on cords. These are little attentions that must not be neglected; one cannot be too thoughtful when giving succor to our fellowmen. Let us adopt this maxim; it is imprinted in all benevolent minds; the heart dictates it, and charity commands it.

This is the time to consider a chapel, or at least an oratory.

A chapel is necessary in a household of any size, in order that the duties of religion may be performed in all circumstances and that the Masters may set a good example. Where it is impossible, for any particular reason, to have one, it will be replaced by an oratory. We have spoken of this in discussing the palace of a Prelate. We shall here pursue the same ideas and observe that the place must be conducive to meditation and inspire the profoundest respect. Severe forms, segmental arches, ceilings a little low, profiles with few moldings, a half-light, an altar in the shape of a tomb, a good picture hung in a recess and lit from unseen windows, all would contribute to this precious illusion. Such devices draw their force from the scholarly rules of perspective; their application is a matter of genius and taste. Well applied, they arouse the sensations and produce the effects that may rightly be expected. Such a room, open at particular times, is a stimulus and incitement to piety. What could be more conducive to the maintenance of good order?

Where architecture produces such effects, in alliance with painting and sculpture, it engenders a magic that acts upon the soul, imparting to it sentiments, impressions, and especially those tender sensations that we savor with such delight.

The true Artist is known by his way of apprehending the objects with which he works; he manifests his skill, his adroitness, and his discretion by setting everything in its right place and treating it in accordance with its true character.

Fitness must always be his guide; this is a principle from which he may not depart; this is the basis of his success and the object of the present work.

The yards and even the stables have a character that is proper to them, one which we shall seek to define and to detail.

The aspect, the lighting, the dimensions, nothing is immaterial, and every part has its effect. Convenience, ease of communication, distribution, and even the detail of every object must concern us. The Architect charged with instituting order must take in all of his operations at a glance. He must in no way neglect the harmony that relates to the character and also the use of the part that he wishes to consider. This is as true of stable yards and their appurtenances, as it is of every other part of a fabric. Let us turn to the details.

STABLE YARDS

Of Stables and Carriage Houses

The exposure of the stables must be to the East and that of the carriage houses to the North. This observation is useful because with any other aspect the horses will grow thin, as they do with a Southern exposure in particular. As for the carriage houses, the value of a Northerly aspect will be obvious, because from this quarter they will never get any sun, and the carriages will be out of the sunlight, which inevitably occasions cracks.

The stable yards in general should face North; they should give direct access to the street; their water should also drain away without passing into the main forecourt of the House. It is convenient to have the stable yard at some distance from the main fabric, because of the noise and the smell. However, a direct communication between the forecourt and the stable yard is indispensable. This service gate must be opened only as necessary, and its key should be in the hands of the Head Groom or such other person as is charged with keeping good order.

All these locations and the carriage houses will be paved with split setts; the stable yards themselves will be cobbled. It is well to place in these yards several stone troughs and faucets to give water; there cannot be too much of this, for washing maintains cleanliness.

The provision of horse ponds has hitherto been neglected in the building of our great town houses, but would nevertheless be of great advantage, as all the horses might be led there once in every day; in case of fire, this would be a valuable resource indeed.

The execution would not be difficult, for the idea itself is simple.

All the clean water from the roofs would be collected; even those in the forecourt would serve, the pitch of the roofs permitting. Such a pond would have every advantage if it were to be arranged and constructed in such a way that it could be drained below, like a basin. In this case, in building it, make the ground adjacent to it higher by five feet, at least, than the gutter in the street; then the head of water will be four or four and a half feet, and by a valve or even a well-placed faucet the water may be discharged at will. Where flooding is apprehended in case of storm, an overflow can be made. There is an answer to all objections; with a little intelligence and some knowledge of hydraulics, the thing can be done. The only difficulty lies in finding the necessary space, which is most often wanting. It may nevertheless be observed that a horse pond of four toises by five will suffice to wash and clean a large number of horses. Besides, can there be too much water in an extensive household? A reservoir of this kind, which requires no maintenance, would be a real treasure. A horse pump might perhaps be necessary in case of drought. The expense is slight, especially for a household of any consequence, and bears no relation to the advantages.

Stables

There must be four stables, which will be larger or smaller in relation to the number of horses.

The first is for the carriage horses; the second is for the riding horses; the third, which is smaller, is for sick horses; and the fourth is for visiting horses, such as those of the Custodians of the country seats, or of the tenant Farmers, or of such friends as may come to dine or sup. Such a practice becomes more and more necessary as the size of the capital increases, and its various quarters grow more remote from each other. As there is no knowing whether the horses of others are healthy or sick, it is best to keep them apart. No prudent Head Groom would allow it to be otherwise.

Stables may be made in four ways, as determined by their position: single, double, triple, and quadruple.

Double stables are those that are most often used and are the most convenient to work. They are also the most pleasant; all that is happening can be seen at a glance.

A single stable must be some twelve feet wide within; a double stable must be at least twenty-two feet wide. When such stables reach a certain length, they are made wide in proportion, thirty feet and sometimes more. A triple stable must be thirty feet wide, and a quadruple, forty. In giving these measurements, we refer to the least possible widths; anything more will be all the better. It will readily be understood that in the two last-named forms the boards above must be carried on joists supported for the most part by posts or pillars, masked for part of their height by the racks and mangers.

Vaulted stables are the best: but in any event they must be of a good height, because of the horses' breath, which, augmented by their numbers, might become harmful. Boards above would not last long, unless lined with a thick ceiling.

We shall describe only single and double stables; the two other kinds are not in common use; they entail difficulties. The general rules are the same.

Where daylight falls directly on the horses' eyes, it will make them liable to shy; it must fall on their hindquarters. To this end, in a single stable, the troughs and the hayrack will be on the wall opposite that from which the light comes. As for the double stable, as there is no choice but to place horses along the wall in which the window openings are made, it is essential that the light should enter no less than ten feet above the ground. Then the light falls at an angle at which it cannot strike the horse except on its rump, and there is nothing to fear; all is in order. The door is usually in the center, which is convenient for the service; but it may be at one end of this same side wall, and always facing East. This is the only favorable aspect. Should more grandeur and greater perfection be desired, the stables might be made with doors in the two gable ends, to set up a through draft; but it must be observed that each of these doors must communicate with a kind of porch that opens to the East. These porches must be of the same width as the stables, for greater ease of unharnessing and placing the harness on wooden pegs built into the walls for that purpose. These doors in the two gable ends have the advantage that they reveal the whole length of the stable as one enters, and this is the finest view. It is a pleasure to observe good order, handsome arrangement, and great cleanliness; it is rare for these qualities to be wanting in such places, and most particularly where a Head Groom is in charge. They are old soldiers, for the most part, and they know the meaning of discipline.

Ten feet away from the walls, on either side, there will be a gutter, and along the center will be a causeway, so that those who visit the stable can go dryshod and walk at their ease. This will be done by making the width greater than necessity would require.

The slope of the paving, from the wall to the gutter, is to be two inches in every toise. From the gutter course to the wall, many Head Grooms have the paving omitted and saltpeter rammed into the ground; and then the fall is five

inches in ten feet. The gutter itself needs very little slope; half an inch in every
toise will suffice; otherwise, the horses would be on an incline that would prevent
them from standing straight. There is no animal more apt to acquire bad habits.
The whole length of the stable is divided in two, for the purposes of the slope: half
falls away to the South and half to the North; which should give, in accordance
with the position we have given, on a length of twenty-five toises, a drop of six
and a quarter inches at each end. This must be borne in mind in setting up the
mangers and the racks, especially when the lengths are great, although they rarely
become so when several stables are in use, as we have shown to be necessary. It
will be noted, nevertheless, that if the fall were to be only two or three inches,
there would be no need to make the racks and mangers out of plumb. The mangers are to be made of boards three inches thick and edged with strips of iron,
so that the horses who have tics do not destroy them and cleanliness may be maintained.

The manger is to be one foot deep by one foot wide at the bottom
and fifteen inches wide at the top, which should be three and a half feet from the
ground.

There should be timber supports every twelve feet, passing through
the depth of the mangers. These should follow the same incline as the mangers
attached to them; the lower edge should be rounded, the arrises chamfered, lest
the horses hurt themselves. Sometimes round poles are inserted between squared
timbers.

The racks are made of battens, with turned oak bars. Sometimes service wood is used; although not so handsome, it is superior in quality. The racks
are three feet high, and they must slope away from the wall. Where the slope is too
great, the horses' manes are ruined; where it is too little, it becomes hard for them
to get the hay, and there are some parts that the horses cannot reach at all. It is for
the Head Groom to determine how this is to be done. In general, one-quarter, or
one-third at the most, of the height of the rack will suffice for the outward slope.
The rail along the top of the rack must be seven and one-quarter feet above the
level of the stable floor below the manger.

The dust from the hay, which falls on the horses' manes and fouls them,
formerly inspired the notion of placing the racks almost upright; to this effect the
base was closed off by a feedbox, and matchboarding covered the interval between this and the trough, which was placed about six inches away from the wall,
so that all the dust fell harmlessly to the ground. The air of cleanliness which then
prevailed was pleasing; but the ill consequences soon caused this practice to be
abandoned in the light of experience. The horses grew visibly thinner, as if they

were not being fed at all. Much time was spent in looking for the cause, and after the most rigorous examination it was seen that the dust was carrying away with it the seeds of the grass; the hay, which is a coarse food in itself, lacked both savor and the necessary salts to keep the horses in good condition. It no longer had that prime quality, that essential virtue, the source of the precious gloss that proclaims their health; and so, in a number of places, careful and attentive Head Grooms have caused this innovation to be discarded. This is one more task for the stableman: he is obliged to take up his comb and serge cloth more often to keep the mane clean and free the horse's neck of the grime that is caused by the accumulation of dust.

Such is the construction and the manner of installation of racks and mangers. Let us proceed to the space allotted to each horse and observe that a wider space is required for a carriage horse than for a saddle horse. Allow four feet for a carriage horse and three and a half for a saddle horse; each division is to be marked by two posts, well rounded and turned, topped with a ball and planted with the ball four feet clear of the floor. There will be two iron rings, to fix one end of the bar that completes the division and is attached to another ring on the manger. Well aligned and perfectly level, these posts are a token of good order and a pleasing sight to see. In each section there must be three rings on the manger to tether the horse; on the crossbeam above and in the center of each stall will be an inscription bearing the horse's name: a precaution required not so much to satisfy curiosity as to preserve good order and ease of working. Such a label, and the similar one placed above the peg for the harness, serve to prevent mistakes. A horse must never change its harness, or its saddle and bridle. This ensures that it stays well mouthed and cannot be hurt; besides, this is a great way to be promptly served, by indicating to the stableman the horses that one desires to use. All is well where there is no confusion. Order and harmony are the ground and principle of Architecture, which allows of no negligence.

At either end of such a stable must be a gallery for the stablemen in attendance; horses require to be watched night and day, because they may entangle themselves, or be taken with a colic, or be subject to any number of accidents. These galleries will be in the form of platforms, reached by a loft ladder behind a partition at the back of each porch. Beneath this ladder will be a large bin for oats, secured either by its own lock or by a padlock; the day's supply of oats is passed into it by means of a hopper. This is the only means to avert a number of abuses and to keep the oats always dry; there is no fear of damp in transit or of theft, and the work is more easily done.

These stables are to be illuminated from either end by means of reflecting lamps lit from outside; this is done from the stablemen's galleries. One lamp illuminates both the gallery and the stable. The platform on which the stableman's bed stands must be so constructed that there is no fear of fire. It is an advantage to have it of brick, as it would be if a vault were to be made. Four feet suffice for the width, and the bedding consists of a simple mattress placed on top; servants of this sort are not to be enclosed, lest they neglect, through drowsiness or through idleness, to observe what goes on.

Stables for Saddle Horses

The same attention should be paid to the other stables, but especially to those of the saddle horses. The size is determined by the number of horses to be accommodated. It will be recalled that three and a half feet suffice for the stabling of a saddle horse; for the rest, all the same precautions must be taken and the same dimensions used. We omitted to say that the trough must be divided by boards, to right and left, corresponding to the width of each compartment. This precaution is rendered the more necessary by the fact that horses frequently fight over their oats; some are greedier than others, and having eaten their portion more quickly, they fall upon those of their neighbors, which must be prevented. In this way, one can tell the state of a horse's appetite and know when it is sick.

Stables for Visitors' Horses

In stables for visitors' horses, some of these precautions may be dispensed with; note, however, that in general the trough must be a little lower, as must the rack. Different horses are received there from one day to the next, and all are not of the same stature; some are very small. It is better, furthermore, to pave this stable throughout, for the sake of cleanliness; it can then be washed down more easily; this is a necessity. If desired, a little less space may be given to each horse, and this may be adjusted by moving the rings that are attached to the manger. Posts may be dispensed with altogether; in this case, if rails are still to be placed between the horses, a beam with chamfered edges may be suspended from the boards above, with ropes descending to support one end of each rail, the other end being attached to the trough.

Stables for Sick Horses

The same principles may be applied to the stabling of sick horses; let there be room for five or six horses, and that will suffice.

Carriage Houses

Carriage houses should be placed to the North, and so constructed that they may be partitioned to hold no more than two carriages each. Some will hold only one; this is an essential provision for the best carriages. Allow sixteen feet in width for two carriages; nine at least for one. In depth, allow twenty or twenty-one feet: the shaft is not to be raised, as this ruins the undercarriage and causes much inconvenience. Where space is restricted and the inconvenience is to be overlooked, fifteen feet of depth will suffice for an ordinary carriage house.

Each house must have full doors, reinforced by bars and diagonal braces; make a wicket in one leaf, which is convenient for the inspection of the carriages.

As there are some carriages of lesser value, they can be placed in open houses, which obviates any confusion of doors and facilitates the work; indeed, closed and open carriage houses may alternate, and by this means the wickets will not catch on each other.

A carriage house needs to be twelve feet high. Carriages vary, and this height will be adequate for any eventuality. Inside the carriage house there must be guides, so that the carriage is guided into its proper place. These guides are wooden structures in the form of isosceles triangles with the angles held by posts and the forward point rounded off to a width of fifteen inches. The base of the triangle is five feet long. It will be seen from these dimensions that once the carriage has started in the right direction, it is guided in such a way that it cannot deviate, however unskillful the coachman. The crossbeam at the back, which forms the base of the triangle, serves to arrest the wheels and prevent the carriage from striking the wall; the distance from barrier to wall is to be eighteen inches clear.

The height of this guide is eight inches at the front and sixteen at the back. Any greater height would break the running boards; this requires close attention, as many mistakes are made. At the entrance of each carriage house, there should be stumps no more than one foot high, so that the axles of the smaller wheels pass over them; these stumps serve to guide the carriage into place and to prevent damage to the door panels from the doors of the carriage house.

Adjoining the stables there must be two locations, one to keep the harnesses and the other for the saddles and bridles; the exposure here is immaterial.

Harness Room

This will be tiled and ceiled; otherwise, it would be too subject to dust. The need for cleanliness demands such a precaution. Every three feet, there must be pegs built into the walls six and a half feet above the floor. These pegs are four-inch timbers rounded at the top and projecting from the walls by about two feet. They serve as hangers for the harness, and two sets are normally placed on a single peg. In this way, the various teams are distinguished; board partitions are placed on either side, projecting from the wall to very much the same distance as the harnesses themselves. Above is a platform of similar boards, especially when the room is high, and to the front of this is attached a bar to hold two curtains, which cover the whole. Above the bar is an inscription bearing the name of the team.

The pegs, mentioned above, in the stable porches are for use in passing; they serve when the harness is removed from the horse or during the preparations for driving out, for the harness room must be locked and there must be no access to it except on necessary business. The windows will be barred, and the two-leaved doors firmly shut. If it were possible to add a little yard containing a lean-to, the harness might be washed under cover; in this case there would need to be a trough and a faucet. Close to the division for each team, there must be a locker with several shelves for the ribbons, cockades, etc., to prevent confusion. In this way, each man answers for whatever may be amiss in his own department. Along the center of this room, there are to be tables, two feet wide and five or six long, with an equal space between them; they will be supported by iron legs fixed well into the floor. These rooms are sometimes paved, but tiles are better, easier of upkeep, and less subject to dust.

It would be well to include a separate room to serve as a kind of workshop for the Harness Maker; a table and a few stools will suffice.

Saddle Room

The place where the saddles for the riding horses are kept should not be far removed; this must also be tiled and ceiled; the windows will have iron bars outside, and the doors will lock securely. All around the walls there will be presses, four feet wide or thereabouts, each with a pair of doors. Sometimes these are set in rows; this is more convenient in that they take up less of the room, but one is then deprived of the pleasure of seeing everything at a glance. These may have glazed doors to enforce the utmost cleanliness and maintain good order. Each press will contain three saddles, each on a sort of triangular sloping bracket, the bridles above, hanging on pegs or wooden clothes racks, and beneath these one or two shelves for the housings, cockades, ribbons, etc.; the taste and care of a conscientious Head Groom will make itself felt here. They may be assembled like trophies, so that each bridle seems to emerge from a knot of ribbon, and above will be written the name of the horse to which it belongs. This arrangement may be varied and rendered more interesting by the variety of forms and outlines; it is for genius and taste to make their mark.

Along the center of the room there will be a table on which to lay the saddles and bridles that are to be put away or required for use.

The size of the saddle room will depend on need, but there must be a side room in which two or three saddlers may work on occasion; this will also serve for the harness room, unless a separate workshop be desired. A table in the middle and several stools are required; this room will be tiled as to the floor, ceiled, and lit by one or two windows; its exposure is of no consequence, and it would be convenient to arrange it as a Saddler's shop, so that it would be easier to see what goes on.

Dung Yard

Adjoining the stable and carriage yards, there will be the dung yard, which is necessary for the cleanliness of the former, where nothing must be left lying. For the best, this yard must lie to the North; with this aspect, a large shed will be set up to keep the carts and the heavy country coaches. It is here, and beneath this same shed, that the trave must be set up for shoeing restive horses and for performing on them any other operations for which restraint is necessary.

In the same quarter, there must be a forge and an anvil: in short, a Farrier's shop.

In this yard, or rather in a little particular area, there will be the latrines for the servants; take care to arrange them in such a way that they are obliged to keep them clean. These latrines must be open at the front, with divisions every three feet, and closed by a wooden door four feet high. The seats, with hoppers, one foot wide only, will be formed by a piece of wood, rounded at the front, placed sixteen inches high, and to avoid any untoward accident, there will be inside the seat an iron bar, thirteen to fourteen lines in thickness, placed diagonally, in such a way that the matter may not rest on it. Pray excuse this detail; the Architect must neglect nothing.

All these parts should be cobbled, and the way out of the dung yard should be to the street; but as we have already said, this will be used only as needed, the keys being with the Porter, or some other person appointed to that effect, as the maintenance of good order requires.

It is by this gate that the wagons will enter with hay, straw, and other supplies for the stable yards, for, once again, all possible care must be taken to keep the main forecourt free of obstruction. Take heed, also, that the water from the stable yards, kitchens, stables, and even the carriage houses must pass directly to the outside. Rather drain the service yards into cesspools than have the inconvenience of water in the forecourt.

With the stables, there must be separate lofts for hay, for straw, and for oats.

Lofts for Hay

The haylofts must be of a considerable size; they are commonly incorporated in the roofs, and for greater convenience, care is taken to let the outside walls rise three feet above the loft floor. By this means, the whole area is freed for use, and damage and disturbance to the roof is avoided. All these lofts will be tiled underfoot, and at intervals there will be dormers, closed by shutters in which there will be a glazed oval opening. In the center there must be a principal dormer with a projecting platform of boards for hoisting the hay. This platform will have an iron framework, three feet high, with two corner bars forming an iron arch to support a beam that ends in a block and tackle.

We have said that the oats must fall through a hopper into the bin in the stables without having to be taken out-of-doors; it would be advisable to make a similar hopper, but larger, for the hay. This would avert many mishaps, and the hay would always be drier and cleaner. These hoppers might be at the ends of the stable porches, and in such a case there would be a space cut out in the loft floor.

Lofts for Straw

The same will apply to the lofts for straw.

Lofts for Oats

The lofts for oats require more precautions. They must be close to the loft stairs, tiled, and wainscoted; take care to leave no hole for the rats and mice. Make dormer openings, as in the other lofts, closed by shutters set with a pane of glass. If it were desired to have one dormer with a projecting platform to raise the sacks, then you might place a winch there, as Bakers do.

Lodging of the Head Groom

The Head Groom's apartment must not be far from the stable yards; he must overlook them for the sake of good order. He is one of the foremost Officers of the household, and he needs a respectable and decent lodging, suited to his position, and so he is to have two anterooms, a dining room, a salon, a cabinet, a bedroom, a kitchen, and two or three other rooms to lodge his servants and attend to his private business.

As for his furnishings, they should be much the same as those of the Steward and the Secretary.

Under Groom

The Under Groom's lodging is similar to that of the Under Secretary, to which we refer; but he will require one additional room to keep the trappings and other articles of value entrusted to his care.

There must also be a large number of chambers for sundry Stablemen, Footmen, and Coachmen; but these are all separate rooms without fireplaces, lit by a single window, built like cells, in which the only furnishings are a bed, two chairs, and a table.

Upholsterer

We have overlooked the matter of the Upholsterer to the household, but he has no fixed location; accommodate him where you can.

He requires four rooms: an anteroom, a workroom, a bedroom, and a cabinet. All these will be tiled and ceiled. Give him two fireplaces; or one will suffice, if need be, in which case this would be the one in the bedroom. All the other rooms are to be heated by stoves, and the back of the bedroom fire would lend heat to the cabinet.

It is well to note that this lodging must be close to the depository. This room is indispensable. Here all the old furnishings are placed, and others found as required for seasonal use; here, also, the Upholsterer makes ready the furniture in his charge, repairs it, and oversees the work that is done on it.

Depository for Furniture

This will always be placed within reach of an easy and convenient staircase: the North is its most favorable aspect; it will be tiled and ceiled. Around the walls, there will be several rows of shelves; and on one side there will be large and deep presses to store all the stuffs and the folding furniture that is out of season but demands to be kept with great care. In the center, there will be a large table on iron supports, and this will serve to spread out, scrub, and clean those objects that require it.

Nearby, there will be one or two rooms to keep the large pieces of furniture; it is important to maintain these in perfect order, and a list must be made; each piece will be designated by its name, its quality, its dimensions, and a number: a sort of inventory. Every class of furniture will be assigned a separate location, so that when need arises what is sought can be found without delay. The

Upholsterer alone will have the key, since this is all in his charge and he is responsible for it, most particularly so if monies have been advanced to him on account.

Note, in addition, that all the Footmen are to be lodged: each will have a room without a chimneypiece; indeed, it would be dangerous to give them such a thing. A bed, a table, and two chairs will suffice. All the keys of these rooms will be different; but the locks will be so contrived that there is a master key, which the Steward alone will have in his keeping. This precaution is necessary for good order's sake and in case of unforeseen circumstances.

Riding School

Before leaving the stables and stable yards, might this not be the place to speak of a riding school? This is a feature that ought to be of great concern, one which our young Noblemen neglect. They owe it to their station in life to love horses; this is a noble pastime, and its usefulness is clear.

What an occasion to show their skill and develop their graces! Perhaps there would be fewer races run; but would there not be more merit, for a young Nobleman in winning his wager himself than in leaving the palm to be carried off by some Jockey who is often a cheat? Might there not be contests for a certain number of rounds and detours, passing alternately through different arches or intercolumniations? This would be a real trial of skill; this would be proof positive that a man had learnt to manage a horse. How gratifying to see two young Noblemen start out together on opposite sides and seek to overcome, in the briefest time, obstacles determined by themselves with due taste and judgment! What a pleasure to spy them at another moment pistol in hand, shooting at a head of Medusa and hitting it several times in the course of a single ride! Movements in combination make difficult accomplishments; and it would be an admirable sight to see them, after a succession of repeated caracoles, hit a hat thrown into the air for them and in a single movement pick it up from the ground! What a variety of occasions might be found to try their skill, since this same skill can furnish the means of defence and of overcoming an enemy! Their sports and amusements would fan the flames of patriotic zeal. They would appear to be the tutelary deities of the nation, exercising to defend it.

The Ancients well knew the value of these noble exercises: their hippodromes were places of the greatest magnificence. What effects must have been produced by such exercises! What sensations of greatness and courage they must have aroused in the soul, which they naturally elevated to heroism! Let no one liken those interesting exercises to our own jousts and old tournaments; these were splendid in truth but dangerous and deadly. We know this from melancholy experience in the case of Henry II.[50] The exercises that we propose here are those that form part of the education of young Noblemen, and they are inseparable from that rank. It is a matter that deserves the closest attention, as conducive to the glory of the nation. We might justly blame our own age for attending too much to frivolities and not enough to all that kindles emulation and trains able military men. Worthy examples and the principles imbibed in youth often ripen the seed of the greatest talents and of the virtues themselves.

Let us simply observe that in association with a fine apartment designed for a military man, a well-composed and tastefully designed riding school would be both useful and agreeable. It would suitably terminate the view along one of the principal avenues of the garden. Aloft, on a triumphal car harnessed to four horses, the god Mars would seem ready to join the course on the hippodrome that we propose.

In the decoration of this building, Doric columns would be used; for that is the warrior's Order: its noble and austere proportions suit him well.

This colonnade would be crowned by the entablature appropriate to it and, most suitably, by one with mutules and perfectly square metopes. Above would be a fine balustrade designed in accord with the proportions and character of the whole.

The bases of the columns might be omitted; indeed, it would be prudent to do so to avoid accidents, as projecting corners are dangerous when exercises are in progress. In such a case, to give the column its proportionate height, the base would be replaced by a drum stouter than the rest of the shaft by one-sixth, thus making a cincture. Such columns, cinctured alternately for the rest of their height, like those of the Palais du Luxembourg, would make a fine effect, in keeping with the genre appropriate to such a place.

The entire roof of the covered portion of the riding school would form a terrace, which would add to the delights of the apartment. It might be decorated with orange and myrtle trees in tubs and with vases: might not the boudoir and the dressing room be so disposed that this would form their garden? No situation could be happier, for Mars and Venus always agree. Observe, however, that the exposure of these two rooms must be to the East; and from this aspect, which is favorable to compositions, the grandest effects might be derived; the part of the colonnade that faces the windows, and thus the West, would be lit picturesquely by the rays of the setting Sun. The contrast of light and shade would produce the effect of a theatrical scene. Let us assume two rows of columns: those behind will be overshadowed in part by the soffit and by the entablature of those closest to the arena; this first row, on the other hand, will be lit from capital to base; the light will be softened by the roundness of the shafts, but it will fall plentifully on the ground within the peristyle, which will reflect it brightly. It will strike full on the entablature and will pick out each member with great distinctness; it will be so distributed that the shadows form a contrast that becomes more effective as the daylight grows stronger. At another time, the Sun's enfeebled rays will still illuminate the lateral parts, when all above is shrouded in the first shades of evening. What beauties! What charms! It is from effects such as these that painting derives the scholarly rules of perspective and optics that contribute to the magic of its art. Why should a skillful Architect neglect to profit by them, unless by cruel force of necessity? For a work that is magnificent in itself often comes to seem frigid; and what is the cause? It is the exposure, the lack of contrasts of light and shade. It may be that no one has ever given sufficient thought to this. It has been too common to decry certain works without knowing the reason. This is unjust; the Artist is not always free to determine his site. The river front of the Hôtel des Monnaies[i] is a striking example of this. Although finely conceived, well composed, and harmonious to a degree, this work seems monotonous: the result fails to answer our expectations. Take due note of the cause: it lies solely in the Northerly exposure of the building. There is no variety in the shadows of the projecting portions; the same tone prevails throughout.

Let us look at the colonnade of the Louvre,[51] with its Easterly exposure, and it will supply proof of our argument. The effect of light and shadow gives it a relief of which the grand facade of the Hôtel des Monnaies is unfortunately deprived.

Let us return to the colonnade of our riding school.

Stone vases, agreeably formed and proportioned in relation to the Order, might be placed above the pedestals that mark the bays of the balustrade.

In the central portions, projections might be formed and the columns coupled, in which case the pedestals above them would be crowned with groups of figures or with such trophies as are appropriate for a riding school.

Here you may let your imagination take flight to reach the tone of grandeur, of nobility, and of magnificence. All must be in keeping with the character and the nature of the place; the least lapse would be unpardonable.

The appearance of a building of this kind must inspire a noble feeling.

i. By M. Antoine of the Academy of Architecture. The first stone was laid on 30 April 1771, on behalf of the King, and the workmen of the Mint were moved to the new building in March 1775.

The sound of the trumpet animates the warrior and even his horses; and the tone, the proportions, and the harmony of Architecture have the same power over our souls.

A riding school conceived and executed in accordance with its essential nature would make the happiest conclusion to the apartment of a young Nobleman, for whom its exercises must be one of the prime objects of his education; they contribute to his health and his strength of temperament: precious qualities, for a military man above all.

Such is the ensemble of a great and splendid house; such is the character that every room must have in itself and in relation to the nature of the persons for whom it is intended. In its compositions, there cannot be too much harmony, always in relation to the mass. Any defect in the dimensions produces an unpleasing impression, through a jarring contrast which often obscures even the image of the forms. Everything in Architecture has a genre that is proper to it. The intelligent Architect must make his presence felt, even in the smallest particulars of his art.

Such is the magnificence of the present age that we are obliged to include in our plans many rooms that our forefathers had no notion of; they appear at the prompting of pleasure, of luxury, and of the refined taste that in former times was unknown. Plain shelves and presses were enough. Our needs increase; an example is set; and we are carried along with it. To be convinced of this, it is enough to consider the new buildings on our boulevards, at the Chaussée-d'Antin, along the Champs-Elysées, and in a number of other parts of our capital.[52] These are not houses; properly speaking, they are palaces, although most are the dwellings of private persons. There, magnificence is conjoined to the greatest comfort; nothing is lacking, either in respect of opulence or of art. The sight of them amazes, but do they satisfy the soul? That is the question. Very often, we see nothing more than vast constructions in which the different genres and characters of building have been confounded. Nothing is relative to the persons who occupy them: at every step, we see that the Artist has not worked with a single coherent aim in mind. We see glimmers of good taste but seldom a well-considered and happily conceived ensemble. These are flashes of light, which are lost in immensity and leave only the semblance of a clear sky, soon to be clouded over.

The genre most in demand has been that of elegant frivolity, and this is far from deserving any such preeminence. Often the sequence of rooms in an apartment is lacking in the necessary relations between the various parts. These rooms have no harmony because of the contrasts of character that are apparent in them. Could it have been done otherwise? No. Most of those who have built thus have done so as a speculation without knowing for whom the house might be intended. What is necessary, on the contrary, is to settle upon a course of action and to have a clear intention. The apartment of a Minister is not the same as that of a lady of fashion; that of a lady of fashion is not suitable for a Magistrate, and so forth. But let us not enter upon any longer discussions; our aim has been to make known the relation that exists between Architecture and our sensations. And thus, in speaking of distribution, we have been at pains to develop the character proper to the various rooms. We have indicated the demands imposed by the luxury of the present day and the need for a progression of opulence within a single apartment. We have explained the concord of the masses, the details, and the profiles: everything that can tend to create a fine ensemble and to maintain harmony, the foundation of that true beauty that touches the soul and excites the sensations. But as the principles are the same as those of exterior decoration, it is to those that we refer the reader.

This might be the time to speak of public buildings, their uses, the sensations that they must arouse, each in its own kind, and the resources to be employed to these ends. We should have much to say on the grand structures that must mark this epoch for the future and will characterize the taste of this century by embodying the genius of a nation. But that would be too vast an undertaking, and it is wise to await the verdict of the public on the essay that we now place before it. If the principles stated herein have the good fortune to please, we shall conceive it our duty to enlarge on our ideas and to continue the work in its several parts.

APPROBATION

I have read, on the orders of my Lord Keeper of the Seals, a Work having as its title *The Genius of Architecture; or, The Analogy of That Art with Our Sensations,* and I have found nothing in it that might prevent its being printed. Paris, this 10th day of February 1780.

MAUDUIT.

ROYAL PRIVILEGE

*L*OUIS, BY THE GRACE OF GOD, KING OF FRANCE AND OF NAVARRE; To our trusty and well-beloved Counselors, the Persons keeping our Courts of Parliament, Masters of the Pleas in ordinary to our Household, Great Council, Provost of Paris, Bailiffs, Seneschals, their Civil Lieutenants, and other of our Justiciaries to whom this may come: GREETINGS. Our well beloved Sieur LE CAMUS DE MÉZIÈRES, Architect, has given Us to understand that he would wish to cause to be printed and given to the Public a Work of his own composition entitled *The Genius of Architecture; or, The Analogy of That Art with Our Sensations,* if it were to please us to grant him the necessary Letters of Privilege to that end. WHEREFORE, being disposed to treat the Petitioner with favor, We have permitted and now permit him to cause the said Work to be printed as many times as he may think fit and to sell it or to cause it to be sold in all parts of our Kingdom. We desire that he shall remain in enjoyment of the effect of the present Privilege, for him and for his heirs in perpetuity, provided that he make no assignment of it to any person; and if he should nevertheless think fit to make such an assignment, the Deed thereof to be registered in the Syndical Chamber of Paris, on pain of nullity both of the Privilege and of the assignment; and then, by virtue of registration of the said assignment, the duration of the present Privilege is to be reduced to that of the life of the petitioner, or to that of ten years from this day, if the Petitioner decease before the expiry of the said ten years. The whole in conformity with Articles IV and V of the Order in Council of the thirtieth day of August 1777, regulating the duration of Privileges in the trade of Bookselling. We PROHIBIT all Printers, Booksellers, and other persons, of whatsoever quality and condition, from introducing any foreign impression of the Work into any place subject to our jurisdiction; and also from printing, selling, or causing to be sold, issued, or counterfeited the said Work, on any pretext whatever, without the express consent given in writing of the said Petitioner or of his representative, on pain of seizure and confiscation of the counterfeit Copies and of a fine of six thousand pounds, which may not be abated, for the first offence; of a like fine and loss of standing in the case of any further offence, and of all costs, damages, and interest, in conformity with the Order in Council of the thirtieth of August 1777, concerning counterfeiting. Providing that these present letters be registered in full in the Register of the Community of Printers and Booksellers of Paris within three months of the date of same; that the printing of the said Work shall be done in our Kingdom and not elsewhere, on good paper and in clear type, in conformity with the Regulations of the Book Trade, on pain of forfeiture of the present Privilege: and that, before placing it on sale, the Manuscript that has served as copy for the printing of the said Work be lodged, in the same state in which the Approbation was given, with our trusty and well beloved Knight Keeper of the Seals of France, Sieur HUE DE MIROMENIL, and that two Copies be then placed in our public Library, one in that of our Château du Louvre, one in that of our trusty and well-beloved Knight Chancellor of France, Sieur de MAUPEOU, and one in that of the said Sieur HUE DE MIROMENIL: and all this on pain of incurring the nullity of these Present Letters. Of which we command and direct that the said Petitioner and his heirs have full and undisturbed enjoyment without let or hindrance. IT IS OUR WILL that a copy of these Present Letters, printed in full at the beginning or at the end of the said Work, be treated as full notification of the same, and that credence be given to the copies collated by one of our trusty and well-beloved Counselor Secretaries, as to the original. WE COMMAND our principal Usher or Sergeant charged with this matter to take all requisite and necessary measures for the execution of the present letters, without need of further authorization, and notwithstanding Clameur de Haro, Norman Charter, and any Letters contrary to this effect. For such is our pleasure. Given at Paris, on this nineteenth day of April, in the year of grace one thousand seven hundred and eighty, and the sixth of our Reign.

BY THE KING IN COUNCIL.
LE BEGUE.

Registered on Register XXI *of the Royal and Syndical Chamber of Booksellers and Printers of Paris, No. 1202, folio 280, in conformity with the dispositions stated in the present Privilege; and on condition of conveying to the said Chamber the eight Copies stipulated by Article* CVIII of the Regulation of *1723. Paris, this 21st day of April 1780.*

A.M. LOTTIN *Senior, Syndic.*

Notes Prepared by Robin Middleton

1. Claude-Henri Watelet (1718–1786), the son of a tax collector, inherited a considerable fortune at the age of twenty-two and dedicated himself thereafter to the role of gifted amateur. He drew, he painted, he engraved. He was clearly a charming host and entertained a large circle of artistic friends, in particular at his small country house, Moulin-Joli, on the banks of the Seine near Bezons. There, he contrived a picturesque garden of sorts, though much of the effect depended on calculated neglect, for the layout of the paths on the related island was really quite formal. Horace Walpole was scathing as to the handling of the picturesque there, but Marie-Antoinette was inspired in part by Watelet's garden to lay out the Hameau at the Petit Trianon at Versailles. Watelet was the author of the first French study of the picturesque garden, the *Essai sur les jardins* (Paris: Prault, 1774), which laid emphasis on the delights of the farm as opposed to the landscaped garden. See Maurice Henriet, "Un amateur d'art au XVIIIᵉ siècle: L'académicien Watelet," *Gazette des beaux-arts* 6 (1922): 173–94; and Dora Wiebenson, *The Picturesque Garden in France* (Princeton: Princeton Univ. Press, 1978).

2. See Introduction, 23–25; Jennifer Montagu, "Charles Lebrun's *Conférence sur l'expression générale et particulière*" (Ph.D. diss., Warburg Institute, Univ. of London, 1959); and Stephanie Ross, "Painting the Passions: Charles LeBrun's *Conférence sur l'expression*," *Journal of the History of Ideas* 45 (January–March 1984): 25–47.

3. Jean-Nicolas Servandoni (1695–1766) was a flamboyant personality, one of the most celebrated designers of stage sets of the eighteenth century. He was also the architect of the west front of Saint-Sulpice in Paris. He was born in Florence; his mother was Italian, but his father, Jean-Louis-Claude Servan, was French and thought to be a coachman from Lyons. Servandoni made his debut as a designer in France in 1726 with sets for *Pyrame et Thisbe* for the Académie Royale de Musique (the Opéra). He at once became famous and in the following years designed a succession of splendid decors, the likes of which had not been seen before in France. In 1737 Servandoni resigned his position as principal designer at the Académie Royale de Musique, although he did continue to be intermittently employed there until François Boucher was appointed principal designer in 1744.

The change, however, by no means signaled the end of his enterprise in this sphere. He had resigned to indulge in yet grander illusions. In 1737 the king leased him the great Salle des Machines in the north wing of the Tuileries, the acoustics of which were intolerable. Between 1738 and 1742 (at which time he was forced to return to work with the Académie Royale de Musique to pay off his debts) and then from 1754 to 1758, Servandoni staged a series of stunning spectacles, altogether surpassing in illusionistic effect his earlier stage designs. Architects were greatly influenced by his work—in particular Charles de Wailly, who studied under him—for Servandoni's trick was to expand the spatial effects to the rear of the stage using the *scena per angola* with perspectives vanishing to the left and right of the stage rather than in the center or to one side alone. This technique had been developed in Italy by the Bibiena family for their theater designs.

Many of the stage sets mentioned here by Le Camus de Mézières are attributable to Servandoni, but not to Servandoni alone, for sets were used again and again and adapted by other designers. The inventory of sets held by the Académie Royale de Musique in 1748, for instance, included a palace of Armida, an abode of Pluto, a temple of the sun, a prison, various apartments, and a forest of Dodona. Two of these descriptions could possibly refer to examples of Servandoni's most stirring designs—his "Palais du Soleil" from act 4 of *Phaëton*, 1730, and his "Forêt de Dodonne" from act 3 of *Issé*, 1741—but one cannot be sure that they are the sets referred to by Le Camus de Mézières. Servandoni also designed a "Palais d'Armide," though the most impressive version of this to be produced in the eighteenth century was that designed for the production of *Armide* in 1761 by his successor Pietro Algieri. François Boucher had designed the palace itself, which appears first in act 5, though this was none too well liked by the critics; it was Algieri's setting for the destruction of the palace in the following scene that caused the sensation. This was in fact painted by Jean-Baptiste Lallemand, with stage machinery by Louis-Alexandre Girault, and costumes by Louis-René Boquet. One can scarcely doubt that this palace, rather than Servandoni's, was the set that so stirred Le Camus de Mézières.

See C. Di Matteo, "Servandoni décorateur d'opéra," Mémoire de Maîtrise, September 1970, Bibliothèque, Direction Patrimoine, Palais-Royal, Paris, 4° Doc. 143; Christel Heybrock, "Jean-Nicolas Servandoni: Eine Untersuchung seiner Pariser Bühenwerke" (Ph.D. diss., Universität Köln, 1970); Jérôme de La Gorce, "Décors et machines à l'Opéra de Paris au temps de Rameau: Inventaire de 1748," *Recherches sur la musique française classique* 21 (1983): 145–57; Charles Malherbe, "Les costumes et décors d'*Armide*," *Bulletin de la Société de l'histoire du théâtre* 1, no. 2 (April 1902): 5–38; and Bert O. States, "Servandoni's Successors at the French Opera: Boucher, Algieri, Girault," *Theatre Survey* (American Society for Theatre Research, Brandeis University) 3 (1962): 41–58.

4. Servandoni's presentation of 1741 in the Salle des Machines at the Tuileries was "Les aventures d'Ulisse," taken from Homer. Godfrey's camp appeared only in 1754 in Servandoni's staging of "La forêt enchantée" from Torquato Tasso's *Gerusalemme liberata*. The most memorable presentation of a sun-parched realm in the estimation of contemporary critics, however, was the entry "Les Incas du Pérou," in Rameau's *Indes galantes*, first produced by Servandoni for the Académie Royale de Musique in 1735 and restaged in 1736, 1743, and 1744. Le Camus de Mézières's memory might, perhaps, have played him false.

5. Père Louis-Bertrand Castel, though he might have opposed Isaac Newton in many things, fully accepted Newton's notion that there was a direct correspondence between

color intervals and the seven notes of the musical scale (Newton, *Opticks* [London: S. Smith and B. Walford, 1704–1730], bk. 1, pt. 2, prop. 6, prob. 2). Castel worked for years on the making of a color organ, a light-and-sound machine, that might coordinate the harmonies of music and colored lights. Voltaire devoted chapter fourteen—"Du rapport des sept couleurs primitives avec les sept notes de la musique"—of the second part of his *Elémens de la philosophie de Neuton* (Amsterdam: Etienne Ledet et Compagnie, 1738), to what he termed Castel's *"clavecin-oculaire."* And Diderot, in his *Lettre sur les sourds et muets a l'usage de ceux qui entendent et qui parle* (n.p., 1751), imagined that a deaf-mute might comprehend the nature of music by watching the lights and the reactions of an audience to a performance on the *"clavecin-oculaire"* (see Denis Diderot, *Oeuvres complètes,* ed. Yvon Belaval, Robert Niklaus, Jacques Chouillet, Raymond Trousson, and John S. Spink [Paris: Hermann, 1978], 4: 145–47). Two concerts were staged in Saint-Germain-des-Prés, Paris, on 21 December 1754 and on New Year's day following, to demonstrate the final form of the instrument. The results were spectacular, if not altogether successful. Amédée-François Frézier and the Abbé Marc-Antoine Laugier both disparaged it but not Le Camus de Mézières. See Louis-Bertrand Castel, *L'optique des couleurs* (Paris: Briasson, 1740); Donald Stephen Schier, *Louis-Bertrand Castel, Anti-Newtonian Scientist* (Cedar Rapids, Iowa: The Torch Press, 1941); and Anne-Marie Chouillet-Roche, "Le clavecin oculaire du P. Castel," *Dix-huitième siècle,* no. 8 (1976): 141–66.

6. Amphion was the son of Antiope and Zeus in Greek mythology. He was given a lyre by Hermes and became a famed musician. With his brother, Zethus, who was married to Thebe, he built the walls of Thebes, drawing the stones into place with the magical sounds of his lyre. The ancient source of the story is Euripides (D. L. Page, trans., *Select Papyri,* The Loeb Classical Library no. 360 [Cambridge Mass.: Harvard Univ. Press; London: William Heinemann Ltd., 1970], 3: 69), though Le Camus de Mézières no doubt derived it from Horace (*Ars poetica* 94).

7. René Ouvrard's treatise, *Architecture harmonique; ou, Application de la doctrine des proportions de la musique à l'architecture* (Paris: R.-J.-B. de La Caille, 1679)—inspired by Marin Mersenne's *Questions harmoniques: Dans lesquelles sont contenues plusieurs choses remarquables pour la physique, pour la morale et pour les autres sciences* (Paris: J. Villery, 1634)—has not been much studied, though the themes explored therein have been taken up repeatedly by architectural theorists, surfacing even in the twentieth century in one form in the *Bauhaus* magazine (1929) and in another in Le Corbusier's *Le Modulor I* (Boulogne-sur-Seine: Editions de l'Architecture d'Aujourd'hui, 1950). Ouvrard's ideas were firmly opposed by Claude Perrault in the *Ordonnance des cinq espèces de colonnes selon la méthode des anciens* (Paris: J.-B. Coignard, 1683), for Perrault was unable to accept the traditional notion of a system of universal harmony with the harmonies of music related directly to the proportional harmonies of architecture. In France, Perrault's Cartesian stance was generally accepted to undermine the clas-

sical system of belief that had sustained theories of architecture from the Renaissance onward. He was firmly supported by Augustin-Charles Daviler and Sebastien Leblond. Perrault was opposed, however, by Charles-Etienne Briseux in the *Traité du beau essentiel dans les arts* (Paris: Author and Chereau, 1752), and by another Frenchman, Antoine Derizet, an architect from Lyons who taught at the Accademia di San Luca in Rome from 1728 onward. He is known to have written a treatise in imitation of Ouvrard's, which remained unpublished. Derizet probably brought these notions to the attention of Bernardo Vittone, who studied at the Accademia di San Luca and later pursued such theories in his treatises, issued in 1760 and 1766 at Lugano. Le Camus de Mézières's reversion to the earlier system of belief is part of his aim to recover a world of mystery. See André Pirro, *Descartes et la musique* (Paris: Fischbacher, 1907); Wolfgang Herrmann, *The Theory of Claude Perrault* (London: A. Zwemmer, 1973); Werner Oechslin, *Bildungsgut und Antikenreception im frühen Settecento in Rom* (Zurich and Freiburg i. Br.: Atlantis Verlag, 1972), 122–24; and Werner Szambien, *Symétrie, goût, caractère: Théorie et terminologie de l'architecture à l'âge classique, 1550–1800* (Paris: Picard, 1986), 26, 43.

8. The Spanish Jesuits Jeronimo de Prado and Juan Bautista Villalpanda published a three-volume commentary on the book of the prophet Ezekiel—*In Ezechielem explanationes* (Rome: A. Zanetti, 1596–1602)—which included a reconstruction of Solomon's Temple in Jerusalem. It was claimed that the design and proportions of the temple had been drawn either by God's own hand or by Solomon at his dictate. This represented the origin and the perfect form of the orders, transmitted to later generations through the remains of ancient architecture and the writings of Vitruvius. These established proportions thus became not only an image of divine harmony but an essential feature of a Christian, rather than a pagan, realm. The notion was, inevitably, taken up throughout Europe in the years that followed in treatises on architecture and in biblical commentary. A large wooden model of Villalpanda's temple design was made by Johann Jakob Erasmus of Hamburg in 1694 and exhibited later in various European capitals. See Wolfgang Herrmann, "Unknown Designs for the 'Temple of Jerusalem' by Claude Perrault," in *Essays in the History of Architecture Presented to Rudolf Wittkower*, ed. Douglas Fraser, Howard Hibbard, Milton J. Lewine (London: Phaidon, 1967), 143–58; Joseph Rykwert, *The First Moderns: The Architects of the Eighteenth Century* (Cambridge, Mass., and London: MIT Press, 1980); and Hans Reuther, "Das Modell des Salomonischen Tempels im Museum für Hamburgische Geschichte," *Niederdeutsche Beiträge zur Kunstgeschichte* 19 (1980): 161–98.

9. On Perrault's notions on proportions, see Introduction, 19–20, and, at greater length, Herrmann (see note 7).

10. See Introduction, 47–51, and, at greater length, Wiebenson (see note 1).

11. Nicolas-Marie Potain's *Traité des ordres d'architecture*, published in Paris in May 1767 by Charles-Antoine Jombert, was not generally highly esteemed, though it was dedicated

to the Marquis de Marigny. The committee—consisting of Etienne-Louis Boullée, Antoine-Matthieu Le Carpentier, Julien-David Leroy, and Jacques-Germain Soufflot—that was appointed by the Académie Royale d'Architecture to examine the work reported on 10 March 1766 that Potain's system was somewhat indeterminate and that he might have done better to have explained the rationale for his rules and those of his rival proponents. Nonetheless, Potain published this report in full in his treatise (pp. xi–xii). The book was reviewed briefly in the *Mercure de France*, no. 171 (May 1768) and judged to be both important and finely illustrated. See also M. Henry Lemonnier, ed., *Procès-verbaux de l'Académie royale d'architecture, 1671–1793* (Paris: J. Schemit, 1922), 7: 237–38, 241–43.

12. The history of the quest to design a French order is outlined by Jean-Marie Pérouse de Montclos in "Le sixième ordre d'architecture; ou, La pratique des ordres suivant les nations," *Journal of the Society of Architectural Historians* 36, no. 4 (December 1977): 223–40.

13. The motto *nec pluribus impar* means literally "not unequal to many," but it is usually rendered as "I suffice for more worlds than one." This motto in conjunction with the emblem of the sun is thought to have been devised for Louis XIV by the antiquary Louis Douvrier on the occasion of the Grand Carrousel held in 1662 to honor the birth of the dauphin. According to Edouard Fournier, however, the symbol and the motto had been used a century before by Philip II of Spain, for whom it would have been more appropriate as he was also the king of the Indies (see *L'esprit dans l'histoire: Recherches et curiosités sur les mots historiques*, 3rd ed. [Paris: E. Dentu, 1857], 198n.). Nonetheless, the device is invariably associated with Louis XIV. He himself offered an interpretation of it in the *Mémoires de Louis XIV pour l'instruction du Dauphin*, ed. Charles Dreyss (Paris: 1860), 2: 570, Appendix 2: 1662. The Académie des Inscriptions offered yet another interpretation in 1663 in "Médailles sur les principaux événements," fol. 74. See in general, Agnès Joly, "Le Roi-Soleil: Histoire d'une image," *Revue de l'histoire de Versailles* 38 (1936): 213–35, and, in particular, E. H. Kantorowicz, "Oriens Augusti-Lever du Roi," *Dumbarton Oaks Papers* 17 (1963): 172.

14. See Introduction, 32–33. Augustin-Charles Daviler, in his "Explication des termes" at the end of the second volume of his *Cours d'architecture* (Paris: N. Langlois, 1691), defines the enfilade as "*l'alignement de plusieurs portes de suite dans un apartement*" ("the ranging of several doors in a line in an apartment").

15. The Rococo style, to which Le Camus de Mézières refers here, reached its fullest expression in France during the years 1730 to 1735. It was largely the creation of Nicolas Pineau, a sculptor, and Juste-Aurèle Meissonnier, a silversmith born in Turin. The reaction to their style of decoration was almost immediate. In 1737 Jacques-François Blondel advised architects to ignore "*tout ce que les caprices de la nouveauté ont introduit depuis quelques années*" ("all that the capriciousness of novelty has introduced in recent years"); see *De la distribution des maisons de plaisance* [Paris: Charles Antoine Jombert, 1737], 1: xv. During his stay in Rome in 1740 Charles de Brosses, president of the parliament in Dijon, wrote to a

friend, M. de Quintin, to remark that "*Les Italiens nous reprochent qu'en France, dans les choses de mode, nous redonnons dans le goût gothique, que nos cheminées, nos boîtes d'or, nos pièces de vaiselle d'argent sont contournées, et recontournées comme si nous avions perdu l'usage du rond et du carré*" ("The Italians reproach us in France, in matters of fashion, for having reverted to a Gothic taste, our chimneypieces, our gold boxes, our silver table services are twisted and twisted again, as if we had lost the use of the round and the square"). See *Lettres d'Italie*, ltr. 41.

It was the clear-cut geometry of the round and the square associated with the antique that the critics missed. The Comte de Caylus (who had himself ventured to Greece in 1716, seeking the site of Troy) together with his circle of collectors and connoisseurs—Pierre-Jean Mariette, the Abbé Jean-Jacques Barthélemy, and the Abbé Jean-Bernard Leblanc—was in large measure responsible for the strong reaction to the more extravagant, wildly assymetrical confections of the Rococo that occurred in the middle years of the century. The Abbé Leblanc dismissed the Rococo in 1745 in his *Lettres d'un françois . . .* (The Hague: J. Neaulme), ltr. 36, but the most scathing attacks were delivered by Charles-Nicolas Cochin. His "Supplication aux orfèvres, ciseleurs, sculpteurs en bois pour les appartemens et autres, par une société d'artistes" was published in the *Mercure de France* in December 1754; his own ironical response to this "Supplication" appeared in the issue of February 1755, "Lettre a M. l'Abbé R^{xx} sur une très-mauvaise plaisanterie qu'il a laissé imprimer dans le Mercure de Décembre 1754; par une société d'architectes, qui pourroient bien prétendre être du premier mérite et de la premiere réputation, quoiqu'ils ne soient pas de l'Académie." Both of these pieces were reprinted in Cochin's *Recueil de quelques pièces concernant les arts* (Paris: Charles-Antoine Jombert, 1757; reprint, Geneva: Minkoff, 1972). In the first of these articles the Rococo was characterized as an artichoke, or a stick of celery. The identification with chicory, the Chinese plant to which Le Camus de Mézières presumably refers, comes only later. The Marquis de Marigny, writing to Jacques-Germain Soufflot in 1760, made clear that, "*Je ne veux point de chicorée moderne*" ("I want none of the modern chicory"); see Jean Locquin, *La peinture d'histoire en France de 1747 à 1785: Etude sur l'évolution des idées artistiques dans la seconde moitié du XVIIIe siècle* (Paris: H. Laurens, 1912; reprint, Paris: Arthena, 1978), 16 n. 6. Locquin also suggests (p. 16 n. 3) that Jean-Bernard Leblanc used the term "*chicorée*" in 1747 in his *Lettre sur l'exposition des ouvrages de peinture, sculpture, etc. de l'année 1747*, but the reference is incorrect and the term does not seem to have been used in that book. See Wolfgang Herrmann, *Laugier and Eighteenth Century French Theory* (London: A. Zwemmer, 1962), 221–34; Svend Eriksen, *Early Neo-Classicism in France* (London: Faber, 1974), 25–36, 226–50; and Marianne Roland Michel, *Lajoue et l'art rocaille* (Neuilly-sur-Seine: Arthena, 1984), 154–66.

16. The name of Jean-Antoine Watteau (1684–1721), the greatest painter of the *fête galante*, was invoked often enough after the middle years of the eighteenth century to mark the decline and lack of seriousness in art. It is unusual, and odd, however, to find his name

linked with early seventeenth-century artists such as Jacques Callot (1592–1635), the etcher from Lorraine, remembered chiefly for his two suites on the miseries of war, *Les Misères de la guerre,* and the burlesque writer Paul Scarron (1610–1660), who, though horribly crippled through most of his life, was irrepressibly wry and sardonic, refusing, almost, to take anything seriously. See Marianne Roland Michel, *Watteau: An Artist of the Eighteenth Century* (London: Trefoil Books, 1984), esp. 297–312 on Watteau's posthumous reputation; Daniel Ternois, *L'art de Jacques Callot* (Paris: F. de Nobele, 1962); and Naomi Forsythe Phelps, *The Queen's Invalid: A Biography of Paul Scarron* (Baltimore: Johns Hopkins Press, 1961).

17. The account offered appears to be yet another variant of the famous story of the painting of the portrait of Helen that Zeuxis of Heraclea executed for the citizens of Croton in Italy. He selected five of the most beautiful local maidens as models, combining their individual perfections in the portrait (Cicero, *De inventione* 2.1.1–3). Another account of this incident, set in Girgenti, is given by Pliny, though he too limits the number of models to five (*Natural History* 35.36.64). Later references to this event are made by Boccaccio (*Il commento alla divina commedia*, ed. Domenico Guerri [Bari: G. Laterza e Figli, 1918], 2: 128–29) and Leon Battista Alberti (*De pictura* 3.56).

18. Themis was the second consort of Zeus, the mother of the Horae and Moerae, she was also respected as a goddess who foretold the future; but it is clearly in her role as a symbol of justice that Le Camus de Mézières refers to her here.

19. See note 1.

20. Pliny the Younger's villas, Laurentum and Tuscum, are described in his letters to Gallus and to Domitius Apollinaris (*Letters* 2.17.5,6). Vicenzo Scamozzi essayed a reconstruction of the most famous of these, the Laurentum on the Roman coast near Ostia, in *L'idea dell'architettura universale* (Venice: Privately printed, 1615), bk. 3, ch. 12, 265–68. But Le Camus de Mézières was no doubt familiar rather with that of Jean-François Félibien des Avaux, *Les plans et les descriptions de deux des plus belles maisons de campagne de Pline le Consul, avec des remarques sur tous ses bâtimens, et une dissertation touchant l'architecture antique et l'architecture gothique* (Paris: Florentin et Pierre Delaulne, 1699; 2nd ed., Amsterdam: Estienne Roger, 1706). Félibien's illustrations had been prepared initially for Claude Le Pelletier's *Comes rusticus, ex optimis latinae linguae scriptoribus excerptus* (Paris, 1692–1695). As might be imagined, though Félibien found Scamozzi's restoration study unsatisfactory and redrew his plans to accord better with Pliny's text, his own reconstruction was conceived in the image of a contemporary French country house rather than an antique villa, of which he knew no authentic model.

Le Camus de Mézières's misconceptions spring directly from Félibien's study, which was much admired in eighteenth-century France, taken up most notably by Bernard de Montfaucon in *L'antiquité expliquée* (Paris: Florentin Delaulne, 1722), 3: 125–29, and in the "Délices des maisons de campagne appelées le Laurentin et la maison de Toscane," included, it seems, in an edition of Pliny's letters by Parfait of 1736. The only other illustrated restorations to have been published at that time—Robert Castell's *The Villas of the Ancients Illustrated* (London: Privately printed, 1729), and Friedrich-August Krubsacius's *Wahrscheinlicher Entwurf von des Jüngern Plinius Landhause, Laurens Genannt, nach Anzeige de 17ten Briefes des II Buches, an den Gallus* (Leipzig, 1760)—do not seem to have been known in France. See Helen Henriette Tanzer, *The Villas of Pliny the Younger* (New York: Columbia Univ. Press, 1924); and Institut Français d'Architecture, *La Laurentine et l'invention de la villa romaine* (Paris: Editions du Moniteur, 1982).

21. Building plots in France were usually designated in terms of the width of the frontage; *hôtels* were thus referred to and categorized. The French toise, originally a local Parisian measure promoted by Henry IV as a national standard, was divided into six *pieds*, each roughly equivalent to an English foot. A toise was thus about six feet, or two yards. *Pieds* were further divided into twelve *pouces*, each *pouce* into twelve *lignes*. See Horace Doursther, *Dictionnaire universel des poids et mesures, anciens et modernes* (Brussels: M. Hayez, 1840; reprint, Amsterdam: Meridian Publishing Co., 1965).

22. See Introduction, 32–33.

23. Though Le Camus de Mézières describes each possible space in the *hôtel* in precise detail, he is somewhat cavalier in his handling of the staircase, a feature of considerable concern, as a rule, to architectural theorists and one that occasioned some controversy, in particular as to its position. Augustin-Charles Daviler discussed the design of the staircase at some length in his *Cours d'architecture* (see note 14), 1: 176, but did not deal with the matter of its placement, though in the chapter added by Sebastien Leblond to the 1710 edition, the right-hand side of the vestibule was recommended (p. 14; see Introduction, 39). Michel de Frémin in his *Mémoires critiques d'architecture* (Paris: Charles Saugrain, 1702) had already recommended that it be placed to the right of the entrance vestibule, this being the direction, he said, to which one turned naturally (p. 46). Jean-Louis de Cordemoy in the *Nouveau traité de toute l'architecture* (Paris: Jean-Baptiste Coignard, 1706) was not so specific, noting only that staircases were no longer placed centrally, where they might interrupt movement from the entrance court to the garden, but in the wings (pp. 162–63). Germain Boffrand took it as axiomatic that the staircase should be set to the right of the vestibule (*Livre d'architecture* [Paris: Guillaume Cavelier Père, 1745], 31), as did Jacques-François Blondel, both in his *Architecture françoise* (Paris: Charles-Antoine Jombert, 1752), bk. 1, 39, and in his *Cours d'architecture* (Paris: Le Veuve Desaint, 1773), 4: 297–98. "*Il semble en effet,*" he wrote in the latter text, "*que la nature nous porte à chercher nos besoins de ce côté; et nous estimons, que pour se dispenser de ce préjugé ou de cette habitude, il faut avoir des raisons essencielles, telles que l'expression ou la situation d'un édifice*" ("It seems that nature leads us to follow our bent to this side, and I believe that to reject this prejudice or custom, one must have vital reasons, such as the appearance or siting of a building"); see p. 298. This usage, he explained, derived from Louis Le Vau's

arrangement in the Palais des Tuileries. At the Hôtel de Toulouse, he noted disapprovingly, the stair was to the left of the vestibule. Marc-Antoine Laugier, surprisingly, thought this the best position (*Essai sur l'architecture* [Paris: Duchesne, 1753], 167; 2nd ed. [Paris: Duschesne, 1755], 148).

French architects clearly had strong feelings on this matter, yet it was the Francophile King Frederick II of Prussia, rather than his French architect, Jean-Laurent Legeay, who, according to D. Thiébault, was to take issue on the subject most famously. Legeay's design of 1763 for the Neues Palais and Communs at Sanssouci, Potsdam, included a grand entrance vestibule with an equally grand staircase to match, all on the central axis. The king wanted an entry of lesser magnificence with an enclosed staircase to the left, permitting a direct route through to the garden. Legeay refused to revise his drawings. During the argument that ensued Legeay is said to have placed his hand on his sword. In another account of the quarrel Hans Kania related it to a question of proper recompense. At all events, Legeay was packed off on extended leave to Aix-la-Chapelle, not to return to Berlin. See Gilbert Erouart, *L'architecture au pinceau: Jean-Laurent Legeay, un piranésien français dans l'Europe des Lumières* (Paris: Electa Moniteur, 1982), 64–66.

24. Built to the design of Pierre Contant d'Ivry between 1764 and 1765, the covered carriage entrance and the related vestibule and staircase at the Palais-Royal were unequaled in Paris for their magnificence and were praised by many critics of the period. See Emile Dupezard, *Le Palais Royal de Paris* (Paris: C. Eggimann, 1911), for fine illustrations; more recently, see Gabrielle Joudiou, "Constructions et projets de Contant d'Ivry à Paris," *Bulletin de la Société de l'histoire de Paris* (Paris: Librairie d'Argences, 1986), 73–114; idem, "Pierre Contant d'Ivry," in *Chevotet-Contant-Chaussard: Un cabinet d'architectes au siècle des Lumières,* ed. Jean-Louis Baritou and Dominique Foussard (Lyons: La Manufacture, 1987), 86–182.

25. Voltaire's *Temple du goût,* published in 1733, though well enough known, has not been much studied by historians of architectural taste. Theodore Besterman has, however, indicated that it was one of the earliest thrusts against the Rococo style, a harbinger of late eighteenth-century classicism. See his "Art in the Age of Reason" in *Studies on Voltaire and the Eighteenth Century* (Banbury, Oxfordshire: The Voltaire Foundation, 1972), 87: 20–24; and idem, *Voltaire on the Arts: Unity and Paradox* (Oxford: Clarendon Press, 1974), 11–15.

26. The Château de Clagny, situated to the northeast of the Château de Versailles, was begun in 1674, according to the designs of Antoine Le Pautre, as a residence for Louis XIV's bastard children. Even before its completion it was judged by Mme de Montespan, the king's mistress, to be lacking in dignity, and the commission was passed instead to Jules Hardouin-Mansart, his first significant work for the crown. He completed it in 1678, adding two wings to flank the entrance court, but the great double-height salon in the center— opening on one side directly onto the entrance court, on the other onto the garden—was based on Le Pautre's initial arrangement. The *château* was in use for only a few decades and

was demolished at the end of the eighteenth century, clearly before the publication of Le Camus's book, though part seems to have survived up to the time of the Revolution. See Alfred and Jeanne Marie, *Mansart à Versailles*, Versailles: Son histoire 2 (Paris: Editions Jacques Fréal, 1972), 1: 2–72.

27. The Salons of War and Peace, one at each end of the spectacular Hall of Mirrors overlooking the gardens of the Château de Versailles, were built between 1679 and 1682 to the designs of Jules Hardouin-Mansart. The great plaster reliefs by Antoine Coysevox and the ceiling paintings by Charles Le Brun, however, were only completed in 1687. See Marie (see note 26), 2: 435–77.

28. The central oval salon appears in domestic architecture in the Palazzo Barberini in Rome, construction of which began in 1628, while Carlo Maderno was still in charge of the work there. The design of the salon itself has been attributed variously to Maderno and to his assistants Francesco Borromini and Gianlorenzo Bernini. The earliest surviving drawing for it is by Borromini. Bernini designed a similar salon for the Barberini casino at Mompecchio, the drawing for which is dated 14 September 1633. In neither case is the oval form expressed externally; nor indeed is it in Louis Le Vau's first true use of the form in France, his remodeling of the Château de Meudon, dating from 1654 to about 1657, or in his design for the east front of the Louvre, dating from 1662 or 1663. Bernini gave the fullest external expression to the oval salon in his design of 1664 for the Louvre facade; it should be noted, however, that Le Vau had designed an oval salon of "sorts"—in fact a rectangle with semicircular ends—for the first floor of the Château du Raincy, erected in the early 1640s. Here the curves determined the form of both the entrance and garden facades. At Vaux-le-Vicomte, Le Vau's design for which is dated uncertainly between 1661 and 1664, the curve of the oval salon dominates the garden facade alone. The Château du Raincy was demolished in the early years of the nineteenth century, that at Vaux survives resplendent.

The central salon of the Château de Marly, though apparently inspired by the arrangement of Palladio's Villa Rotonda at Vicenza, is octagonal in plan. It was designed by Jules Hardouin-Mansart. Work on the *château* began in 1677 with the erection of the twelve related pavilions, and it continued through to 1686 when Charles Le Brun conceived his designs for painting the facades with ornamental motifs. Pilasters and sculptures were added to the *château* elevations only later. The buildings were not often in use during the eighteenth century, and though they survived the Revolution to serve as a cotton mill, they had almost all disappeared by the time Napoleon bought the estate in 1811.

Jacques-François Blondel, it is worth remarking, cited the salons of the *châteaux* of Marly, Clagny, Vaux, Raincy, and Meudon as exemplars of the double-height salon, or *salon à l'italienne*, in his *Architecture françoise* (see note 23), bk. 1, 30. In his *Cours d'architecture* he added the salon of the Château de Montmorency but omitted that at Vaux (see note 23), 4: 215. See Patricia Waddy, *Seventeenth-Century Roman Palaces: Use and the Art of the Plan* (New

York: Architectural History Foundation; Cambridge, Mass.: MIT Press, 1990); Robert W. Berger "Louis Le Vau's Château du Raincy," *Architectura* 6, no. 1 (1976): 36–46; Jean Cordey, *Vaux-le-Vicomte* (Paris: A. Morance, 1924); and Jeanne and Alfred Marie, *Marly* (Paris: Editions "Tel," 1947).

29. See Introduction, 33.

30. The bed *à la polonaise* was not clearly defined in the eighteenth century and was often confused with others of a somewhat exotic origin—*à l'italienne, à la turque, à la chinoise.* Several of these, though none labeled *à la polonaise,* are illustrated in the first and second *cahiers* of Jules-François Boucher's first suite of engravings of furnishings, dating from the early 1770s. What they all have in common is a draped and decorated canopy smaller in area than the bed itself. However, the correct canopy for a bed *à la polonaise* seems to have been that illustrated in Diderot and d'Alembert's *Encyclopédie; ou, Dictionnaire raisonné des sciences, des arts et des métiers* (Paris: Briasson, 1771), 9 (plates): s.v. "Tapissier," pl. v, fig. 1. The most sumptuous representation of a bed of this type is Pierre-Antoine Baudoin's engraving after the younger Moreau, *Le coucher de la mariée,* 1768, reproduced in Pierre Verlet, *La maison du XVIIIᵉ siècle en France: Société, décoration, mobilier* (Paris: Baschet, 1966); Verlet's text has been translated by George Savage as *The Eighteenth Century in France: Society, Decoration, Furniture* (London and Rutland, Vt.: Charles E. Tuttle Co., 1967), pl. 200. The references to illustrations of beds by André-Jacob Roubo in this work are inaccurate.

31. Though the woman's role and position in French society was recognized as of significant and independent import from at least the late seventeenth century onward and though, as we have seen, the mistress of the house had long been accorded a separate apartment, the first room designated specifically for women—different from, though no doubt distantly related to, the harem—was the boudoir. This term is not listed in Diderot and d'Alembert's *Encyclopédie* (see note 30) of 1751 onward. It is used early by Jean-François de Bastide in *La petite maison,* said to have been published first in the *Journal économique* in 1753, certainly published five years later in the *Nouveau spectateur* and in its final form in 1763 in the *Contes de M. de Bastide* (Paris: L. Cellot) from which it was reprinted in a limited edition by Paul-Lacroix Jacob in 1879 (Paris: Librairie des Bibliophiles). In Bastide's usage the room is not devoted exclusively to women. Many of the decorative details and arrangements described by Bastide, however, were taken over entirely by Le Camus. The word is defined first in volume 1 of Charles-François Roland Le Virloys's *Dictionnaire d'architecture, civile, militaire et navale* (Paris: Les Librairies Associés, 1770): "*Boudoir: est dans la distribution d'un appartement, un petit cabinet à cheminée, pres de la chambre à coucher, et du cabinet de toilette, dont la vue doit etre agréable, et qui doit etre bien eclaire. On l'a appelle boudoir, parce que c'est dans cet endroit où une femme se retire pour mediter, ou pour lire, ou pour travailler, en un mot, pour etre seule*" ("Boudoir: in the planning of an apartment is a small room with a fireplace, alongside the bedroom and dressing room, from which there is a pleasant view and which is well lit. One

calls it a boudoir, because here a woman may retire to think, or read, or work, or, in a word, be alone"). This usage is confirmed in the first volume of Antoine-Chrysostome Quatre-mère de Quincy's dictionary of architecture in the *Encyclopédie méthodique* (Paris: Panckouke; Liège: Plomteux, 1788), 312.

On the social role of women in the seventeenth and eighteenth century, see Carolyn C. Lougee, *Le paradis des femmes: Women, Salons, and Social Stratification in Seventeenth Century France* (Princeton: Princeton Univ. Press, 1976); Joan B. Landes, *Women and the Public Sphere in the Age of the French Revolution* (Ithaca: Cornell Univ. Press, 1988); and D. Goodman, "Enlightenment Salons: The Convergence of Female and Philosophic Ambitions," *Eighteenth-Century Studies* 22, no. 3 (1989): 329–50.

32. The deities referred to were all involved in famous amorous encounters. Amphitrite, one of the sea nymphs, was seduced and married by Poseidon (Neptune to the Romans), the god of earthquakes and water, especially the seas. Amphitrite was usually depicted riding in triumph with Poseidon, accompanied by nereids, tritons, dolphins, and sea horses (Hesiod, *Theogony* 930–33). The story of Cupid and Psyche is related most engagingly—and at greatest length—in Apuleius's *The Golden Ass* (bks. 4–6). So beautiful was Psyche that she was worshiped as an equal of Venus, the goddess of love, beauty, and fertility. Angered by this mortal rival, Venus sent her son Cupid to exact revenge. Instead, Cupid fell in love with Psyche and eventually married her. The wedding was blessed by the gods, Psyche was made immortal, and even Venus was appeased in the end.

Venus was in origin an Italian goddess of vegetation but was invested by the Romans with the attributes of the Greek goddess Aphrodite. She was married to Vulcan (in Greek mythology Hephaestus), the god of fire and the underworld. She nonetheless had an affair with Mars, the god of war (see note 36). Vulcan ensnared the lovers in an embrace and exhibited them thus to the asssembled gods, who in Ovid's account were amused rather than shocked by this spectacle (*Metamorphoses* 4.167–89).

33. Paphos, off the west coast of Cyprus, is the site of the most famous of temples dedicated to Aphrodite, or Venus, and it is there that she is said to have risen from the sea. Paphos is also described in Ovid's *Metamorphoses* (10.245–60) as the daughter of Pygmalion and his statue bride who was brought to life by Venus—perhaps an oblique reference on the part of Le Camus to Condillac's conceit of the statue brought slowly to life.

34. Flora (see note 48), formerly the nymph Chloris, was seduced and married by Zephyrus, the god of the west wind (Ovid, *Fasti* 5.195–212).

35. Diana, an Italian goddess of the woods, was identified by the Romans with Artemis, the Greek goddess of women. She is usually characterized as the goddess of the hunt. One day while bathing in a grotto in the forest, she was surprised by Actaeon, a keen hunter. She was so outraged that she turned him into a stag, and he was torn to pieces by his own hounds (Ovid, *Metamorphoses* 3.155–252).

36. Mars was the god of war, betokened as a rule by his sacred spears; Themis (see note 18) is referred to by Le Camus de Mézières as an incarnation of justice.

37. Plutus was the god of wealth, originally and more properly responsible for the abundance of crops.

38. Le Camus de Mézières would seem to be referring here to Etienne-Louis Boullée's extraordinary grottolike chapel of Sainte-Geneviève in the transept of Saint-Roch, of 1763, in which mystery and drama are both sustained by a single source of concealed lighting. See Jean-Marie Pérouse de Montclos, *Etienne-Louis Boullée 1728–1799: De l'architecture classique à l'architecture révolutionnaire* (Paris: Arts et Métiers Graphiques, 1967) 55–58, pl. 15.

39. Le Camus de Mézières describes more often than one might expect the use of iron elements and fittings in his interiors. Some indication of the knowledge and intensive activity in relation to iron production in eighteenth-century France is revealed in Georges-Louis-Leclerc Buffon's *mémoire* "Expériences sur la tenacité et sur la décomposition du fer," and the chapter "Le fer," both in volume 5 of his *Histoire naturelle des minéraux* (Paris: Imprimerie Royale, 1783–1788) and also in the article "Serrurerie" in Diderot and d'Alembert's *Encyclopédie* (see note 30). Something of the range of iron rods, straps, hangers, railings, hinges, and door furniture in general use is in evidence in Pierre Patte's chapter "De la serrurerie" in Jacques-François Blondel's *Cours d'architecture* (Paris: La Veuve Desaint, 1777), 6: 402–35, pls. 133–36. Patte deals with iron as a structural material in several of his other writings.

40. Lucullus's costly and carefully orchestrated dining arrangements are recounted by Plutarch in his *Lives* (Lucullus 51.1–5). The cost allowed for meals in his household was set on a fixed scale, and they were served in settings appropriate to their cost. The most elaborate entertainments took place in the Apollo apartment. Lucullus would give notice to his servants as to the nature of the occasion required simply by naming the dining room of his choice.

41. Hebe, the daughter of Zeus and Hera, was the cupbearer of the gods; Bacchus, in his Lydian origins, was a god of fertility, but in later classical times was identified as a god of wine. Comus too was a personification of revelry as a deity, usually represented as a young man crowned with flowers. Traditionally his statue was placed at the entrance to the apartment of newlyweds; but in *La petite maison* Jean-François de Bastide also invoked Bacchus and Comus as deities of the dining room.

42. Cloris, or rather Chloris, was a nymph in classical mythology (see note 34), but Le Camus de Mézières probably refers here also to one of the many women seduced by Hylas, whose amorous adventures added a certain piquancy to Honoré d'Urfé's long and suffocating pastoral novel *Astrée*, published between 1607 and 1619. Hilas was the name chosen by Le Camus for the amorous shepherd in his own novel, *Aaba* (see Introduction, 61).

43. Petronius, master of the emperor Nero's pleasures, is generally assumed to be the

author of the *Satyricon*, a fragmentary, picaresque novel that centers on a feast in the house of Trimalchio. Petronius describes a ceiling in the dining room there that opens up to allow a large hoop to descend from which are suspended golden crowns and alabaster jars of perfumes, gifts for Trimalchio's guests (*Satyricon* 60). Suetonius in his *Lives of the Caesars* describes an even more elaborate ceiling in one of the dining rooms of Nero's celebrated Golden House, which no doubt served as Petronius's source of inspiration. It included panels of fretted ivory that folded back to shower down cascades of flowers and incorporated pipes from which guests were sprinkled with perfumes. The main banqueting hall there had a ceiling that revolved like the heavens (Nero 31.1, 2).

44. Plutarch's treatise on the control of anger, *De cohibenda ira*, alludes only in passing to Alexander's slaying of Clytus (458B). The incident is recounted in full, however, in Plutarch's "Life of Alexander" (50–51), though Le Camus de Mézières would seem to have taken it rather from Seneca's treatise on anger, *De ira* (3.17.1).

45. I have been unable to trace this reference in Aristotle's writings on music; nor does it have a ring of authenticity. It might derive from pseudo-Aristotelian writings.

46. The three modes of Greek music and their effects are described by Plato (*Republic* 398c–399c) and Aristotle (*Politics* 8.1339a–1342b, in particular 1340b and 1342a, b). The Lydian mode was somewhat languid, suitable for dirges and laments; the Phrygian mode was livelier but still inspiring of firmness of purpose and sobriety; while the Dorian mode was the noblest of all, stern, sedate, and uplifting. Le Camus de Mézières's account of Tyrtaeus rousing his Spartan troops by switching from a Lydian to a Phrygian mode is not included in the obvious ancient sources for his life and activity (Plato, *Laws* 1.629a–630d, Diodorus Siculus 8.27, Strabo 8.362, Pausanias 4.15.6–16.6, Athenaeus, *Deipnosophistai* 11.YV.630d–631b). Tyrtaeus was a Spartan general, perhaps of Athenian origin, active in the seventh century B.C. He was also an elegiac poet, who led his troops into battle to the sound of the flute, singing his songs. The battle to which Le Camus de Mézières makes reference was the second Messenian War, described by Strabo and, with greater elaboration, by Pausanias, who would seem to have been Le Camus de Mézières's source, although an even more obvious source is Horace (*Ars poetica* 402). See Cecil Maurice Bowra, *Early Greek Elegists* (Cambridge, Mass.: Harvard Univ. Press, 1938), 39–70.

47. The number, names, and attributes of the muses vary considerably in classical literature, but the canonic number, laid down by Hesiod, was generally accepted to be nine—Calliope (muse of the heroic epic), Clio (muse of history), Euterpe (muse of wind instruments), Erato (muse of lyric poetry), Melpomene (muse of tragedy), Polyhymnia (muse of singing or mimicry), Terpsichore (muse of dance), Thalia (muse of comedy), and Urania (muse of astronomy).

48. The classical deities to whom Le Camus de Mézières refers, as must by now be evident, were all readily known to his eighteenth-century readers. They are all presented in

their Roman rather than in their Greek guise and most are to be found in Ovid's works, either in his *Fastes*, first translated into French in 1660, or in the far more popular *Metamorphoses*, first translated in 1532, and repeatedly thereafter. The French translation with which we may assume Le Camus de Mézières would have been familiar was that of Fontanelle, issued first in 1767 and again in 1770. Flora was a Latin goddess of flowering or blossoming plants; Pomona, once again of Roman origin, was the goddess of tree-borne fruits, in particular apples; while Bacchus, as already noted, was by late classical times identified as the god of wine.

49. The *hôtel* in question is that of Marie-Madeleine Guimard, *première danseuse* at the Comédie Française from 1756 and at the Opéra from 1762. At the height of her fame she had many rich and influential admirers, most notably the banker Jean-Benjamin de La Borde, who is thought to have introduced her to Claude-Nicolas Ledoux, the architect of her small but costly and highly celebrated *hôtel*, begun in June 1770. The largest room was the *salle à manger*, top-lit, with windows along one wall opening onto a small, completely enclosed conservatory. See Michel Gallet, *Claude Nicolas Ledoux 1736–1806* (Paris: Picard, 1980), 84–90.

50. Henri II was lanced accidentally in the eye by the Comte de Montgomery on 30 June 1559, during the jousts organized to celebrate the twin wedding of his daughter Elizabeth to the King of Spain and his sister Marguerite to the Duc de Savoie; he died after ten days in agony. The site of the tournament was that of the future Place des Vosges in Paris.

51. The east front of the Louvre, known to contemporaries as the portico or colonnade, was largely built between 1667 and 1678, to the designs of a small committee consisting of Louis Le Vau, Charles Le Brun, and Claude Perrault with the latter's brother Charles, Jean-Baptiste Colbert's factotum, acting as secretary. Claude Perrault, however, is usually credited with the design. This was quite remarkable. For though the traditional French compositional scheme was clearly in evidence, with a central pavilion linked to two outlying ones, the emphases throughout had changed. The outline of the whole was almost rectangular, and even in plan scarcely any stress was laid on the individual units. The focus of attention, moreover, was not on the pavilions, not even the central pavilion, but on the link elements, which consisted of colonnades of freestanding, coupled columns. The aim, as Claude Perrault made clear in his translation of Vitruvius, was that the column should resume its antique role as a structural element rather than a mere decorative motif that could be applied to a surface, as evidenced in the facades of the courtyard behind, the so-called Cour carré.

The Louvre colonnade was at once acclaimed, and though it was often enough subjected to criticism, its reputation remained extraordinarily high throughout the following century. Critics as diverse as Florent Le Comte, Jean-Louis de Cordemoy, Amédée-François Frézier, Jean-Bernard Leblanc, La Font de Saint-Yenne, Marc-Antoine Laugier, Charles-Nicolas Cochin, Julien-David Leroy, Pierre Patte, Jacques-François Blondel, Pierre-

Joseph Antoine, and even that doctrinaire classicist Antoine-Chrysostome Quatremère de Quincy, all recognized it as the exemplar of a new style. Quatremère de Quincy, sharper than the rest, however, noted in the first volume of his *Encyclopédie méthodique* (see note 31) that the proportioning of the columns was not at all correct and did not accord with Perrault's own recommendations. Perrault, he remarked, seems, almost, to have known the Palmyra colonnades when he designed his own. A.-A.-J. Feutry, who disliked the Louvre facade, had suggested as early as 1767 that Palmyra should be regarded as the source of inspiration; yet points of judgment were constantly referred to it. Whole buildings even, were designed in emulation of it. In Paris Ange-Jacques Gabriel adopted its general arrangement in 1753 for the buildings on the Place Louis xv, now the Place de la Concorde, while at Rouen, Antoine-Matthieu Le Carpentier suggested a paraphrase for the Hôtel de Ville in 1757. See Florent Le Comte, *Cabinet des singularitez d'architecture, peinture, sculpture et gravure* (Paris: Picart, 1699), vol. 1, *Sommaire historique d'architecture*, s.v. "Louis Le Vau," "Messire Jean-Baptiste Colbert," and, esp., "Claude Perrault"; Jean-Louis de Cordemoy (see note 23), 135–36, 143–44, 148, 176, 196–98; Amédée-François Frézier, *Dissertation sur les ordres d'architecture* (Strasbourg: J.-D. Doulsseker, 1738), 11-12, 37–38; Jean-Bernard Leblanc, 1745 (see note 15), ltr. 36; La Font de Saint-Yenne, *L'ombre du grand Colbert, le Louvre et la ville de Paris* (The Hague: n.p., 1749); rev. ed (Paris: n.p., 1752), esp. 150–52; and idem, *Le génie du Louvre aux Champs-Elysées: Dialogue entre le Louvre, la ville de Paris, l'ombre de Colbert et Perrault* (Paris: n.p., 1756); Marc-Antoine Laugier, 1753 (see note 23), 3, 21–22, 57; idem, 1755 (see note 23), 3, 17, 52; and idem, *Observations sur l'architecture* (Paris and The Hague: Desaint, 1765), 79–80; two letters on the Louvre colonnade in *Mercure de France* 2 (April 1755): 167, and 2 (June 1755): 144–55. Charles-Nicolas Cochin "Mercure du mois de Juin de l'année 2355," in *Recueil de quelques pièces concernant les arts* (see note 15), 70–87, esp. 72–75, 77–80, 85; Julien-David Leroy, *Histoire de la disposition et des formes différentes que les chrétiens ont données à leurs temples* (Paris: Desaint et Saillart, 1764), 59–61 (Leroy, like Le Camus de Mézières later, deals with the Louvre colonnade specifically in terms of light and shade); Pierre Patte, *Mémoires sur les objets les plus importans de l'architecture* (Paris: Rozet, 1769), 268–93, 319–41; Jacques-François Blondel, *Cours d'architecture*, innumerable references, but see esp. (Paris: La Veuve Desaint, 1772), 3: 11–12, 64–69 and (Paris: La Veuve Desaint, 1773), 4: xlvi–xlvii; Pierre-Joseph Antoine, *Série de colonnes* (Dijon: L. N. Frantin; Paris: Alexandre Jombert, 1782), 24–25; Antoine-Chrysostome Quatremère de Quincy (see note 31), s.v. "Accouplement," "Colonnade" and "Balbek," esp. 7–9, 721–22.

52. For a detailed study of the development of the Parisian *hôtel* in the eighteenth century and the expansion of Paris along the Champs-Elysées and in the Chaussée-d'Antin, see Michel Gallet, *Paris: Domestic Architecture of the Eighteenth Century* (London: Barrie and Jenkins, 1972); and Pascal Etienne, ed., *Le Faubourg Poissonnière: Architecture, élégance et décor* (Paris: La Délégation, 1986).

Appendix A

The following illustrations have been reproduced from Nicolas-Marie Potain's *Traité des ordres d'architecture* (1767). In his discussion of the classical orders, Le Camus refers to Potain's treatise as a "model . . . thoughtful and composed with taste." *Le génie de l'architecture* was originally published with a single illustration showing the relative proportions of the five orders. That illustration—which is comparable in content, but not in quality, to "figure a" in this appendix—has not been reproduced in this volume.

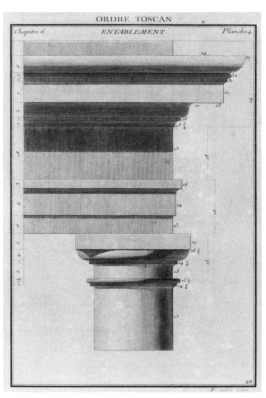

a. *The five orders and their proportional relationship. Illustrated in Nicolas-Marie Potain,* Traité des ordres d'architecture *(Paris: Charles-Antoine Jombert, 1767), ch. 2, 12, pl. 1. Middleton Collection.*

b. *Tuscan entablature and capital. Illustrated in Nicolas-Marie Potain,* Traité des ordres d'architecture *(Paris: Charles-Antoine Jombert, 1767), ch. 6, 49, pl. 4. Middleton Collection.*

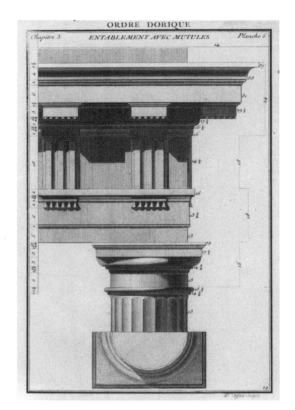

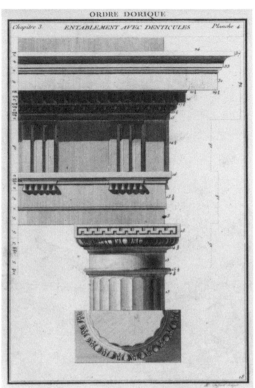

c. *Doric entablature and capital, with mutules. Illustrated in Nicolas-Marie Potain,* Traité des ordres d'architecture *(Paris: Charles-Antoine Jombert, 1767), ch. 3, 19, pl. 5. Middleton Collection.*

d. *Doric entablature and capital, with dentils. Illustrated in Nicolas-Marie Potain,* Traité des ordres d'architecture *(Paris: Charles-Antoine Jombert, 1767), ch. 3, 18, pl. 4. Middleton Collection.*

e. *Ionic entablature and capital, antique style. Illustrated in Nicolas-Marie
Potain,* Traité des ordres d'architecture *(Paris: Charles-Antoine Jombert,
1767), ch. 4, 32, pl. 9. Middleton Collection.*
f. *Ionic entablature and capital, modern style. Illustrated in Nicolas-Marie
Potain,* Traité des ordres d'architecture *(Paris: Charles-Antoine Jombert,
1767), ch. 4, 34, pl. 11. Middleton Collection.*

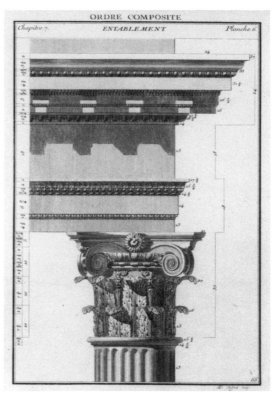

g. *Corinthian entablature and capital. Illustrated in Nicolas–Marie Potain,*
Traité des ordres d'architecture *(Paris: Charles-Antoine Jombert, 1767),*
ch. 5, 43, pl. 6. Middleton Collection.
h. *Composite entablature and capital. Illustrated in Nicolas-Marie Potain,*
Traité des ordres d'architecture *(Paris: Charles-Antoine Jombert, 1767),*
ch. 7, 55, pl. 6. Middleton Collection.

Appendix B

Schedule of Works for the Building of the Hôtel de Beauvau, Paris, 1768,
with an *Addition to the Schedule Attached to the Lifetime Lease Assigned by M. Camus, Advocate,*
to Monsieur le Prince and Madame la Princesse de Beauvau

Archives Nationales, Paris
Minutier central des notaires
Etude Bronod, LXXXVIII, 715

Introduction

The Hôtel de Beauvau, 96 rue du Faubourg Saint-Honoré, Paris, now the Ministère de l'Intérieur, was built to the design and under the supervision of Nicolas Le Camus de Mézières between 1768 and 1770 (figs. *i*, *ii*). The owner of the site was Armand Gaston Camus (1740–1804), a lawyer, later a deputy to the Convention, who agreed to build the *hôtel* upon a prior loan of 200,000 *livres* (on which he would pay an annual interest of 8,000 *livres*) and an annual payment of 12,000 *livres* and to cede it for life to Charles Juste, Prince de Beauvau (1720–1793) and his second wife, née Marie-Charlotte de Rohan-Chabot (1729–1807). The contract documenting this transaction, now in the Archives Nationales in Paris, was drawn up by the lawyer L.-L. Bronod and registered on 2 July 1768. The annexes to this contract, together with three drawings, describe the *hôtel* to be built by Le Camus de Mézières.

Préfet Honoraire Paul Bouteiller is responsible for the first substantial investigation into the history of the property, published in two articles in the review of the Ministère de l'Intérieur, *L'administration*, no. 150 (15 January 1991) and no. 151 (15 April 1991). The contract documents, which were first published in the second of these articles, have been translated and reproduced here with the permission of the Archives Nationales in Paris.

The written description of the principal rooms can be followed on the ground-floor plan (fig. *iii*). The main entrance to the *hôtel* proper is at the far left corner of the entrance court, leading into a square vestibule. This is not described. The Prince de Beauvau's apartment leads off this, to the left, into the first anteroom and continues along the length of the garden front in the sequence of second anteroom, audience chamber, bedchamber, and cabinet or dressing room; the latter has two related closets for clothing, the one on the garden front, the other, awkwardly shaped, set more or less internally with a single window opening onto a hexagonal court. The third anteroom, which leads off the entrance vestibule to the right, serves also as a dining room but is effectively the second anteroom to the princess's apartment, which stretches along the entrance court front in the sequence of salon, bedchamber, and cabinet or dressing room, which leads to the prince's second closet at the rear, thus linking the apartments. The princess's apartment continues into a circular boudoir, overlooking the internal hexagonal court, with a closet of ease alongside and a bath chamber on the garden front.

The kitchen and offices are on the left-hand side of the plan. The attic floor plan is not illustrated here.

—R.M.

VUE DE L'HOTEL DE BEAUVEAU.

i. *F. D. Née after Jean-Baptiste Lallemand,* Hôtel de Beauvau, *engraving.*
Paris, Bibliothèque Nationale, Cabinet des Estampes, VA 2816 fol. E VI.
Photo: Bibliothèque Nationale, Paris.

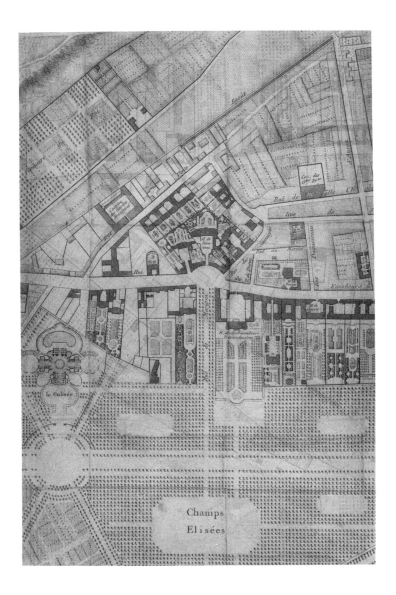

ii. *Site plan of the Hôtel Beauvau, a detail taken from section 5, "Plan du quartier du Palais Royal," of 1773. Illustrated in the* Atlas *to Jaillot [Jean-Baptiste-Michel Renou de Chavigné],* Recherches critiques, historiques et topographiques sur la ville de Paris, *5 vols. (Paris: Author and Aug. Mart. Lottin, 1772–1782). Middleton Collection.*

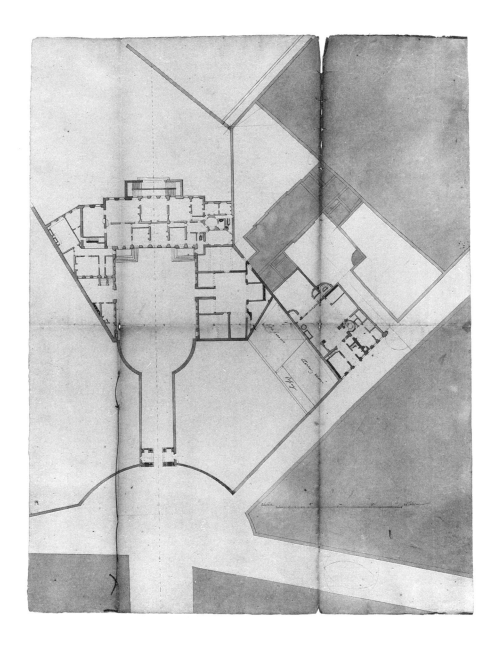

iii. *Plan of the Hôtel de Beauvau. Paris, Archives Nationales, Minutier central des notaires, Etude Bronod, LXXXVIII, 715.*

SCHEDULE OF WORKS FOR THE BUILDING OF THE HOTEL DE BEAUVAU, PARIS, 1768

*D*escription of the mansion to be built for Monsieur le Prince and Madame la Princesse de Beauvau on land belonging to Sieur Camus, having access from the Grande Rue du Faubourg Saint-Honoré, opposite the Rue de Marigny, which contains an area of about fourteen hundred toises.

The said mansion to be preceded by an avenue facing and on the alignment of the Rue de Marigny and terminated at the Grande Rue du Faubourg Saint-Honoré by a fine peristyle with the inscription "Hôtel de Beauvau," with wrought iron gates, to the right of which shall be the porter's lodge with bedchamber above, incorporated in the neighboring house.

This avenue, which shall receive no encumbrance from the neighboring houses, apart from a drain to carry off rainwater and the overhanging cornice, shall be planted with linden trees fronted with posts; it shall be thirty feet in width and shall lead to a grand forecourt, twelve toises in width by approximately twenty in length, bounded at the near end by two segments of a circle; stone posts with a rail to be placed along both sides of the avenue and all around the forecourt.

To the right of this forecourt shall be the courtyard for the stables and carriage houses. The stables shall contain thirty-two horses, and the carriage houses shall be for eight carriages; there shall be a well and a trough.

Above these carriage houses and stables shall be the lodgings of the officers and servants employed therein, together with the infirmary.

The lofts shall serve as a granary for fodder.

To the left of the forecourt shall be a courtyard containing the kitchens, pantries, and subordinate offices, together with the lodgings of the officers and servants employed therein. A well and a trough shall be provided.

The pastry kitchen and roasting chamber for occasional use shall be accommodated in part of the basement of the main fabric.

The main fabric shall consist of a ground floor and an attic story.

There shall be cellars and basements along the whole length of the ground floor of the main fabric and also beneath the wing containing the boudoir and the bathroom.

This main fabric shall be approximately sixteen toises in length on the garden side, not including the bath and kitchen wings, which shall flank it; it shall be two rooms deep, about eight toises. On the side facing the forecourt, it shall be raised by three steps, as necessary, and on the garden front there shall be a fine double flight of steps, which shall correspond to the whole length of the projecting bay.

The height of the ground floor, to the ceiling, shall be sixteen feet, and entresols shall be placed above the bathrooms, closets, and kitchens, such entresols being about seven feet in height.

The height of the upper or attic story, to the ceiling, shall be ten feet, and part of the lofts shall be wainscoted to form servants' rooms.

As for the garden, Madame de Beauvau shall supply the design and provide the fruit trees; the box and arbor trees only shall be the responsibility of the landlord, to the exclusion of any decoration; a well shall be sunk, and a trough and pump supplied.

The decorations shall be as follows:

Ground Floor of the Main Fabric

The first anteroom shall be paved with freestone in lias. It shall be wainscoted throughout to its full height. There shall be a niche to hold a stove.

The second anteroom shall be parqueted and wainscoted to its full height. There shall be a chimneypiece with a marble architrave, a fireplace and covings, and a frame with a looking glass in two parts, six feet and a half in height by three feet and a half in width for each. The opening made for the stove in the first anteroom shall be broken through but without a niche, so that a single stove may heat both rooms at once.

The third anteroom or dining room shall be paved with freestone with black marble dressings. A flue shall be provided for a stove; and the entire room shall be decorated in stucco at the expense of Monsieur and Madame de Beauvau.

The staircase shall be in masons' and carpenters' work with single balusters and fillet. The said staircase not to be a principal feature, the master apartments being on the ground floor.

The room adjoining the second anteroom, serving as a reception chamber for the Prince, shall be parqueted and with wainscoting to dado height throughout. There shall be a recess at the far end with frames covered in tapestry, which shall serve to make a press for linen and for clothes, and there shall be a glass over the mantel in two pieces, each approximately nine feet in height by four feet in width, the frame to be carved and the moldings around the glass gilt.

The following chamber, which is to be the bedchamber of the Prince, shall be parqueted and with wainscoting to dado height throughout, a rich marble chimneypiece, a fireplace with covings, and three carved frames for looking glasses. That above the fireplace shall contain two pieces of glass, eight feet in height overall and each approximately four feet in width; the two others shall each also contain two pieces, six feet in height overall and likewise four feet wide; the framing with noble and simple carvings; only the moldings holding the glass to be gilt. The two overdoors also to be carved and gilt.

The ceiling shall have a carved cornice with a rose in the center finished with a hook.

The cabinet shall be parqueted, with wainscoting to its full height, marble chimneypiece, and carved frame for glass above, but the glasses shall be provided by the Prince and shall form no part of the present contract.

The adjacent closet shall be paved with freestone with black marble dressings and wainscoted to dado height throughout.

As for the back closets, they shall also be paved with freestone and marble dressings.

Salon

The salon shall be parqueted and wainscoted to its full height, with a sculptured frieze and keystones, a rich marble chimneypiece, cast-iron fireplace and covings, a sculptured frame for a glass above the mantel, glasses in two pieces, approximately nine feet in height and each approximately four feet in width; in addition, two other glasses, one opposite the fireplace and the other at the back of the room, to face the windows; the said glasses each to be in two pieces each ten feet in height by four feet, the frame sculptured, the molding holding the glass alone to be gilt. If Monsieur le Prince de Beauvau also desires to have two glasses between the windows, these to be of the same dimensions as the foregoing, these shall be supplied by him, outside the contract, and the frames by the landlord; the overdoors shall be ornamented with sculpture and shall leave vacant spaces for the paintings, which shall be provided by the Prince. Only the moldings holding the glasses, as above, and the frames of the paintings, to be gilt; in addition, a cornice with sculptural ornament and a rose in the ceiling fitted with a ring.

The bedchamber of Madame la Princesse shall be parqueted and wainscoted to dado height throughout. The chimneypiece in rich marble, cast-iron fireplace and covings. In this room, three looking glasses of the same height and width as those in the salon, the overdoors with sculptural ornaments but without paintings. For the rest, this room, that of Monsieur de Beauvau, and the salon shall be painted in broken white distemper with the moldings around the glasses and overdoors gilt.

The dressing room shall be parqueted with wainscoting to full height throughout, painted in the color to be elected by the Princess. At the back of the room, a press shall be let into the wainscoting. The ceiling shall have a sculptured cornice; the overdoors to be sculptured to receive paintings, which the Prince shall supply. The landlord shall supply two looking glasses, suited to the location, with sculptured frames and gilt moldings.

The boudoir shall also be parqueted with wainscoting to dado height, the chimneypiece with a marble architrave as in the dressing room, fireplace and covings, the mirror frame sculptured, the molding around the glass gilt, and the glass in two pieces, at the landlord's expense.

The bathroom and the water closet shall be tiled in black and white, wainscoting to dado height. If Monsieur le Prince and Madame la Princesse desire stucco, the value of the wainscoting shall be deducted, and in that case the said Lord and Lady shall be responsible for the decoration of the said bathroom.

The baths, pipes, and utensils necessary for the said bathroom shall be provided by the said Lord and Lady and set in place by the landlord.

All the enfilading doors on the ground floor of the principal fabric shall consist of two leaves, four feet in width by nine feet in height, with double architrave and embrasures.

Joinery panels shall be placed above the doors of the first anteroom, and paintings above those of the second and the third.

The windows leading to the garden on the ground floor of the principal fabric and those giving onto the forecourt, with the exception of the two anterooms and the closet, shall be of Bohemian glass; those of the boudoir and bathroom likewise. All of the other windows shall be in ordinary glass. There shall be double casements with Bohemian glass and espagnolettes on the garden face of the ground floor.

All the joinery used shall be of fully matured and seasoned wood; and, if the said wood were to split or to part from its veneer, the landlord would be required to make it good at his own expense.

All the door and window hardware shall be well fitting and of well-polished iron or bronze, except for that of the salon, of the two bedchambers, and of the boudoir, which shall be of iron with gilt moldings.

In addition, all the windows on the ground floor shall have wickets made to fit.

All the rooms on the entresol shall be floored with small quarry tiles; chimneypieces with architraves of freestone, fireplaces and covings, and solid doors with iron hardware.

The attic story shall contain four complete apartments, consisting of a small anteroom lit by fanlights, a large chamber with a fireplace, and a cabinet. The chambers shall be wainscoted to dado height, and two of them shall be parqueted. In addition, in two of the apartments, two anterooms shall be made with fireplaces, and care shall be taken to allow for two closets in which a servant may sleep. Each of these apartments to have its own closet. In addition, the Princess reserves the right to alter this story to make an adequate apartment out of three of the four rooms whose use has yet to be decided upon. But the entire expense of this variation, if it be made, shall be borne by her, and an allowance shall be made for the expense that would otherwise have been required.

This story shall also contain three private chambers with fireplace, and access to the whole of the said story shall be by means of a corridor, running the whole length of the building, which shall be lit by two large windows.

The whole of the said story shall be floored in small quarry tiles with the exception of two rooms, which shall, as aforesaid, be parqueted. Four of the chimneypieces shall be provided with marble architraves and with fireplaces and covings; the other fireplaces shall have freestone architraves.

All the doors shall be paneled with the exception of those of the closets, which may be glazed to admit light.

The window sashes, with the exception of those of the chambers in the four apartments, shall be in dormers, for the sake of a clear view and lest the sashes take up too much space within the apartments. In addition, the principal rooms of the four apartments shall have sashes in walnut with the usual hardware.

One part of the lofts shall be wainscoted, as aforesaid, to make rooms for servants. There shall be ten of these, five with fireplaces without architraves but with cast-iron fireplaces.

Each of these rooms shall be lit by a small dormer or circular window, which shall as far as possible be concealed from view by the balustrade or plinths. The said rooms shall be floored with small quarry tiles.

All the rooms adjacent to the kitchen and stable courtyard, whether for the lodgings of officers or other servants, or for the kitchen, or for the stables, shall be floored with small quarry tiles.

The windows shall be in dormers with ordinary glass, the doors shall be solid, and two of the chimneypieces shall be made with freestone architraves and with iron fireplaces and covings; the others without architraves but with cast-iron fireplaces.

There shall be closets of ease and closestools in the said kitchen and stable yard, and there shall also be a closestool in the attic story or wainscoted loft of the principal fabric.

All the work of distribution and embellishment shall be performed with care and neatness and in accordance with the rules of art.

All the paintings and moldings on wainscoting, doors, and windows shall be such as to render the rooms noble and well fitted to their intended use.

Signed and paraphed by the undersigned, under the lifetime lease granted in the presence of the said notary in Paris, on this second day of July, one thousand seven hundred and sixty-eight.

Le Prince de Beauvau; Camus; Chabot;
Princesse de Beauvau; Le Camus de Mézières
Bronod

Addition to the schedule attached to the lifetime lease assigned by M. Camus, advocate, to Monsieur le Prince and Madame la Princesse de Beauvau

Whereas it has been agreed that certain changes be made, notably to the second anteroom, dining room, kitchen, servants' hall, laundry, with lobbies; and additionally for a second stable yard to incorporate a gate to the Rue des Saussaies and a garden door to the Rue de la Ville l'Evêque: a new plan has been drawn up in which all these items are shown, and they shall be put into execution as follows.

Dining Room

The said room shall be paved with freestone with black marble dressings, ceiled, and with a cornice. The said room shall be in stucco, but the expense of the stucco shall be borne by the Prince.

A portion of the first anteroom shall be set aside for a sideboard and closet.

This operation is at the Prince's charge with the exception of the partition between the first and second anterooms.

The kitchen shall be tiled and ceiled. The passage shall also be tiled and ceiled, as shall the servants' hall and laundry.

It has also been agreed that an additional back courtyard shall be made for the carriage houses, opening onto the Rue des Saussaies by way of a carriage entrance; that the said courtyard shall comprise a surface area, including the passageway, of seventy toises; that the whole of the said area shall be paved and walled around; and that a saddle room shall be placed there, supplementary to the first saddle room, and a shed to house two carriages.

There shall also be a passageway or egress from the garden, along the garden wall of the Hôtel Saint-Florentin to the Rue de la Ville l'Evêque, the said passageway to contain a surface area of forty-two toises and to be bounded laterally by walls and at either end, both at the garden end and at the Rue de la Ville l'Evêque, by gates.

Signed and paraphed under the memorandum of agreement signed in the presence of the notaries undersigned in Paris, on this seventeenth day of July, one thousand seven hundred and sixty-nine, being a schedule appended to a lifetime lease granted in the presence of Maître Bronod, one of the notaries undersigned, who has kept the record thereof, and his confrere, on the second of July, one thousand seven hundred and sixty-eight.

Le Prince de Beauvau; Chabot;
Princesse de Beauvau; Camus;
Le Camus de Mézières
Bronod

List of Nicolas Le Camus de Mézières's Publications

With F. A. Babuty-Desgodetz. *Dissertation de la compagnie des architectes-experts des bâtimens à Paris, en réponse au mémoire de M. Paris du Verney, . . . sur la théorie et la pratique des gros bois de charpente.* Paris: Babuty fils, 1763.

Le génie de l'architecture; ou, L'analogie de cet art avec nos sensations. Paris: Author and Benoit Morin, 1780. Reprint, Geneva: Minkoff, 1972.

Le guide de ceux qui veulent bâtir: Ouvrage dans lequel on donne les renseignemens nécessaires pour réussir dans cet art, et prévenir les fraudes qui pourroient s'y glisser. 2 vols. Paris: Author and Benoit Morin, 1781. 2nd ed., 1786. Reprint of 2nd ed., Geneva: Minkoff, 1972.

Mémoire sur la manière de rendre incombustible toute salle de spectacle. Paris: Benoit Morin, 1781.

Traité de la force des bois: Ouvrage essentiel qui donne les moyens de procurer plus de solidité aux édifices, de connoître la bonne et la mauvaise qualité des bois, de calculer leur force, et de ménager près de moité sur ceux qu'on emploie ordinairement, et qui enseigne aussi la manière la plus avantageuse d'exploiter les forèts, d'en faire l'estimation sur pied, etc. Paris: Author and Benoit Morin, 1782.

[Wolf d'Orfeuil, pseud.] *L'esprit des almanachs: Analyse critique et raisonnée de tous les almanachs tant anciens que modernes.* Paris: Vve. Duchesne, 1783.

Description des eaux de Chantilly et du hameau. Paris: Author, B. Morin, and Belin, 1783.

Aaba; ou, Le triomphe de l'innocence, suivi de: La Vallée de Tempé. Paris: Gueffier jeune [1784]. 2nd ed., Paris: Vve. Gueffier, 1802.

Recueil des différens plans et dessins, concernant la nouvelle Halle aux grains, située au lieu et place de l'ancien Hôtel de Soissons.
This folio is usually dated 1769, but the book was never published and the eight copies thus far recorded are all different; they are made up with varying numbers of plates in different states of completion and are bound in irregular order. These copies were clearly issued at different times, all after 1769, but there can be no certainty as to dates.

The copies recorded are held in the following collections:

AV   Avery Library, Columbia University, New York
          (AA 531 L492 L49)

BN   Bibliothèque Nationale, Paris (V. 81)

BHVP   Bibliothèque Historique de la Ville de Paris (M F 4022)

CCA   Centre Canadien d'Architecture, Montreal, Canada
          (WM6119 Cage)

M   Middleton Collection, New York

RIBA   Royal Institute of British Architects, London EW 725.26 (44S)

SM   Sir John Soane's Museum, London (AL30)

V   Vitry Collection, Montfort-l'Amaury, France

A description of the most complete copy, if such existed, would be as follows:

Recueil / Des differens Plans et Dessins, / Concernant / La Nouvelle Halle Aux
Grains, / Situee Au Lieu Et Place / De L'Ancien Hotel De Soissons / [rule: 8.6 cm] /
Par N. le Camus De Mézieres, Architecte du Roi. / Et de son Universite, Expert des
Batimens. / A Paris / 1769
Engr. t.-pl., engr. port., [ms. dedication], [23] engr. pls.; 62 cm (folio).

T.-pl.:   [Lettered only, as above; engraving unsgd.; pl.: 31.2 x 25.5 cm]

Port.:   [Portrait of Armand-Jérome Bignon set in oval frame above tablet in-
           scribed with his name and titles; engraving, sgd. bottom left *F. Drouais
           Effigiem Pinx 1758*; bottom right *N. De Launay Sculp 1769*; pl.: 44.7 x
           30 cm]

Ms.:   [Dedication, see below.]

[1]   Plan / de Halle couverte et incombustible / en l'Emplacement de l'Hotel

de / Soissons [cutaway plan/section lettered thus top left; 'Remarques' A–M top right; engraving, sgd. bottom left *Inv: et delin: le Camus / de Mezieres Expertus / Regis Academiae que tudiis / Parisiensis Architectus*; bottom right *Dien scr.*; pl.: 58 x 44 cm]

[2]   Plan / Des Halles couvertes et incombustibles / pratiquées pour les Grains Farines et Grenail / les, en l'emplacement de l'ancien Hotel de Soissons, / Quartier de St. Eustache [site plan lettered thus top right with three notes explaining cross-hatching, key to letters A–G in plan, and inset elevation and cross-section of Halle with vignette of monumental column; engraving, sgd. bottom right *C. Poulleau sculp.*; pl.: 62.8 x 46.6 cm]

[3]   Plan / Des Caves / Et Fondations [engraving, sgd. bottom right *G: T: / Taraval sculp*; pl.: 70 x 62 cm]

[4]   Plan / Du Rez-De-Chaussée [with scale; engraving, sgd. bottom right *L G F / Taraval sculp*; pl.: 70 x 62 cm]

[5]   Plan / De L'Etage D'Entre-Sol [engraving, unsgd.; pl.: 69.5 x 62 cm]

[6]   Plan / Du P.^er Etage [engraving, unsgd.; pl.: 62 x 69.5 cm]

[7]   Élévation Extérieure [engraving, unsgd.; pl.: 28.3 x 43.8 cm]

[8]   Élévation Extérieure / Avec une Coupe [engraving, unsgd.; pl.: 28.2 x 43.5 cm]

[9]   Coupe De La Halle / Le mur extérieur seulement supprimé [engraving, sgd. bottom right *L G Taraval sculp*; pl.: 28.5 x 43.6 cm]

[10]   Projet pour couvrir l'interieur de la Nouvelle Halle aux grains de Paris, présenté et dédié lors de la / construction à Monsieur Bignon, ancien prevost des marchands, par M. Le Camus de Mézieres architecte, / sous la conduite et sur les Dessins de qui ce monument INCOMBUSTIBLE a été elevé. [engraving, sgd. bottom right *Le Camus de Mezieres Inv: et del: Taraval Sculp.*; pl.: 26.7 x 40 cm]

[11]   Plan de la Coupole, une par dessous et par dessus [engraving, sgd. bottom right *Taraval sculp*; pl.: 26.5 x 40 cm]

[12]   Coupe de la partie circulaire couverte [engraving, unsgd.; pl.: 42.8 x 28 cm]

[13]   Plan de l'Escalier au Rez-de-Chaussée, vers la Rue de Grenelle [engraving, unsgd.; pl. 42.7 x 28 cm]

[14]   Plan de l'Escalier vers la Rue de Grenelle / à la hauteur des Entresols [engraving, unsgd.; 42.7 x 27.9 cm]

[15]   Plan de l'Escalier vers la Rue de Grenelle / à l'Etage du Grenier [engraving, unsgd.; pl.: 43 x 28 cm]

[16]   Coupe de l'Escalier, vers la Rue de Grenelle sur la ligne A. B. [engraving, unsgd.; pl.: 42.4 x 27.4 cm]

[17]   Coupe de l'Escalier, vers la Rue de Grenelle, sur la ligne C. D. [engraving, unsgd.; pl.: 42.5 x 27.5 cm]

[18]   Coupe de l'Escalier, vers la Rue de Grenelle, sur la ligne E. F. [engraving, unsgd.; pl.: 42.3 x 27.7 cm]

[19]   Coupe de l'Escalier, vers la Rue de Grenelle [engraving, sgd. bottom right *Michelinot sculp.*; pl.: 41.1 x 26.6 cm]

[20]   Plan de l'Escalier, vers la Rue du Four, au Rez-de-Chaussée [engraving, unsgd.; pl.: 42.5 x 27.5 cm]

[21]   Plan de l'Escalier, vers la Rue du Four, au Premier Etage [engraving, unsgd.; pl.: 42.4 x 26.5 cm]

[22]   Coupe de l'Escalier, vers la Rue du Four [engraving sgd. bottom right *Michelinot sculp.*; pl.: 41.4 x 26.5 cm]

[23]   Plan de la Guerite à l'Etage du Grenier / servant de Bureau / Plan de la Guerite au Rez-de-Chaussée / servant de Bureau [mislabeled? — actually

front elevation and partial plans of booths, one domed with a pineapple finial, the other flat topped; engraving, unsgd.; pl.: 27.5 x 41.1 cm]

Ms. dedications in Avery Library and Sir John Soane's Museum copies.

A Monsieur / Bignon, / Seigneur et Patron de la Meaufle, Sémilly, Le Saussay, Lillebelle et autre Lieux, Commandeur Prevôt des Ceremonies des ordres / du Roi, Conseiller d'Etat, Bibliothécaire de sa Majesté, l'un des quarante de l'Academie Francaise et honoraire de celle des / Inscriptions et Belles Lettres Prevôt des Marchands. / Monsieur / Si l'idée de [SM pouvoir] former un Edifice public inconbustible, si les Plans qu j'en ai donné pour la nouvelle Halle aux grains, dont / j'ai été honoré de l'exécution, ont pu [AV animer mon zèle, et] flatter mon amour propre, une chose cependant m'est aussi precieuse, c'est / d'en former un recueil de tous les dessins et de vous le présenter; J'ose esperer, Monsieur, que vous voudrez bien agréer cet / ouvrage, il vous est offert pour la reconnoissance et il vous est dû à cause de l'intérêt que vous prenez au bien public. Amis et / Protecteurs des Arts et des Sciences Les Bignons se font de tous tems et pour toûjours couronnés de gloire. Les places les / distinctions particulières qu'ils on recus d nos Rois, le choix successif qu'on en a fair pour présider à la collection de la / plus belle Bibliotheque de l'Univers complettent leur éloge; Aussi, Monsieur, je ne chercherai point a entrer dans aucun détail / des raisons de ce choix si mérité, votre modestie s'y oppose, et je sens d'ailleurs la faiblesse de mon pinceau, je me contenterai / d'exalter mon bonheur, puisque vôtre nom à la tête de mon ouvrage en fera le plus bel ornement, et que ce sera pour moi / une occasion de vous donner un Témoignage public du profond respect avec le quel j'ai l'honneur d'être / Monsieur / votre très humble et très / obéissant Serviteur, Le Camus de Mezieres

This description is based on one compiled by Nicholas Savage, librarian to the Royal Academy, London, who inspected the RIBA and SM copies. I am most grateful to him.

Only four of the recorded copies have an engraved title plate (BHVP, CCA, RIBA, SM), but two of these (CCA, RIBA) lack the portrait and the ms. dedication, making the BHVP and the SM copies, seemingly, the most complete. However, the BHVP copy, though its plates are in as fully lettered a state as is to be found, lacks the plate 6 "Plan Du P.^{er} Etage"; while the SM copy has three of the plates, 4, 5, and 21, in an unlettered state. It has plate 16 in both its lettered and unlettered state. The BHVP copy has a duplicate of plate 23.

The AV copy, sometimes thought to have been Le Camus de Mézières's own (though the pencil note on the flyleaf recording this fact may be no more than a dealer's surmise), lacks the engraved title plate. The title is written in ink. The portrait and ms. dedication and twenty-three plates are present. The titles and lettering on plates 3, 4, 6, 9, 11, 12, 13, 14, 15, 16, 17, 18, 20, 21, 23 are all in manuscript, both ink and pencil; the titles on plate 10 are partly engraved, partly in manuscript. M. Arnaud de Vitry's copy (V) has the title page and dedication in manuscript and all twenty-three plates, some unlettered, some with titles in manuscript (both ink and pencil), but it lacks the portrait. The Middleton copy (M), lacking both title page and dedication, has the portrait and all twenty-three plates, though, plate 2 apart, all are in an unlettered state, except for some of the engravers' names. The BN copy is the least complete, no doubt the earliest, lacking title page, portrait, and dedication and including only eighteen plates. It lacks in particular plates 10 and 11 illustrating the project for covering the court with a dome.

It must be stressed that the plate numbers referred to in the notes above are those that would appear in the "ideal" copy described here; they do not reflect the order in which the plates are actually bound together in the various copies analyzed.

Armand-Jérome Bignon (1711–1772), to whom the book is dedicated, was, like his much more famous uncle the Abbé Jean-Paul Bignon, his brother Jérome (IV) Bignon de Blanzy, and his own son Jérome-Frédéric (alias Jean-Frédéric) Bignon, the king's librarian (*Bibliothécaire du Roi*)—though it was hinted that he could barely read. But from 1764, in succession to Camus Pontcarré de Viarmes, he served also as *Prévôt des Marchands* in Paris. His principal contribution to the improvement of the city, according to his obituarist in the *Histoire de l'Académie Royale des Inscriptions et Belles-Lettres* (Paris: L'Imprimerie Imperiale, 1780), 40: 187–97, was the building of a quay to serve the rue la Huchette. No mention is made therein of his support for the Halle au Blé, promoted most vigorously and begun by his predecessor. For Bignon's biography, see Michel Prevost and Jean-Charles Roman d'Amat, *Dictionnaire de biographie française* (Paris: Librairie Letouzey et Ané, 1954), 6: 434, and Simone Balayé, *La bibliothèque nationale des origines à 1800* (Geneva: Droz, 1988).

Index

THE GENIUS OF ARCHITECTURE; OR,
THE ANALOGY OF THAT ART WITH OUR SENSATIONS

Introduction by Robin Middleton
Translation by David Britt

Born and educated in South Africa, Robin Middleton received his Ph.D. from Cambridge in 1958, after completing a study on Eugène-Emmanuel Viollet-le-Duc and nineteenth-century French theory. An architect; technical editor of *Architectural Design*; consultant to Thames and Hudson, Cambridge University Press, and *Daidalos*; faculty member at the University of Cambridge, the Architectural Association, Bartlett School of Architecture, and Columbia University, Robin Middleton will always be remembered by at least one student of architectural history (and I suspect others) for the persuasive and scholarly power of a single essay, "The Abbé de Cordemoy and the Graeco-Gothic Ideal." —HFM

David Britt graduated in modern languages at Cambridge in 1961 and taught briefly before accepting an editorial position with Thames and Hudson, London, ultimately becoming a senior editor specializing in art and illustrated books. Since 1987 he has worked as a free-lance editor and translator. His most recent translations include: *Egon Schiele and His Contemporaries* (Royal Academy of Arts), *Japonisme in Western Painting, from Whistler to Matisse* (Cambridge University Press), *Joseph Beuys* (Abbeville Press), *Toulouse-Lautrec* (South Bank Centre), and *German Expressionism 1915–1925: The Second Generation* (Los Angeles County Museum of Art). Currently, he is translating works by J.-N.-L. Durand, Aby Warburg, and Johann Joachim Winckelmann for the Getty Center's TEXTS & DOCUMENTS series. He lives with his wife, Sue, and their three children in Muswell Hill, North London.

Designed by Lorraine Wild
Composed by Andresen Graphic Services, Tucson
in Cochin type (introduction), Fournier type (translation).
Printed by The Castle Press, Pasadena,
on Mohawk Superfine 80 lb, white and off-white.
Bound by Roswell Book Bindery, Phoenix.

TEXTS & DOCUMENTS
Series designed by Laurie Haycock Makela and Lorraine Wild

LIBRARY OF CONGRESS CATALOGING-IN-PUBLICATION DATA

Le Camus de Mézières, Nicolas, 1721–1789.
[Génie de l'architecture. English]
The genius of architecture, or, The analogy of that art with our
sensations / Nicolas Le Camus de Mézières ; introduction by
Robin Middleton ; translation by David Britt.
p. cm. - (Texts & documents)
Translation of : Le génie de l'architecture, ou, L'analogie de cet
art avec nos sensations.
Includes bibliographical references and index.
ISBN 0-89236-234-0 : $29.95.
ISBN 0-89236-235-9 (pbk.) : $19.95
1. Architecture — Philosophy. 2. Aesthetics, French — 18th century.
3. Architecture — Early works to 1800. I. Title. II. Title: Genius
of architecture. III. Title: Analogy of that art with our
sensations. IV. Series.
NA2515.L4513 1992
720 ' .1 — dc20   92-875
                                                                          CIP